THE COST OF DISCIPLESHIP

Other works of Dietrich Bonhoeffer
published by SCM Press

LIFE TOGETHER
LETTERS AND PAPERS FROM PRISON
ETHICS

Dietrich Bonhoeffer

THE COST OF DISCIPLESHIP

Complete Edition

SCM PRESS LTD

Translated from the German *Nachfolge*
first published 1937 by Chr. Kaiser Verlag, Munich
by R. H. Fuller, with some revision by Irmgard Booth

334 00259 1

Abridged English translation published October 1948
Complete edition published October 1959
by SCM Press Ltd
26–30 Tottenham Road, London N1 4BZ

Thirteenth impression 1984

Printed in Great Britain by
Richard Clay (The Chaucer Press) Ltd,
Bungay, Suffolk

CONTENTS

Foreword by Bishop G. K. A. Bell — 7

Memoir by G. Leibholz — 9

INTRODUCTION — 29

I GRACE AND DISCIPLESHIP — 33

   1 Costly Grace — 35
   2 The Call to Discipleship — 48
   3 Single-minded Obedience — 69
   4 Discipleship and the Cross — 76
   5 Discipleship and the Individual — 84

II THE SERMON ON THE MOUNT — 93

Matthew 5: Of the 'Extraordinariness' of the Christian Life

   6 The Beatitudes — 95
   7 The Visible Community — 104
   8 The Righteousness of Christ — 109
   9 The Brother — 115
  10 Woman — 119
  11 Truthfulness — 122
  12 Revenge — 126
  13 The Enemy – the 'Extraordinary' — 131

Matthew 6: Of the Hidden Character of the Christian Life

  14 The Hidden Righteousness — 139
  15 The Hiddenness of Prayer — 145
  16 The Hiddenness of the Devout Life — 151
  17 The Simplicity of the Carefree Life — 154

Matthew 7: The Separation of the Disciple Community

  18 The Disciple and Unbelievers — 162
  19 The Great Divide — 169
  20 The Conclusion — 175

CONTENTS

III THE MESSENGERS 177

21 The Harvest 179
22 The Apostles 182
23 The Work 184
24 The Suffering of the Messengers 190
25 The Decision 194
26 The Fruit 197

**IV THE CHURCH OF JESUS CHRIST AND
THE LIFE OF DISCIPLESHIP** 199

27 Preliminary Questions 201
28 Baptism 205
29 The Body of Christ 212
30 The Visible Community 223
31 The Saints 245
32 The Image of Christ 269

Index of Subjects 279

Index of Biblical References 281

FOREWORD

by G. K. A. Bell, *late Bishop of Chichester*

'WHEN Christ calls a man', says Dietrich Bonhoeffer, 'he bids him come and die.' There are different kinds of dying, it is true; but the essence of discipleship is contained in those words. And this marvellous book is a commentary on the cost. Dietrich himself was a martyr many times before he died. He was one of the first as well as one of the bravest witnesses against idolatry. He understood what he chose, when he chose resistance. I knew him in London in the early days of the evil régime: and from him, more than from any other German, I learned the true character of the conflict, in an intimate friendship. I have no doubt that he did fine work with his German congregation: but he taught many besides his fellow-countrymen while a pastor in England. He was crystal clear in his convictions; and young as he was, and humble-minded as he was, he saw the truth, and spoke it with a complete absence of fear. In Stockholm when he came so unexpectedly to see me in 1942, as an emissary from the Opposition, he was exactly the same, completely candid, completely regardless of personal safety, while deeply moved by the shame of the country he loved. Wherever he went, with whomever he was, with students, with those of his own age, or with his elders, he was undaunted, detached from himself, devoted to his friends, to his home, to his country as God meant it to be, to his Church, to his Master. I am very glad that the full text of *Nachfolge* appears in this latest edition of *The Cost of Discipleship*. The book will show men by what fire this young German churchman was possessed. It will also show the cost at which discipleship, in all nations, is to be won.

G. K. A. BELL

January 1958   Bp.

ACKNOWLEDGEMENTS

The poems 'Who am I?' on p. 15 and 'New Year 1945' on p. 16 are quoted by kind permission of *Time and Tide* and *The New English Review*.

MEMOIR
by G. Leibholz

DIETRICH BONHOEFFER was born in Breslau on February 4th, 1906, the son of a university professor and leading authority on psychiatry and neurology. His more remote ancestors were theologians, professors, lawyers, artists. From his mother's side there was also some aristocratic blood in his veins.

His parents were quite outstanding in character and general outlook. They were very clear-sighted, cultured people and uncompromising in all things which matter in life. From his father, Dietrich Bonhoeffer inherited goodness, fairness, self-control and ability; from his mother, his great human understanding and sympathy, his devotion to the cause of the oppressed, and his unshakable steadfastness.

Both his father and mother brought up their son Dietrich with his three brothers, his twin-sister and three other sisters, in Breslau and (from 1912) in Berlin, in that Christian, humanitarian and liberal tradition which to the Bonhoeffers was as native as the air they breathed. It was that spirit which determined Dietrich Bonhoeffer's life from the beginning.

Bonhoeffer was as open as any man could be to all the things which make life beautiful. He rejoiced in the love of his parents, his sisters and brothers, his fiancée, his many friends. He loved the mountains, the flowers, the animals – the greatest and the simplest things in life. His geniality and inborn chivalry, his love of music, art and literature, the firmness of his character, his personal charm and his readiness to listen, made him friends everywhere. But what marked him most was his unselfishness and preparedness to help others up to the point of self-sacrifice. Whenever others hesitated to undertake a task that required special courage, Bonhoeffer was ready to take the risk.

Theology itself was somehow in his blood. On his mother's side Bonhoeffer's grandfather, von Hase, had been a chaplain to the Emperor, whose displeasure he incurred when he allowed himself to differ from his political views. When the Emperor stopped attending his services, Hase was urged to tender his resignation. His great-grandfather was Carl von Hase, the most distinguished Church historian in the Germany of the nineteenth century, who tells us in his autobiography of his visit to Goethe in Weimar in 1830, and who (just as Dietrich Bonhoeffer's grandfather on his father's side) was himself imprisoned for his subversive liberal views in the fortress of the High Asperg in 1825.[1] On his father's side he belonged to an old Swabian family which had been living in Württemberg since 1450 and which was also able to claim not a few theologians in previous generations.

This tradition of the Bonhoeffer family may explain why Dietrich Bonhoeffer had already made up his mind at the age of fourteen, when he was still at school, to read theology. At the age of seventeen he entered Tübingen University. A year later he attended courses at Berlin University, and sat at the feet of Adolf von Harnack, R. Seeberg, Lietzmann and others. Harnack soon formed a very high opinion of his character and abilities. Later he came under the influence of Karl Barth's theology which, though he never went to his lectures or studied under him, left its mark on Bonhoeffer's first book, *Sanctorum Communio*. In 1928 he went as a curate to Barcelona for a year and in 1930 at the age of twenty-four he became a lecturer in Systematic Theology in Berlin University. But before actually starting with his academic career he went to Union Theological Seminary in New York as 'a brilliant and theologically sophisticated young man'.[2] His writings[3] quickly gave him a firm reputation in the theological world,

---

[1] For further details on C. von Hase, cf. *Encyclopaedia Britannica*, vol. 11, p. 241. Von Hase has made Jena an attractive place for theology and men of learning all over the world.

[2] Niebuhr in *Union Seminary Quarterly Review*, vol. 1, no. 3, March 1946, p. 3.

[3] *Sanctorum Communio: eine Dogmatische Untersuchung zur Soziologie der Kirche*, 1930; *Akt und Sein*, 1931; *Schöpfung und Fall*, 1933 (Eng. trans.: *Creation and Fall*, 1959); *Nachfolge*, 1937 (Eng. trans.: *The Cost of Discipleship*, 1948); *Versuchung*,

especially his *Nachfolge* which through his death has gained a new and deep significance; this book greatly impressed theologians throughout the world at the time when it first made its appearance. Some of his other books, especially his *Ethics*, written by him in prison, are published in English, and others will appear before long.

A splendid career in the realm of theological scholarship lay thus open before him. In the light of his achievement and in the prospect of what he might have achieved, his death is a great tragedy. But worldly standards cannot measure the loss adequately. For God had chosen him to perform the highest task a Christian can undertake. He has become a martyr. 'And seekest thou great things for thyself? Seek them not. For behold, I will bring evil upon all flesh; but thy life will I give unto thee for a prey in all places whither thou goest.' 'I cannot get away from Jeremiah 45,' wrote Bonhoeffer from the prison cell.

2

Dietrich Bonhoeffer was a great realist. He was one of the few who quickly understood, even before Hitler came to power, that National Socialism was a brutal attempt to make history without God and to found it on the strength of man alone. Therefore in 1933, when Hitler came to power, he abandoned his academic career, which seemed to him to have lost its proper meaning. He was not however expelled from the University until 1936 and even lectured there in the summer and winter of 1935-36. As late as February 1933 he denounced on the wireless a political system which corrupted and grossly misled a nation and made the 'Führer' its idol and God. In October 1933, after six months of the Church struggle, he decided to leave Berlin for London, where, as a pastor, he ministered to two congregations and tried to explain to his British friends, among them especially the Bishop of Chichester, the true character of the German Church struggle. He quickly realized that in the situation in which the world and

1937 (Eng. trans.: *Temptation*, 1955); *Gemeinsames Leben*, 1939 (Eng. trans.: *Life Together*, 1954); *Ethik*, 1943 (Eng. trans.: *Ethics*, 1955).

the Churches found themselves in the 'thirties nothing was gained any longer for the Churches by citing their old credal statements. The ecumenical movement seemed to him to offer the only way of reuniting the various members of the body of Christ. This explains why Bonhoeffer considered it the duty of the Churches to listen anew to the message of the Bible and to put themselves in the context of the whole Church. Therefore no wonder that Bonhoeffer soon played a remarkable *rôle* in the ecumenical movement[1] and that it was he who, more than any other teacher in a German university or theological seminary, had made German students familiar with the life, the history and development of the non-Lutheran Churches.

In 1935 Bonhoeffer, already one of the leaders of the Confessional Church, returned to Germany. He went to Pomerania to direct an illegal Church Training College, first in a small peninsula in the Baltic, later on in Finkenwalde near Stettin. This College was not formed after any existing model. It was not an order comprising men living in ascetic seclusion; nor was it a Training College in the ordinary sense of the word. The attempt was made here to live the 'community life' of a Christian as described in one of Dietrich Bonhoeffer's shorter writings. Young ministers who came from all over the Reich learned here what is so sorely needed to-day – namely, how in the twentieth century a Christian life should be lived in a spirit of genuine brotherhood, and how such a life could naturally and freely grow if there were only men who entirely belonged to the Lord and, therefore, in brotherly love to one another. It was not until 1940 that the College was finally closed down by the Gestapo.

When war seemed inevitable, Bonhoeffer's friends abroad wanted him to leave Germany to save his life, for he was unalterably opposed to serving in the Army in an aggressive war. When asked by a Swede at the Ecumenical Conference at Fanö, Denmark, in 1934, 'What will you do when war comes?' he answered:

[1] He was a member of the Youth Commission of the World Council of Churches and of the World Alliance for International Friendship through the Churches. He was elected (with Präses Koch) to be a member of the Ecumenical Christian Council for Life and Work at Fanö, Denmark, in 1934.

'I shall pray to Christ to give me the power not to take up arms.'
In June 1939, American friends got him out of Germany. But soon
he felt that he could not stay there, but that he had to return to
his country. When he came to England on his return from the
United States, his friends quickly realized that Bonhoeffer's heart
belonged to his oppressed and persecuted fellow Christians in
Germany and that he would not desert them at a time when they
needed him most.

The reasoning which brought Bonhoeffer to his decision belongs, as Reinhold Niebuhr[1] says, 'to the finest logic of Christian
martyrdom'. 'I shall have no right', Bonhoeffer wrote to Niebuhr
before leaving America, 'to participate in the reconstruction of
Christian life in Germany after the war if I do not share the trials
of this time with my people. . . . Christians in Germany will face
the terrible alternative of either willing the defeat of their nation
in order that Christian civilization may survive, or willing the
victory of their nation and thereby destroying our civilization.
I know which of these alternatives I must choose; but I cannot
make this choice in security.' Dietrich Bonhoeffer never regretted
this decision, not even in prison, where he wrote in later years: 'I
am sure of God's hand and guidance. . . . You must never doubt
that I am thankful and glad to go the way which I am being led.
My past life is abundantly full of God's mercy, and, above all sin,
stands the forgiving love of the Crucified.'

At the outbreak of the war friends in Germany managed to
spare him the ordeal of serving in the Army, so that he was able
to go on with the work for the Confessional Church and to
combine it with some activity for the political underground
movement to which the war had given its chance. Bonhoeffer,
qualified both by character and general outlook, soon belonged to
the few who had a strong spiritual influence on the growing
opposition in Germany.

Bonhoeffer (together with his sister Christel and her husband,
Hans von Dohnanyi) was arrested by the Gestapo in the house of

[1] Niebuhr, op. cit., p. 3. Cf. also Niebuhr, 'Death of a Martyr', in *Christianity
and Crisis*, June 25th, 1945.

his parents on April 5th, 1943. In prison and concentration camps, Bonhoeffer greatly inspired by his indomitable courage, his unselfishness and his goodness, all those who came in contact with him. He even inspired his guards with respect, some of whom became so much attached to him that they smuggled out of prison his papers and poems written there, and apologized to him for having to lock his door after the round in the courtyard.

His own concern in prison was to get permission to minister to the sick and to his fellow prisoners, and his ability to comfort the anxious and depressed was amazing. We know what Bonhoeffer's word and religious assistance meant to his fellow prisoners, especially during their last hours (even to Molotov's nephew Kokorin, who was imprisoned with Bonhoeffer in Büchenwald and to whom the teaching of Christ was brought home); we know what Bonhoeffer's practical aid meant in prison (Tegel) during political trials to those men of whom ten or twenty were sentenced to death by a military court every week in 1943 and 1944. Some of these (among them a British soldier), charged with sabotage, were saved by him (and his father and solicitor[1]) from certain death. We have heard that his fellow prisoners were deeply impressed by the calmness and self-control which Bonhoeffer displayed even in the most terrible situations. For instance, during the very heavy bombings of Berlin, when the explosions were accompanied by the howling of his fellow prisoners, who beat with their fists against the locked doors of their cells clamouring to be transferred to the safe bunkers, Bonhoeffer stood, we have been told, like a giant before men.

But this is only the one side of the picture. The other side is that Bonhoeffer was a man who lived in, and loved, this world. He, a giant before man, was but a child before God. While he was in the body, the fight between flesh and spirit, Adam and Christ, was going on in him. Sometimes he seemed to have become a riddle to himself. One day he gave expression to this conflict in his soul in a moving poem written from the prison-cell and entitled:

[1] Kurt Wergin, Berlin.

WHO AM I?[1]

Who am I? They often tell me
I stepped from my cell's confinement
calmly, cheerfully, firmly,
like a Squire from his country house.

Who am I? They often tell me
I used to speak to my warders
freely and friendly and clearly,
as though it were mine to command.

Who am I? They also tell me
I bore the days of misfortune
equably, smilingly, proudly,
like one accustomed to win.

Am I then really that which other men tell of?
Or am I only what I myself know of myself?
Restless and longing and sick, like a bird in a cage,
struggling for breath, as though hands were compressing my throat,
yearning for colours, for flowers, for the voices of birds,
thirsting for words of kindness, for neighbourliness,
tossing in expectation of great events,
powerlessly trembling for friends at an infinite distance,
weary and empty at praying, at thinking, at making,
faint, and ready to say farewell to it all.

Who am I? This or the Other?
Am I one person to-day and to-morrow another?
Am I both at once? A hypocrite before others,
and before myself a contemptible woebegone weakling?
Or is something within me still like a beaten army
fleeing in disorder from victory already achieved?

Who am I? They mock me, these lonely questions of mine.
Whoever I am, Thou knowest, O God, I am thine!

[1] Translated by J. B. Leishman.

On October 5th, 1944, Bonhoeffer was transferred from Tegel to the main Gestapo prison in the Prinz Albrechtstrasse in Berlin. Although fully aware of what he had to expect there, he was perfectly calm, saying goodbye to his friends as though nothing had happened, but, as a fellow prisoner remarked, 'his eyes were quite unnatural'. The direct contact hitherto maintained with the outside world was now cut. One of the last messages received from him was a poem composed at the Gestapo prison in Berlin during the very heavy air raids on Berlin. It was entitled 'New Year 1945' and reads as follows:[1]

> *With every power for good to stay and guide me,*
> *comforted and inspired beyond all fear,*
> *I'll live these days with you in thought beside me,*
> *and pass, with you, into the coming year.*
>
> *The old year still torments our hearts, unhastening:*
> *the long days of our sorrow still endure.*
> *Father, grant to the soul thou hast been chastening*
> *that thou hast promised – the healing and the cure.*
>
> *Should it be ours to drain the cup of grieving*
> *even to the dregs of pain, at thy command,*
> *we will not falter, thankfully receiving*
> *all that is given by thy loving hand.*
>
> *But, should it be thy will once more to release us*
> *to life's enjoyment and its good sunshine,*
> *that we've learned from sorrow shall increase us*
> *and all our life be dedicate as thine.*
>
> *To-day, let candles shed their radiant greeting:*
> *lo, on our darkness are they not thy light,*
> *leading us haply to our longed-for meeting?*
> *Thou canst illumine e'en our darkest night.*

[1] Translated by Geoffrey Winthrop Young.

When now the silence deepens for our harkening,
grant we may hear thy children's voices raise
from all the unseen world around us darkening
their universal paean, in thy praise.

While all the powers of Good aid and attend us,
boldly we'll face the future, be it what may.
At even, and at morn, God will befriend us,
And oh, most surely on each new year's day!

In February, when the Gestapo prison in Berlin was destroyed by an air raid, Bonhoeffer was taken to the concentration camp of Büchenwald and from there to other places until he was executed by special order of Himmler at the concentration camp at Flossenburg on April 9th, 1945, just a few days before it was liberated by the Allies. This happened just about the time when his brother Klaus and his sisters' husbands, Hans von Dohnanyi and Rüdiger Schleicher, met their execution at the hands of the Gestapo in Berlin and in the concentration camp at Sachsenhausen.

3

The guiding force in Bonhoeffer's life, underlying all that he did, worked and suffered for, was his faith and love of God, in whom he found peace and happiness. From his faith the breadth of vision came which enabled him to separate the gold in life from the dross and to differentiate what was and what was not essential in the life of man. From it came the constancy of mind, persistency of purpose, love of suffering humanity and of truth, justice and goodness. But it was not enough for him to seek justice, truth, honesty and goodness for their own sake and patiently to suffer for them. No, according to Bonhoeffer, we have to do so in loyal obedience to Him who is the source and spring of all goodness, justice and truth and on whom he felt absolutely dependent.

It is the same call of God which also obliges us only to make use of freedom with a deep feeling of responsibility. Bonhoeffer believed in man as a free spiritual being, but this freedom was conferred and inspired by divine grace and granted man, not for his glorification, but for the conservation of the divine ordering of human life. If Christian teaching does not guide us in the use of freedom and God is denied, all obligations and responsibilities that are sacred and binding on man are undermined. A Christian has then no other choice but to act, to suffer and – if it has to be – to die. As he put it in his poem, 'Stations on the Road to Freedom', composed in prison when he realized that his death was certain, the last verse of which runs as follows:

DEATH[1]

Come now, solemnest feast on the road to eternal freedom,
Death, and destroy those fetters that bow, those walls that imprison
this our transient life, these souls that linger in darkness,
so that at last we see what is here withheld from our vision.
Long did we seek you, freedom, in discipline, action and suffering.
Now that we die, in the face of God himself we behold you.

It was his brotherly love of his fellow-men which also caused Bonhoeffer to believe that it was not enough to follow Christ by preaching, teaching and writing. No, he was in deadly earnest when he called for Christian action and self-sacrifice. This explains why Bonhoeffer always acted spontaneously, 'in hiding', far from all publicity, and why he considered self-righteousness and complacency great sins against the Holy Spirit, and regarded ambition and vanity as the start of the road to hell.

Bonhoeffer stood for what is called Christian Humanism to-day. For he offered his life for a new understanding of the personal life which has its roots in the Christian faith. It was he who made true the word that 'the spirit of man is the lamp of the Lord' (Prov. 20.27) and that God's revelation is through man and for man only. To Bonhoeffer, Christianity was not the concern of the believing, pious soul who shuts himself up and keeps himself within the bounds of the sacramental sphere. No, according to him Christianity has its place in this world and the Church as the Body of

---

[1] Translation by J. B. Leishman

Christ, and the fellowship in him can only be the visible Church. Man must follow him who has served and passed through this world as the living, the dying and the risen Lord. Therefore, wherever it pleases God to put man in this world, the Christian must be ready for martyrdom and death. It is only in this way that man learns faith.

As he himself has put it: 'The Christian is not a *homo religiosus*, but simply a man as Jesus (in distinction from John the Baptist) was a man. . . . Not the flat and banal "This-sidedness" of the Enlightened, of the Active, of the Comfortable and the Sluggard, but the deep "This-sidedness" which is full of discipline and in which the knowledge of the Death and Resurrection is always present, this it is that I mean.[1] When a man really gives up trying to make something out of himself – a saint, or a converted sinner, or a churchman (a so-called clerical somebody), a righteous or unrighteous man, . . . when in the fullness of tasks, questions, success or ill-hap, experiences and perplexities, a man throws himself into the arms of God . . . then he wakes with Christ in Gethsemane. That is faith, that is *metanoia* and it is thus that he becomes a man and Christian. How can a man wax arrogant if in a this-sided life he shares the suffering of God?'[2]

The idea that God himself has been suffering through Christ in this world and from its remoteness from him, had occupied Bonhoeffer's mind again and again. Bonhoeffer frequently felt strongly that God himself shared his suffering. In the second verse of the poem 'Christian and Unbeliever', composed by Bonhoeffer a few months before his death, this feeling is expressed as follows:

Men go to God when he is sore bested:
find him poor and scorned, without shelter and bread,
whelmed under weight of the wicked, the weak, the dead.
Christians stand by God in his hour of grieving.[3]

[1] On the term 'this-sidedness' see Schönherr, 'Die Zeichen der Zeit', *Evangelische Monatsschrift*, 1947, pp. 307–12.
[2] The full text in German can be found in *Das Zeugnis eines Boten*, ed. by Visser 't Hooft, Geneva, 1945, pp. 46–47.
[3] Translated by Geoffrey Winthrop Young.

Bonhoeffer's standing with God in his hour of grieving explains, ultimately, why he did not take his own suffering seriously and why his courage was so great and uncompromising.

This steadfastness of mind and preparedness to sacrifice everything has been proved on many occasions. For instance, when in the summer of 1940 despair had seized most of those who were actively hostile to the Nazi régime and when the proposal was made that further action should be postponed so as to avoid giving Hitler the air of a martyr, Bonhoeffer unswervingly and successfully opposed this suggestion: 'If we claim to be Christians, there is no room for expediency.' Thus the group led by him went on with its activities at a time when the world inside and outside Germany widely believed in a Nazi victory. Or when the question arose as to who was prepared to inform the British Government, through the Bishop of Chichester, of the exact details of the German resistance movement, it was again Bonhoeffer who, as early as May 31st, 1942, at the risk of his life, undertook this task at the instigation of his brother-in-law Hans von Dohnanyi in the hope of a sympathetic understanding on the part of the British Government.[1]

Further, in his hearing before the Gestapo during his imprisonment, defenceless and powerless as he then was and only fortified by the word of God in his heart, he stood erect and unbroken before his tormentors. He refused to recant, and defied the Gestapo machine by openly admitting that, as a Christian, he was an implacable enemy of National Socialism and its totalitarian demands towards the citizen – defied it, although he was continually threatened with torture and with the arrest of his parents, his sisters and his fiancée, who all had a helping hand in his activities. We know of another scene in October 1944, when friends made an attempt to liberate him and to take him to safety abroad, and he decided to remain in prison in order not to endanger others.

We also know from the testimony of a British officer, a fellow-

---

[1] The Bishop of Chichester tells us of his conversations in Sweden with Bonhoeffer in an article published in the *Contemporary Review*, 1945, no. 958, pp. 203 ff.

prisoner, of the last service which Dietrich Bonhoeffer held on the day before his death and which 'moved all deeply, Catholics and Protestants alike, by his simple sincerity'. When trying afterwards to keep the imprisoned wives of men executed for their leadership in the plot against Hitler from depression and anxiety, he was taken away. We know that Dietrich Bonhoeffer, who was never tried, went steadfastly on his last way to be hanged, and died with admirable calmness and dignity.

God heard his prayer and granted him the 'costly grace' – that is, the privilege of taking the cross for others and of affirming his faith by martyrdom.

4

Dietrich Bonhoeffer's life and work has far-reaching implications. First, Bonhoeffer's and his friends' political activities show that the still widely-held view that the plot of July 1944 was simply a 'conspiracy of a small clique of reactionaries and discouraged officers', who saw that Hitler was losing the war and had made a mess of their profession, is wrong. There also was in the German opposition movement another strand of uncorrupted spiritual forces which opposed all that Hitler and National Socialism stood for on grounds of Christianity and the basic values of life, of truth, justice, goodness and decency. This trend drew its members from quite different political parties and religious groups. None of these men stood for a special party belief, but for a certain way of life, the destruction of which was the avowed purpose of National Socialism. Here there was the 'other Germany' of which there was so much talk in the 'thirties. These men were in truth the upholders of the European and Western tradition in Germany, and it was Dietrich Bonhoeffer who more than anybody else realized that nothing less than a return to the Christian faith could save Germany. The failure of these men was not only a tragedy for Germany, but for Europe as a whole, and historians may well come one day to the conclusion that the consequences of this failure cannot be made good.

The existence of this strand within the German opposition

movement confirms that the last war was, ultimately, ideological in its basic character and that we are living to-day in a primarily ideological age. Only thus can we fully understand the motives of Dietrich Bonhoeffer's action. No doubt, Bonhoeffer was a great patriot and he loved his country so much that he preferred death to safety. But he was also too astute a political analyst not to see that Germany would be engulfed in the coming catastrophe. The fanatical devilish forces within National Socialism left no alternative. They were aiming at the destruction of Germany as a European and Christian country. By planned political action he hoped to avoid this tragic disaster. As he used to say: it is not only my task to look after the victims of madmen who drive a motor-car in a crowded street, but to do all in my power to stop their driving at all.

Ultimately, it was the allegiance which he owed to God and his master which forced upon him the terrible decision, not merely to make a stand against National Socialism (all the underground movements in the German-occupied countries did that), but also – and this in contrabistinction to all the underground movements which appealed to nationalism – to work for the defeat of his own country, since only thus could Germany as a Christian and European country be saved from extinction. For this very reason Bonhoeffer and his friends were tortured, hanged and murdered. It was Bonhoeffer and his friends who proved by their resistance unto death that even in the age of the nation-state there are loyalties which transcend those to state and nation. They proved that even in this age nationalism stands under God and that it is a sin against him and his call for fellowship with other nations if it degenerates into national egotism and greed. This message, which implies the virtual death sentence of the still prevailing materialistic concept of nationalism, belongs to the spiritual inheritance of Dietrich Bonhoeffer's and his friends' martyrdom. Only from this point of view can it be proved that Hitler and his gang were not only the destroyers of Europe but also traitors to their own country; and, further, that men can lose their country if it is represented by an anti-Christian régime.

True, it cannot be said that the war had actually been waged by the Western countries on these ideological lines. We know that in the later stages of the war, when the regrettable 'unconditional surrender' policy of Casablanca was accepted by the Western countries, the war had gradually lost its ideological character and taken on a more and more nationalistic outlook. This was due to the fact that the West and its political leaders were, ultimately, not confronted with the tragic conflict of loyalties to which Christians in Germany were exposed. Of course, there were in the Western countries outstanding Christians and non-Christians who felt this conflict weighing heavily on their conscience and their thought and courageously refused during the war to bow down to public opinion.[1] These men raised the claims of a higher loyalty than the national, and challenged politicians and churchmen alike. But they had not experienced the full weight of the tragic issue at stake. Only those who paid with their lives for the tragic conflict of loyalties can claim to be the martyrs of a new age.

5

Secondly, the religious implications concern the Protestant Church in Germany especially, but also affect the Church as a whole.

In the earlier stages of his career Bonhoeffer accepted the traditional Lutheran view that there was a sharp distinction between politics and religion. Gradually, however, he revised his opinion, not because he was a politician or because he refused to give Caesar his due, but because he came to recognize that the political authority in Germany had become entirely corrupt and immoral and that a false faith is capable of terrible and monstrous things. For Bonhoeffer Hitler was the Antichrist, the arch-destroyer of the world and its basic values, the Antichrist who enjoys destruction, slavery, death and extinction for their own sake, the Anti-

---

[1] Cf., for instance, the speeches delivered by the late Bishop of Chichester in the House of Lords during the war, his essays and addresses which are now embodied in his book, *The Church and Humanity, 1939-1946* (1947).

christ who wants to pose the negative as positive and as creative.

Bonhoeffer was firmly and rightly convinced that it is not only a Christian right but a Christian duty towards God to oppose tyranny, that is, a government which is no longer based on natural law and the law of God. For Bonhoeffer this followed from the fact that the Church as a living force in this world entirely depends on her *this-sidedness*. Of course, Bonhoeffer understood this term neither in the sense of modern liberal theology nor in the sense of the National Socialist creed. Both modern liberal theology and secular totalitarianism hold pretty much in common that the message of the Bible has to be adapted, more or less, to the requirements of a secular world. No wonder, therefore, that the process of debasing Christianity as inaugurated by liberal theology led, in the long run, to a complete perversion and falsification of the essence of Christian teaching by National Socialism. Bonhoeffer was firmly convinced that 'this side' must be fully related to, and permeated by, Christian love, and that the Christian must be prepared, if necessary, to offer his life for this. Thus all kinds of secular totalitarianism which force man to cast aside his religious and moral obligations to God and subordinate the laws of justice and morality to the State are incompatible with his conception of life.

This explains why Bonhoeffer did not take the pacifist line, although his aristocratic noble-mindedness and charming gentleness made him, at the bottom of his heart, a pacifist. But to refrain from taking any part in the attempt to overcome the National Socialist régime conflicted too deeply with his view that Christian principles must in some way be translated into human life and that it is in the sphere of the material, in state and society, that responsible love has to be manifested.

Again, it was typical of Bonhoeffer that he did not commit the Church by his actions. The responsibility was his and not that of the Church, and therefore he cannot, alas, be said to have represented by his action the Confessional Church as a whole. True, the Barmen Declaration had committed the Church to action in the political as well as in the religious sphere, and Bonhoeffer left no doubt that deciding for or against Barmen was deciding for or against the Confessional Church in Nazi Germany. As he once said: 'He who severs himself from the Confessional Church severs himself from the Grace of God.' But there were only a few of its members who took the Barmen message so seriously that they were prepared courageously to act upon the practical consequence of their conclusions. Therefore we cannot be surprised that Bonhoeffer was filled with increasing sorrow about the course the Confessional Church took in the later years of the National Socialist régime. He felt that the Confessional Church was more concerned with her own existence and inherited rights than with preaching against the war and with the fate of the persecuted and oppressed. Thus it was Bonhoeffer who first brought home the full lesson of the Oxford Conference to the Lutheran Church in Germany, namely, that the life of the Church must be linked with the life of the people. This is the deeper meaning of Bonhoeffer's martyrdom and death for the Protestant Church in Germany. Her future depends on her right understanding of them.

6

Those who attended the service held at Holy Trinity in London at the instigation of the late Bishop of Chichester on July 27th, 1945,[1] felt that, on April 9th, 1945, when Dietrich Bonhoeffer met his death at the hands of the S.S. Black Guards, something had happened in Germany that could not be measured by human standards. They felt that God himself had intervened in the most terrible struggle the world has witnessed so far by sacrificing one of his most faithful and courageous sons to expiate the crimes of a diabolical régime and to revive the spirit in which the civilization of Europe has to be rebuilt.

Indeed, if self-sacrifice is the highest fulfilment of the human being, and if the value of man with his bodily existence depends on the measure of sacrifice he is called to exercise for the sake of responsible love in the material environment in which he has

---

[1] Cf. Bonhoeffer, *Gedenkheft*, Berlin, 1947. Another memorial service was held at Berlin on April 9th, 1946; cf. op. cit., pp. 18-36.

been set, then Bonhoeffer's life and death belong to the annals of Christian martyrdom, or, as Niebuhr said, 'to the modern Acts of the Apostles'. His good fight has been a living symbol that the spiritual has the primacy over the material. His story has become the story of the victory of the spirit of the loving and truly human person over evil, evil which was not able to break the last stronghold of responsible spiritual freedom. 'The life of the spirit is not that which shuns death and keeps clear of destruction: rather it endureth death and in death it is sustained. It only achieves its truth in the midst of utter destruction.'

It has often been said that those of the many who are not directly guilty for the crimes of the former régime in Germany must be punished for their passive attitude towards it. In a modern dictatorship, however, with its subterranean ubiquity and all-embracing instruments of oppression, a revolt means certain death to all who support it. To reproach in a modern tyranny a people as a whole for failing to revolt is as if one would reproach a prisoner for failing to escape from a heavily guarded prison. The majority of the people in all nations alike does not consist of heroes. What Dietrich Bonhoeffer and others did cannot be expected from the many. The future in modern society depends much more on the quiet heroism of the very few who are inspired by God. These few will greatly enjoy the divine inspiration and will be prepared to stand for the dignity of man and true freedom and to keep the law of God, even if it means martyrdom or death. These few perform the law because they 'look not at the things which are seen, but at the things which are unseen: for the things which are seen are temporal, but the things that are unseen are eternal'.

Bonhoeffer often asked himself about the deeper meaning of his life, which seemed to him so disconnected and confused. A few months before his death, when coming events cast their shadows before, he wrote in prison: 'It all depends on whether or not the fragment of our life reveals the plan and material of the whole. There are fragments which are only good to be thrown away, and others which are important for centuries to come be-

cause their fulfilment can only be a divine work. They are fragments of necessity. If our life, however remotely, reflects such a
fragment . . . we shall not have to bewail our fragmentary life,
but, on the contrary, rejoice in it.'

Indeed, we have to rejoice in God's mercy. We have not found
Dietrich Bonhoeffer's grave, but the memory of his life will safely
be guarded, not only in the hearts of those who are indissolubly
united with him, but also in the heart of the Church who draws
her life-blood again and again from those who 'follow him'.

Beyond that we know that the time will come when we shall
have to realize that we owe it to the inspiration of Dietrich Bonhoeffer's life and death, and of those who died with him, that
Western civilization can be saved. For not only in its material
standards, but also in its spiritual vitality, has Western civilization
been falling steadily and with increasing rapidity into ruin and
desolation. The good message of Dietrich Bonhoeffer's life and
death is that Western civilization must not die. It will be born
again to youth. It has already recaptured faith and vitality. What
was said of Moses as he went to his death, 'And the Lord showed
him all the land' (Deut. 34.1), applies to Bonhoeffer and to those
who have given their lives for the new humanity which will arise
through their martyrdom.

Thus Bonhoeffer's life and death have given us great hope for
the future. He has set a model for a new type of true leadership
inspired by the gospel, daily ready for martyrdom and death and
imbued by a new spirit of Christian humanism and a creative
sense of civic duty. The victory which he has won was a victory
for us all, a conquest never to be undone, of love, light and liberty.

INTRODUCTION

REVIVAL of church life always brings in its train a richer under-standing of the Scriptures. Behind all the slogans and catchwords of ecclesiastical controversy, necessary though they are, there arises a more determined quest for him who is the sole object of it all, for Jesus Christ himself. What did Jesus mean to say to us? What is his will for us to-day? How can he help us to be good Christians in the modern world? In the last resort, what we want to know is not, what would this or that man, or this or that Church, have of us, but what Jesus Christ himself wants of us. When we go to church and listen to the sermon, what we want to hear is his Word – and that not merely for selfish reasons, but for the sake of the many for whom the Church and her message are foreign. We have a strange feeling that if Jesus himself – Jesus alone with his Word – could come into our midst at sermon time, we should find quite a different set of men hearing the Word, and quite a different set rejecting it. That is not to deny that the Word of God is to be heard in the preaching which goes on in our church. The real trouble is that the pure word of Jesus has been overlaid with so much human ballast – burdensome rules and regulations, false hopes and consolations – that it has become extremely difficult to make a genuine decision for Christ. Of course it is our aim to preach Christ and Christ alone, but, when all is said and done, it is not the fault of our critics that they find our preaching so hard to understand, so overburdened with ideas and expressions which are hopelessly out of touch with the mental climate in which they live. It is just not true that every word of criticism directed against contemporary preaching is a deliberate rejection of Christ and proceeds from the spirit of Antichrist. So many people come to church with a genuine desire to hear what we have to say, yet they are always going back home with the uncomfortable feeling that we are making it too difficult for them to come to Jesus. Are we determined to have nothing to do with all these people? They are convinced that it is not the Word of Jesus himself that puts them off, but the superstructure of human, institutional, and doctrinal elements in our preaching. Of course we know all the answers to these objections, and those answers certainly make it easy for us to slide out of our responsibilities. But perhaps it would be just as well to ask ourselves whether we do not in fact often act as obstacles to Jesus and his Word. Is it not possible that we cling too closely to our own favourite presentation of the gospel, and to a type of preaching which was all very well in its own time and place and for the social set-up for which it was originally intended? Is there not after all an element of truth in the contention that our preaching is too dogmatic, and hopelessly irrelevant to life? Are we not constantly harping on certain ideas at the expense of others which are just as important? Does not our preaching contain too much of our own opinions and convictions, and too little of Jesus Christ? Jesus invites all those that labour and are heavy laden, and nothing could be so contrary to our best intentions, and so fatal to our proclamation, as to drive men away from him by forcing upon them man-made dogmas. If we did so, we should make the love of Jesus Christ a laughing-stock to Christians and pagans alike. It is no use taking refuge in abstract discussion, or trying to make excuses, so let us get back to the Scriptures, to the word and call of Jesus Christ himself. Let us try to get away from the poverty and pettiness of our own little convictions and problems, and seek the wealth and splendour which are vouchsafed to us in Jesus Christ.

We propose to tell how Jesus calls us to be his disciples. But is not this to lay another and still heavier burden on men's shoulders? Is this all we can do when the souls and bodies of men are groaning beneath the weight of so many man-made dogmas? If we recall men to the following of Jesus, shall we not be driving a still sharper goad into their already troubled and wounded consciences? Are we to follow the practice which has been all too common in the history of the Church, and impose on men demands too grievous to bear, demands which have little to do with the centralities of the Christian faith, demands which may be a pious luxury for the few, but which the toiling masses, with their anxiety for their daily bread, their jobs and their families, can only reject as utter blasphemy and a tempting of God? Is it the Church's concern to erect a spiritual tyranny over men, by dictating to them what must be believed and performed in order to be saved, and by presuming to enforce that belief and behaviour with the sanctions of temporal and eternal punishment? Shall the word of the Church bring new tyranny and oppression over the souls of men? It may well be that this is what many people want. But could the Church consent to meet such a demand?

When the Bible speaks of following Jesus, it is proclaiming a discipleship which will liberate mankind from all man-made dogmas, from every burden and oppression, from every anxiety and torture which afflicts the conscience. If they follow Jesus, men escape from the hard yoke of their own laws, and submit to the kindly yoke of Jesus Christ. But does this mean that we ignore the seriousness of his commands? Far from it. We can only achieve perfect liberty andenjoy fellowship with Jesus when his command, his call to absolute discipleship, is appreciated in its entirety. Only the man who follows the command of Jesus single-mindedly, and unresistingly lets his yoke rest upon him, finds his burden easy, and under its gentle pressure receives the power to persevere in the right way. The command of Jesus is hard, unutterably hard, for those who try to resist it. But for those who willingly submit, the yoke is easy, and the burden is light. 'His commandments are not grievous' (I John 5.3). The commandment of Jesus is not a sort of spiritual shock treatment. Jesus asks nothing of us without giving us the strength to perform it. His commandment never seeks to destroy life, but to foster, strengthen and heal it.

But one question still troubles us. What can the call to discipleship mean to-day for the worker, the business man, the squire and the soldier? Does it not lead to an intolerable dichotomy between our lives as workers in the world and our lives as Christians? If Christianity means following Christ, is it not a religion for a small minority, a spiritual élite? Does it not mean the repudiation of the great mass of society, and a hearty contempt for the weak and the poor? Yet surely such an attitude is the exact opposite of the gracious mercy of Jesus Christ, who came to the publicans and sinners, the weak and the poor, the erring and the hopeless. Are those who belong to Jesus only a few, or are they many? He died on the cross alone, abandoned by his disciples. With him were crucified, not two of his followers, but two murderers. But they all stood beneath the cross, enemies and believers, doubters and cowards, revilers and devoted followers. His prayer, in that hour, and his forgiveness, was meant for them all, and for all their sins. The mercy and love of God are at work even in the midst of his enemies. It is the same Jesus Christ, who of his grace calls us to follow him, and whose grace saves the murderer who mocks him on the cross in his last hour.

And if we answer the call to discipleship, where will it lead us? What decisions and partings will it demand? To answer this question we shall have to go to him, for only he knows the answer. Only Jesus Christ, who bids us follow him, knows the journey's end. But we do know that it will be a road of boundless mercy. Discipleship means joy.

In the modern world it seems so difficult to walk with absolute certainty in the narrow way of ecclesiastical decision and yet remain in the broad open spaces of the universal love of Christ, of the patience, mercy and 'philanthropy' of God (Titus 3.4) for the weak and the ungodly. Yet somehow or other we must combine the two, or else we shall follow the paths of men. May God grant us joy as we strive earnestly to follow the way of discipleship. May we be enabled to say 'No' to sin and 'Yes' to the sinner. May we withstand our foes, and yet hold out to them the Word of the gospel which woos and wins the souls of men. 'Come unto me, all ye that labour and are heavy laden, and I will give you rest. Take my yoke upon you, and learn of me, for I am meek and lowly in heart: and ye shall find rest unto your souls. For my yoke is easy, and my burden is light' (Matt. 11.28 ff).

Part One

GRACE AND DISCIPLESHIP

I   COSTLY GRACE

CHEAP grace is the deadly enemy of our Church. We are fighting to-day for costly grace.

Cheap grace means grace sold on the market like cheapjack's wares. The sacraments, the forgiveness of sin, and the consolations of religion are thrown away at cut prices. Grace is represented as the Church's inexhaustible treasury, from which she showers blessings with generous hands, without asking questions or fixing limits. Grace without price; grace without cost! The essence of grace, we suppose, is that the account has been paid in advance; and, because it has been paid, everything can be had for nothing. Since the cost was infinite, the possibilities of using and spending it are infinite. What would grace be if it were not cheap?

Cheap grace means grace as a doctrine, a principle, a system. It means forgiveness of sins proclaimed as a general truth, the love of God taught as the Christian 'conception' of God. An intellectual assent to that idea is held to be of itself sufficient to secure remission of sins. The Church which holds the correct doctrine of grace has, it is supposed, *ipso facto* a part in that grace. In such a Church the world finds a cheap covering for its sins; no contrition is required, still less any real desire to be delivered from sin. Cheap grace therefore amounts to a denial of the living Word of God, in fact, a denial of the Incarnation of the Word of God.

Cheap grace means the justification of sin without the justification of the sinner. Grace alone does everything, they say, and so everything can remain as it was before. 'All for sin could not atone.' The world goes on in the same old way, and we are still sinners 'even in the best life' as Luther said. Well, then, let the Christian live like the rest of the world, let him model himself on the world's standards in every sphere of life, and not presumptuously aspire to live a different life under grace from his old life under sin. That was the heresy of the enthusiasts, the Anabaptists

35

and their kind. Let the Christian beware of rebelling against the free and boundless grace of God and desecrating it. Let him not attempt to erect a new religion of the letter by endeavouring to live a life of obedience to the commandments of Jesus Christ! The world has been justified by grace. The Christian knows that, and takes it seriously. He knows he must not strive against this indispensable grace. Therefore – let him live like the rest of the world! Of course he would like to go and do something extra-ordinary, and it does demand a good deal of self-restraint to refrain from the attempt and content himself with living as the world lives. Yet it is imperative for the Christian to achieve renunciation, to practise self-effacement, to distinguish his life from the life of the world. He must let grace be grace indeed, otherwise he will destroy the world's faith in the free gift of grace. Let the Christian rest content with his worldliness and with this renunciation of any higher standard than the world. He is doing it for the sake of the world rather than for the sake of grace. Let him be comforted and rest assured in his possession of this grace – for grace alone does everything. Instead of following Christ, let the Christian enjoy the consolations of his grace! That is what we mean by cheap grace, the grace which amounts to the justification of sin without the justification of the repentant sinner who departs from sin and from whom sin departs. Cheap grace is not the kind of forgiveness of sin which frees us from the toils of sin. Cheap grace is the grace we bestow on ourselves.

Cheap grace is the preaching of forgiveness without requiring repentance, baptism without church discipline, Communion with-out confession, absolution without personal confession. Cheap grace is grace without discipleship, grace without the cross, grace without Jesus Christ, living and incarnate.

Costly grace is the treasure hidden in the field; for the sake of it a man will gladly go and sell all that he has. It is the pearl of great price to buy which the merchant will sell all his goods. It is the kingly rule of Christ, for whose sake a man will pluck out the eye which causes him to stumble, it is the call of Jesus Christ at which the disciple leaves his nets and follows him.

Costly grace is the gospel which must be *sought* again and again, the gift which must be *asked* for, the door at which a man must *knock*.

Such grace is *costly* because it calls us to follow, and it is *grace* because it calls us to follow *Jesus Christ*. It is costly because it costs a man his life, and it is grace because it gives a man the only true life. It is costly because it condemns sin, and grace because it justifies the sinner. Above all, it is *costly* because it cost God the life of his Son: 'ye were bought at a price', and what has cost God much cannot be cheap for us. Above all, it is *grace* because God did not reckon his Son too dear a price to pay for our life, but delivered him up for us. Costly grace is the Incarnation of God.

Costly grace is the sanctuary of God; it has to be protected from the world, and not thrown to the dogs. It is therefore the living word, the Word of God, which he speaks as it pleases him. Costly grace confronts us as a gracious call to follow Jesus, it comes as a word of forgiveness to the broken spirit and the contrite heart. Grace is costly because it compels a man to submit to the yoke of Christ and follow him; it is grace because Jesus says: 'My yoke is easy and my burden is light.'

On two separate occasions Peter received the call, 'Follow me.' It was the first and last word Jesus spoke to his disciple (Mark 1.17; John 21.22). A whole life lies between these two calls. The first occasion was by the lake of Gennesareth, when Peter left his nets and his craft and followed Jesus at his word. The second occasion is when the Risen Lord finds him back again at his old trade. Once again it is by the lake of Gennesareth, and once again the call is: 'Follow me.' Between the two calls lay a whole life of discipleship in the following of Christ. Half-way between them comes Peter's confession, when he acknowledged Jesus as the Christ of God. Three times Peter hears the same proclamation that Christ is his Lord and God – at the beginning, at the end, and at Caesarea Philippi. Each time it is the same grace of Christ which calls to him 'Follow me' and which reveals itself to him in his confession of the Son of God. Three times on Peter's way did

37

grace arrest him, the one grace proclaimed in three different ways.

This grace was certainly not self-bestowed. It was the grace of Christ himself, now prevailing upon the disciple to leave all and follow him, now working in him that confession which to the world must sound like the ultimate blasphemy, now inviting Peter to the supreme fellowship of martyrdom for the Lord he had denied, and thereby forgiving him all his sins. In the life of Peter grace and discipleship are inseparable. He had received the grace which costs.

As Christianity spread, and the Church became more secularized, this realization of the costliness of grace gradually faded. The world was christianized, and grace became its common property. It was to be had at low cost. Yet the Church of Rome did not altogether lose the earlier vision. It is highly significant that the Church was astute enough to find room for the monastic movement, and to prevent it from lapsing into schism. Here on the outer fringe of the Church was a place where the older vision was kept alive. Here men still remembered that grace costs, that grace means following Christ. Here they left all they had for Christ's sake, and endeavoured daily to practise his rigorous commands. Thus monasticism became a living protest against the secularization of Christianity and the cheapening of grace. But the Church was wise enough to tolerate this protest, and to prevent it from developing to its logical conclusion. It thus succeeded in relativizing it, even using it in order to justify the secularization of its own life. Monasticism was represented as an individual achievement which the mass of the laity could not be expected to emulate. By thus limiting the application of the commandments of Jesus to a restricted group of specialists, the Church evolved the fatal conception of the double standard – a maximum and a minimum standard of Christian obedience. Whenever the Church was accused of being too secularized, it could always point to monasticism as an opportunity of living a higher life within the fold, and thus justify the other possibility of a lower standard of life for others. And so we get the paradoxical result that monasticism, whose mission was to preserve in the Church of Rome the primitive Christian realization of the costliness of grace, afforded conclusive justification for the secularization of the Church. By and large, the fatal error of monasticism lay not so much in its rigorism (though even here there was a good deal of misunderstanding of the precise content of the will of Jesus) as in the extent to which it departed from genuine Christianity by setting up itself as the individual achievement of a select few, and so claiming a special merit of its own.

When the Reformation came, the providence of God raised Martin Luther to restore the gospel of pure, costly grace. Luther passed through the cloister; he was a monk, and all this was part of the divine plan. Luther had left all to follow Christ on the path of absolute obedience. He had renounced the world in order to live the Christian life. He had learnt obedience to Christ and to his Church, because only he who is obedient can believe. The call to the cloister demanded of Luther the complete surrender of his life. But God shattered all his hopes. He showed him through the Scriptures that the following of Christ is not the achievement or merit of a select few, but the divine command to all Christians without distinction. Monasticism had transformed the humble work of discipleship into the meritorious activity of the saints, and the self-renunciation of discipleship into the flagrant spiritual self-assertion of the 'religious'. The world had crept into the very heart of the monastic life, and was once more making havoc. The monk's attempt to flee from the world turned out to be a subtle form of love for the world. The bottom having thus been knocked out of the religious life, Luther laid hold upon grace. Just as the whole world of monasticism was crashing about him in ruins, he saw God in Christ stretching forth his hand to save. He grasped that hand in faith, believing that 'after all, nothing we can do is of any avail, however good a life we live'. The grace which gave itself to him was a costly grace, and it shattered his whole existence. Once more he must leave his nets and follow. The first time was when he entered the monastery, when he had left everything behind except his pious self. This time even that was taken from him. He obeyed the call, not through any merit of his own, but

39

simply through the grace of God. Luther did not hear the word: 'Of course you have sinned, but now everything is forgiven, so you can stay as you are and enjoy the consolations of forgiveness.' No, Luther had to leave the cloister and go back to the world, not because the world in itself was good and holy, but because even the cloister was only a part of the world.

Luther's return from the cloister to the world was the worst blow the world had suffered since the days of early Christianity. The renunciation he made when he became a monk was child's play compared with that which he had to make when he returned to the world. Now came the frontal assault. The only way to follow Jesus was by living in the world. Hitherto the Christian life had been the achievement of a few choice spirits under the exceptionally favourable conditions of monasticism; now it is a duty laid on every Christian living in the world. The commandment of Jesus must be accorded perfect obedience in one's daily vocation of life. The conflict between the life of the Christian and the life of the world was thus thrown into the sharpest possible relief. It was a hand-to-hand conflict between the Christian and the world.

It is a fatal misunderstanding of Luther's action to suppose that his rediscovery of the gospel of pure grace offered a general dispensation from obedience to the command of Jesus, or that it was the great discovery of the Reformation that God's forgiving grace automatically conferred upon the world both righteousness and holiness. On the contrary, for Luther the Christian's worldly calling is sanctified only in so far as that calling registers the final, radical protest against the world. Only in so far as the Christian's secular calling is exercised in the following of Jesus does it receive from the gospel new sanction and justification. It was not the justification of sin, but the justification of the sinner that drove Luther from the cloister back into the world. The grace he had received was costly grace. It was grace, for it was like water on parched ground, comfort in tribulation, freedom from the bondage of a self-chosen way, and forgiveness of all his sins. And it was costly, for, so far from dispensing him from good works, it meant that he must take the call to discipleship more seriously than ever before. It was grace because it cost so much, and it cost so much because it was grace. That was the secret of the gospel of the Reformation – the justification of the sinner.

Yet the outcome of the Reformation was the victory, not of Luther's perception of grace in all its purity and costliness, but of the vigilant religious instinct of man for the place where grace is to be obtained at the cheapest price. All that was needed was a subtle and almost imperceptible change of emphasis, and the damage was done. Luther had taught that man cannot stand before God, however religious his works and ways may be, because at bottom he is always seeking his own interests. In the depth of his misery, Luther had grasped by faith the free and unconditional forgiveness of all his sins. That experience taught him that this grace had cost him his very life, and must continue to cost him the same price day by day. So far from dispensing him from discipleship, this grace only made him a more earnest disciple. When he spoke of grace, Luther always implied as a corollary that it cost him his own life, the life which was now for the first time subjected to the absolute obedience of Christ. Only so could he speak of grace. Luther had said that grace alone can save; his followers took up his doctrine and repeated it word for word. But they left out its invariable corollary, the obligation of discipleship. There was no need for Luther always to mention that corollary explicitly for he always spoke as one who had been led by grace to the strictest following of Christ. Judged by the standard of Luther's doctrine, that of his follower was unassailable, and yet their orthodoxy spelt the end and destruction of the Reformation as the revelation on earth of the costly grace of God. The justification of the sinner in the world degenerated into the justification of sin and the world. Costly grace was turned into cheap grace without discipleship.

Luther had said that all we can do is of no avail, however good a life we live. He had said that nothing can avail us in the sight of God but 'the grace and favour which confers the forgiveness of sin'. But he spoke as one who knew that at the very moment of his crisis he was called to leave all that he had a second time and follow Jesus. The recognition of grace was his final, radical breach with his besetting sin, but it was never the justification of that sin. By laying hold of God's forgiveness, he made the final, radical renunciation of a self-willed life, and this breach was such that it led inevitably to a serious following of Christ. He always looked upon it as the answer to a sum, but an answer which had been arrived at by God, not by man. But then his followers changed the 'answer' into the data for a calculation of their own. That was the root of the trouble. If grace is God's answer, the gift of Christian life, then we cannot for a moment dispense with following Christ. But if grace is the data for my Christian life, it means that I set out to live the Christian life in the world with all my sins justified beforehand. I can go and sin as much as I like, and rely on this grace to forgive me, for after all the world is justified in principle by grace. I can therefore cling to my bourgeois secular existence, and remain as I was before, but with the added assurance that the grace of God will cover me. It is under the influence of this kind of 'grace' that the world has been made 'Christian', but at the cost of secularizing the Christian religion as never before. The antithesis between the Christian life and the life of bourgeois respectability is at an end. The Christian life comes to mean nothing more than living in the world and as the world, in being no different from the world, in fact, in being prohibited from being different from the world for the sake of grace. The upshot of it all is that my only duty as a Christian is to leave the world for an hour or so on a Sunday morning and go to church to be assured that my sins are all forgiven. I need no longer try to follow Christ, for cheap grace, the bitterest foe of discipleship, which true discipleship must loathe and detest, has freed me from that. Grace as the data for our calculations means grace at the cheapest price, but grace as the answer to the sum means costly grace. It is terrifying to realize what use can be made of a genuine evangelical doctrine. In both cases we have the identical formula – 'justification by faith alone'. Yet the misuse of the formula leads to the complete destruction of its very essence.

At the end of a life spent in the pursuit of knowledge Faust has to confess:

'I now do see that we can nothing know.'

That is the answer to a sum, it is the outcome of a long experience. But as Kierkegaard observed, it is quite a different thing when a freshman comes up to the university and uses the same sentiment to justify his indolence. As the answer to a sum it is perfectly true, but as the initial data it is a piece of self-deception. For acquired knowledge cannot be divorced from the existence in which it is acquired. The only man who has the right to say that he is justified by grace alone is the man who has left all to follow Christ. Such a man knows that the call to discipleship is a gift of grace, and that the call is inseparable from the grace. But those who try to use this grace as a dispensation from following Christ are simply deceiving themselves.

But, we may ask, did not Luther himself come perilously near to this perversion in the understanding of grace? What about his *Pecca fortiter, sed fortius fide et gaude in Christo* ('Sin boldly, but believe and rejoice in Christ more boldly still')? You are a sinner, anyway, and there is nothing you can do about it. Whether you are a monk or a man of the world, a religious man or a bad one, you can never escape the toils of the world or from sin. So put a bold face on it, and all the more because you can rely on the *opus operatum* of grace. Is this the proclamation of cheap grace, naked and unashamed, the *carte blanche* for sin, the end of all discipleship? Is this a blasphemous encouragement to sin boldly and rely on grace? Is there a more diabolical abuse of grace than to sin and rely on the grace which God has given? Is not the Roman Catechism quite right in denouncing this as the sin against the Holy Ghost?

If we are to understand this saying of Luther's, everything depends on applying the distinction between the data and the answer to the sum. If we make Luther's formula a premiss for our doctrine of grace, we are conjuring up the spectre of cheap grace. But Luther's formula is meant to be taken, not as the premiss, but

43

as the conclusion, the answer to the sum, the coping-stone, his very last word on the subject. Taken as the premiss, *pecca fortiter* acquires the character of an ethical principle, a principle of grace to which the principle of *pecca fortiter* must correspond. That means the justification of sin, and it turns Luther's formula into its very opposite. For Luther 'sin boldly' could only be his very last refuge, the consolation for one whose attempts to follow Christ had taught him that he can never become sinless, who in his fear of sin despairs of the grace of God. As Luther saw it, 'sin boldly' did not happen to be a fundamental acknowledgement of his disobedient life; it was the gospel of the grace of God before which we are always and in every circumstance sinners. Yet that grace seeks us and justifies us, sinners though we are. Take courage and confess your sin, says Luther, do not try to run away from it, but believe more boldly still. You are a sinner, so be a sinner, and don't try to become what you are not. Yes, and become a sinner again and again every day, and be bold about it. But to whom can such words be addressed, except to those who from the bottom of their hearts make a daily renunciation of sin and of every barrier which hinders them from following Christ, but who nevertheless are troubled by their daily faithlessness and sin? Who can hear these words without endangering his faith but he who hears their consolation as a renewed summons to follow Christ? Interpreted in this way, these words of Luther become a testimony to the costliness of grace, the only genuine kind of grace there is.

Grace interpreted as a principle, *pecca fortiter* as a principle, grace at a low cost, is in the last resort simply a new law, which brings neither help nor freedom. Grace as a living word, *pecca fortiter* as our comfort in tribulation and as a summons to discipleship, costly grace is the only pure grace, which really forgives sins and gives freedom to the sinner.

We Lutherans have gathered like eagles round the carcase of cheap grace, and there we have drunk of the poison which has killed the life of following Christ. It is true, of course, that we have paid the doctrine of pure grace divine honours unparalleled in Christendom, in fact we have exalted that doctrine to the position of God himself. Everywhere Luther's formula has been repeated, but its truth perverted into self-deception. So long as our Church holds the correct doctrine of justification, there is no doubt whatever that she is a justified Church! So they said, thinking that we must vindicate our Lutheran heritage by making this grace available on the cheapest and easiest terms. To be 'Lutheran' must mean that we leave the following of Christ to legalists, Calvinists and enthusiasts – and all this for the sake of grace. We justified the world, and condemned as heretics those who tried to follow Christ. The result was that a nation became Christian and Lutheran, but at the cost of true discipleship. The price it was called upon to pay was all too cheap. Cheap grace had won the day.

But do we also realize that this cheap grace has turned back upon us like a boomerang? The price we are having to pay to-day in the shape of the collapse of the organized church is only the inevitable consequence of our policy of making grace available to all at too low a cost. We gave away the word and sacraments wholesale, we baptized, confirmed, and absolved a whole nation unasked and without condition. Our humanitarian sentiment made us give that which was holy to the scornful and unbelieving. We poured forth unending streams of grace. But the call to follow Jesus in the narrow way was hardly ever heard. Where were those truths which impelled the early Church to institute the catechumenate, which enabled a strict watch to be kept over the frontier between the Church and the world, and afforded adequate protection for costly grace? What had happened to all those warnings of Luther's against preaching the gospel in such a manner as to make men rest secure in their ungodly living? Was there ever a more terrible or disastrous instance of the Christianizing of the world than this? What are those three thousand Saxons put to death by Charlemagne compared with the millions of spiritual corpses in our country to-day? With us it has been abundantly proved that the sins of the fathers are visited upon the children unto the third and fourth generations. Cheap grace has turned out to be utterly merciless to our Evangelical Church.

This cheap grace has been no less disastrous to our own spiritual lives. Instead of opening up the way to Christ it has closed it. Instead of calling us to follow Christ, it has hardened us in our disobedience. Perhaps we had once heard the gracious call to follow him, and had at this command even taken the first few steps along the path of discipleship in the discipline of obedience, only to find ourselves confronted by the word of cheap grace. Was that not merciless and hard? The only effect that such a word could have on us was to bar our way to progress, and seduce us to the mediocre level of the world, quenching the joy of discipleship by telling us that we were following a way of our own choosing, that we were spending our strength and disciplining ourselves in vain – all of which was not merely useless, but extremely dangerous. After all, we were told, our salvation had already been accomplished by the grace of God. The smoking flax was mercilessly extinguished. It was unkind to speak to men like this, for such a cheap offer could only leave them bewildered and tempt them from the way to which they had been called by Christ. Having laid hold on cheap grace, they were barred for ever from the knowledge of costly grace. Deceived and weakened, men felt that they were strong now that they were in possession of this cheap grace – whereas they had in fact lost the power to live the life of discipleship and obedience. The word of cheap grace has been the ruin of more Christians than any commandment of works.

In our subsequent chapters we shall try to find a message for those who are troubled by this problem, and for whom the word of grace has been emptied of all its meaning. This message must be spoken for the sake of truth, for those among us who confess that through cheap grace they have lost the following of Christ and further, with the following of Christ, have lost the understanding of costly grace. To put it quite simply, we must undertake this task because we are now ready to admit that we no longer stand in the path of true discipleship. We confess that, although our Church is orthodox as far as her doctrine of grace is concerned, we are no longer sure that we are members of a Church which follows its Lord. We must therefore attempt to recover a true understanding of the mutual relation between grace and discipleship. The issue can no longer be evaded. It is becoming clearer every day that the most urgent problem besetting our Church is this: How can we live the Christian life in the modern world?

Happy are they who have reached the end of the road we seek to tread, who are astonished to discover the by no means self-evident truth that grace is costly just because it is the grace of God in Jesus Christ. Happy are the simple followers of Jesus Christ who have been overcome by his grace, and are able to sing the praises of the all-sufficient grace of Christ with humbleness of heart. Happy are they who, knowing that grace, can live in the world without being of it, who, by following Jesus Christ, are so assured of their heavenly citizenship that they are truly free to live their lives in this world. Happy are they who know that discipleship simply means the life which springs from grace, and that grace simply means discipleship. Happy are they who have become Christians in this sense of the word. For them the word of grace has proved a fount of mercy.

2 THE CALL TO DISCIPLESHIP

And as he passed by he saw Levi, the son of Alphæus, sitting at the place of toll, and he saith unto him, Follow me. And he arose and followed him. (Mark 2.14)

THE call goes forth, and is at once followed by the response of obedience. The response of the disciples is an act of obedience, not a confession of faith in Jesus. How could the call immediately evoke obedience? The story is a stumbling-block for the natural reason, and it is no wonder that frantic attempts have been made to separate the two events. By hook or by crook a bridge must be found between them. Something must have happened in between, some psychological or historical event. Thus we get the stupid question: Surely the publican must have known Jesus before, and that previous acquaintance explains his readiness to hear the Master's call. Unfortunately our text is ruthlessly silent on this point, and in fact it regards the immediate sequence of call and response as a matter of crucial importance. It displays not the slightest interest in the psychological reasons for a man's religious decisions. And why? For the simple reason that the cause behind the immediate following of call by response is Jesus Christ himself. It is Jesus who calls, and because it is Jesus, Levi follows at once. This encounter is a testimony to the absolute, direct, and unaccountable authority of Jesus. There is no need of any preliminaries, and no other consequence but obedience to the call. Because Jesus is the Christ, he has the authority to call and to demand obedience to his word. Jesus summons men to follow him not as a teacher or a pattern of the good life, but as the Christ, the Son of God. In this short text Jesus Christ and his claim are proclaimed to men. Not a word of praise is given to the disciple for his decision for Christ. We are not expected to contemplate the disciple, but only him who calls, and his absolute authority.

According to our text, there is no road to faith or discipleship, no other road – only obedience to the call of Jesus.

And what does the text inform us about the content of discipleship? Follow me, run along behind me! That is all. To follow in his steps is something which is void of all content. It gives us no intelligible programme for a way of life, no goal or ideal to strive after. It is not a cause which human calculation might deem worthy of our devotion, even the devotion of ourselves. What happens? At the call, Levi leaves all that he has – but not because he thinks that he might be doing something worth while, but simply for the sake of the call. Otherwise he cannot follow in the steps of Jesus. This act on Levi's part has not the slightest value in itself, it is quite devoid of significance and unworthy of consideration. The disciple simply burns his boats and goes ahead. He is called out, and has to forsake his old life in order that he may 'exist' in the strictest sense of the word. The old life is left behind, and completely surrendered. The disciple is dragged out of his relative security into a life of absolute insecurity (that is, in truth, into the absolute security and safety of the fellowship of Jesus), from a life which is observable and calculable (it is, in fact, quite incalculable) into a life where everything is unobservable and fortuitous (that is, into one which is necessary and calculable), out of the realm of finite (which is in truth the infinite) into the realm of infinite possibilities (which is the one liberating reality). Again it is no universal law. Rather is it the exact opposite of all legality. It is nothing else than bondage to Jesus Christ alone, completely breaking through every programme, every ideal, every set of laws. No other significance is possible, since Jesus is the only significance. Beside Jesus nothing has any significance. He alone matters.

When we are called to follow Christ, we are summoned to an exclusive attachment to his person. The grace of his call bursts all the bonds of legalism. It is a gracious call, a gracious commandment. It transcends the difference between the law and the gospel. Christ calls, the disciple follows; that is grace and commandment in one. 'I will walk at liberty, for I seek thy commandments' (Ps. 119.45).

Discipleship means adherence to Christ, and, because Christ is the object of that adherence, it must take the form of discipleship. An abstract Christology, a doctrinal system, a general religious knowledge on the subject of grace or on the forgiveness of sins, render discipleship superfluous, and in fact they positively exclude any idea of discipleship whatever, and are essentially inimical to the whole conception of following Christ. With an abstract idea it is possible to enter into a relation of formal knowledge, to become enthusiastic about it, and perhaps even to put it into practice; but it can never be followed in personal obedience. Christianity without the living Christ is inevitably Christianity without discipleship, and Christianity without discipleship is always Christianity without Christ. It remains an abstract idea, a myth which has a place for the Fatherhood of God, but omits Christ as the living Son. And a Christianity of that kind is nothing more nor less than the end of discipleship. In such a religion there is trust in God, but no following of Christ. Because the Son of God became Man, because he is the Mediator, for that reason alone the only true relation we can have with him is to follow him. Discipleship is bound to Christ as the Mediator, and where it is properly understood, it necessarily implies faith in the Son of God as the Mediator. Only the Mediator, the God-Man, can call men to follow him.

Discipleship without Jesus Christ is a way of our own choosing. It may be the ideal way, It may even lead to martyrdom, but it is devoid of all promise. Jesus will certainly reject it.

And they went to another village. And as they went in the way, a certain man said unto him, I will follow thee whithersoever thou goest. And Jesus said unto him, The foxes have holes, and the birds of heaven have nests, but the Son of man hath not where to lay his head. And he said unto another, Follow me. But he said, Lord, suffer me first to go and bury my father. But he said unto him, Leave the dead to bury their dead, but go thou and publish abroad the kingdom of God. And another said, I will follow thee, Lord; but suffer me first to bid farewell to them that are at my house. But Jesus said unto him, No man, having put his hand unto the plough, and looking back, is fit for the kingdom of God. (Luke 9.57-62)

The first disciple offers to follow Jesus without waiting to be called. Jesus damps his ardour by warning him that he does not know what he is doing. In fact he is quite incapable of knowing. That is the meaning of Jesus' answer – he shows the would-be disciple what life with him involves. We hear the words of One who is on his way to the cross, whose whole life is summed up in the Apostles' Creed by the word 'suffered'. No man can choose such a life for himself. No man can call himself to such a destiny, says Jesus, and his word stays unanswered. The gulf between a voluntary offer to follow and genuine discipleship is clear.

But where Jesus calls, he bridges the widest gulf. The second would-be disciple wants to bury his father before he starts to follow. He is held bound by the trammels of the law. He knows what he wants and what he must do. Let him first fulfil the law, and then let him follow. A definite legal ordinance acts as a barrier between Jesus and the man he has called. But the call of Jesus is stronger than the barrier. At this critical moment nothing on earth, however sacred, must be allowed to come between Jesus and the man he has called – not even the law itself. Now, if never before, the law must be broken for the sake of Jesus; it forfeits all its rights if it acts as a barrier to discipleship. Therefore Jesus emerges at this point as the opponent of the law, and commands a man to follow him. Only the Christ can speak in this fashion. He alone has the last word. His would-be follower cannot kick against the pricks. This call, this grace, is irresistible.

The third would-be disciple, like the first, thinks that following Christ means that he must make the offer on his own initiative, as if it were a career he had mapped out for himself. There is however a difference between the first would-be disciple and the third, for the third is bold enough to stipulate his own terms. Unfortunately, however, he lands himself in a hopeless inconsistency, for although he is ready enough to throw in his lot with Jesus, he succeeds in putting up a barrier between himself and the Master. 'Suffer me first.' He wants to follow, but feels obliged to insist on his own terms. Discipleship to him is a possibility which can only be realized when certain conditions have been fulfilled.

This is to reduce discipleship to the level of the human under-standing. First you must do this and then you must do that. There is a right time for everything. The disciple places himself at the Master's disposal, but at the same time retains the right to dictate his own terms. But then discipleship is no longer discipleship, but a programme of our own to be arranged to suit ourselves, and to be judged in accordance with the standards of a rational ethic. The trouble about this third would-be disciple is that at the very moment he expresses his willingness to follow, he ceases to want to follow at all. By making his offer on his own terms, he alters the whole position, for discipleship can tolerate no conditions which might come between Jesus and our obedience to him. Hence the third disciple finds himself at loggerheads not only with Jesus, but also with himself. His desires conflict not only with what Jesus wants, but also with what he wants himself. He judges himself, and decides against himself, and all this by saying, 'Suffer me first.' The answer of Jesus graphically proves to him that he is at variance with himself and that excludes discipleship. 'No man, having put his hand to the plough and looking back, is fit for the kingdom of God.'

If we would follow Jesus we must take certain definite steps. The first step, which follows the call, cuts the disciple off from his previous existence. The call to follow at once produces a new situation. To stay in the old situation makes discipleship impos-sible. Levi must leave the receipt of custom and Peter his nets in order to follow Jesus. One would have thought that nothing so drastic was necessary at such an early stage. Could not Jesus have initiated the publican into some new religious experience, and leave them as they were before? He could have done so, had he not been the incarnate Son of God. But since he is the Christ, he must make it clear from the start that his word is not an abstract doctrine, but the re-creation of the whole life of man. The only right and proper way is quite literally to go with Jesus. The call to follow implies that there is only one way of believing on Jesus Christ, and that is by leaving all and going with the incarnate Son of God.

The first step places the disciple in the situation where faith is possible. If he refuses to follow and stays behind, he does not learn how to believe. He who is called must go out of his situation in which he cannot believe, into the situation in which, first and foremost, faith is possible. But this step is not the first stage of a career. Its sole justification is that it brings the disciple into fellowship with Jesus which will be victorious. So long as Levi sits at the receipt of custom, and Peter at his nets, they could both pursue their trade honestly and dutifully, and they might both enjoy religious experiences, old and new. But if they want to believe in God, the only way is to follow his incarnate Son.

Until that day, everything had been different. They could remain in obscurity, pursuing their work as the quiet in the land, observing the law and waiting for the coming of the Messiah. But now he has come, and his call goes forth. Faith can no longer mean sitting still and waiting – they must rise and follow him. The call frees them from all earthly ties, and binds them to Jesus Christ alone. They must burn their boats and plunge into absolute insecurity in order to learn the demand and the gift of Christ. Had Levi stayed at his post, Jesus might have been his present help in trouble, but not the Lord of his whole life. In other words Levi would never have learnt to believe. The new situation must be created, in which it is possible to believe on Jesus as God incarnate; that is the impossible situation in which everything is staked solely on the word of Jesus. Peter had to leave the ship and risk his life on the sea, in order to learn both his own weakness and the almighty power of his Lord. If Peter had not taken the risk, he would never have learnt the meaning of faith. Before he can believe, the utterly impossible and ethically irresponsible situation on the waves of the sea must be displayed. The road to faith passes through obedience to the call of Jesus. Unless a definite step is demanded, the call vanishes into thin air, and if men imagine that they can follow Jesus without taking this step, they are deluding themselves like fanatics.

It is an extremely hazardous procedure to distinguish between a situation where faith is possible and one where it is not. We must first realize that there is nothing in the situation to tell us to which category it belongs. It is only the call of Jesus which makes it a situation where faith is possible. Secondly, a situation where faith is possible can never be demonstrated from the human side. Discipleship is not an offer man makes to Christ. It is only the call which creates the situation. Thirdly, this situation never possesses any intrinsic worth or merit of its own. It is only through the call that it receives its justification. Last, but not least, the situation in which faith is possible is itself only rendered possible through faith.

The idea of a situation in which faith is possible is only a way of stating the facts of a case in which the following two propositions hold good and are equally true: *only he who believes is obedient, and only he who is obedient believes.*

It is quite unbiblical to hold the first proposition without the second. We think we understand when we hear that obedience is possible only where there is faith. Does not obedience follow faith as good fruit grows on a good tree? First, faith, then obedience. If by that we mean that it is faith which justifies, and not the act of obedience, all well and good, for that is the essential and unexceptionable presupposition of all that follows. If however we make a chronological distinction between faith and obedience, and make obedience subsequent to faith, we are divorcing the one from the other – and then we get the practical question, when must obedience begin? Obedience remains separated from faith. From the point of view of justification it is necessary thus to separate them, but we must never lose sight of their essential unity. For faith is only real when there is obedience, never without it, and faith only becomes faith in the act of obedience.

Since, then, we cannot adequately speak of obedience as the consequence of faith, and since we must never forget the indissoluble unity of the two, we must place the one proposition that only he who believes is obedient alongside the other, that only he who is obedient believes. In the one case faith is the condition of obedience, and in the other obedience the condition of faith. In exactly the same way in which obedience is called the consequence of faith, it must also be called the presupposition of faith.

Only the obedient believe. If we are to believe, we must obey a concrete command. Without this preliminary step of obedience, our faith will only be pious humbug, and lead us to the grace which is not costly. Everything depends on the first step. It has a unique quality of its own. The first step of obedience makes Peter leave his nets, and later get out of the ship; it calls upon the young man to leave his riches. Only this new existence, created through obedience, can make faith possible.

This first step must be regarded to start with as an external work, which effects the change from one existence to another. It is a step within everybody's capacity, for it lies within the limits of human freedom. It is an act within the sphere of the natural law (*justitia civilis*) and in that sphere man is free. Although Peter cannot achieve his own conversion, he can leave his nets. In the gospels the very first step a man must take is an act which radically affects his whole existence. The Roman Catholic Church demanded this step as an extraordinary possibility which only monks could achieve, while the rest of the faithful must content themselves with an unconditional submission to the Church and its ordinances. The Lutheran confessions also significantly recognize the first step. Having dealt effectively with the danger of Pelagianism, they find it both possible and necessary to leave room for the first external act which is the essential preliminary to faith. This step there takes the form of an invitation to come to the Church where the word of salvation is proclaimed. To take this step it is not necessary to surrender one's freedom. Come to church! You can do that of your own free will. You can leave your home on a Sunday morning and come to hear the sermon. If you will not, you are of your own free will excluding yourself from the place where faith is a possibility. Thus the Lutheran confessions show their awareness of a situation where faith is a possibility, and of a situation where it is not. Admittedly they tend to soft-pedal it as though they were almost ashamed of it. But there it is, and it shows that they are just as aware as the gospels of the importance of the first external step.

Once we are sure of this point, we must add at once that this step is, and can never be more than, a purely external act and a dead work of the law, which can never of itself bring a man to Christ. As an external act the new existence is no better than the old. Even at the highest estimate it can only achieve a new law of life, a new way of living which is poles apart from the new life with Christ. If a drunkard signs the pledge, or a rich man gives all his money away, they are both of them freeing themselves from their slavery to alcohol or riches, but not from their bondage to themselves. They are still moving in their own little orbit, perhaps even more than they were before. They are still subject to the commandment of works, still as submerged in the death of the old life as they were before. Of course, the work has to be done, but of itself it can never deliver them from death, disobedience and ungodliness. If we think our first step is the pre-condition for faith and grace, we are already judged by our work, and entirely excluded from grace. Hence the term 'external work' includes everything we are accustomed to call 'disposition' or 'good intention', everything which the Roman Church means when it talks of *facere quod in se est*. If we take the first step with the deliberate intention of placing ourselves in the situation where faith is possible, even this possibility of faith will be nothing but a work. The new life it opens to us is still a life within the limits of our old existence, and therefore a complete misapprehension of the true nature of the new life. We are still in unbelief.

Nevertheless the external work must be done, for we still have to find our way into the situation where faith is possible. We must take a definite step. What does this mean? It means that we can only take this step aright if we fix our eyes not on the work we do, but on the word with which Jesus calls us to do it. Peter knows he dare not climb out of the ship in his own strength – his very first step would be his undoing. And so he cries, 'Lord, bid me come to thee upon the waters,' and Jesus answers: 'Come.' Christ must first call him, for the step can only be taken at his word. This call is his grace, which calls him out of death into the new life of obedience. But when once Christ has called him, Peter has no alternative – he must leave the ship and come to him. In the end, the first step of obedience proves to be an act of faith in the word of Christ. But we should completely misunderstand the nature of grace if we were to suppose that there was no need to take the first step, because faith was already there. Against that we must boldly assert that the step of obedience must be taken before faith can be possible. Unless he obeys, a man cannot believe.

Are you worried because you find it so hard to believe? No one should be surprised at the difficulty of faith, if there is some part of his life where he is consciously resisting or disobeying the commandment of Jesus. Is there some part of your life which you are refusing to surrender at his behest, some sinful passion, maybe, or some animosity, some hope, perhaps your ambition or your reason? If so, you must not be surprised that you have not received the Holy Spirit, that prayer is difficult, or that your request for faith remains unanswered. Go rather and be reconciled with your brother, renounce the sin which holds you fast – and then you will recover your faith! If you dismiss the word of God's command, you will not receive his word of grace. How can you hope to enter into communion with him when at some point in your life you are running away from him? The man who disobeys cannot believe, for only he who obeys can believe.

The gracious call of Jesus now becomes a stern command: Do this! Give up that! Leave the ship and come to me! When a man says he cannot obey the call of Jesus because he believes, or because he does not believe, Jesus says: 'First obey, perform the external work, renounce your attachments, give up the obstacles which separate you from the will of God. Do not say you have not got faith. You will not have it so long as you persist in disobedience and refuse to take the first step. Neither must you say that you have faith, and therefore there is no need for you to take the first step. You have not got faith so long as and because you will not take the first step but become hardened in your unbelief under the guise of humble faith.' It is a malicious subterfuge to argue like this, a sure sign of lack of faith, which leads in its turn to a lack of obedience. This is the disobedience of the 'believers';

when they are asked to obey, they simply confess their unbelief and leave it at that (Mark 9.24). You are trifling with the subject. If you believe, take the first step, it leads to Jesus Christ. If you don't believe, take the first step all the same, for you are bidden to take it. No one wants to know about your faith or unbelief, your orders are to perform the act of obedience on the spot. Then you will find yourself in the situation where faith becomes possible and where faith exists in the true sense of the word.

This situation is therefore not the consequence of our obedience, but the gift of him who commands obedience. Unless we are prepared to enter into that situation, our faith will be unreal, and we shall deceive ourselves. We cannot avoid that situation, for our supreme concern is with a right faith in Jesus Christ, and our objective is, and always will be faith, and faith alone ('from faith to faith', Rom. 1.17). If anyone rushes forward and challenges this point in an excess of Protestant zeal, let him ask himself whether he is not after all allowing himself to become an advocate of cheap grace. The truth is that so long as we hold both sides of the proposition together they contain nothing inconsistent with right belief, but as soon as one is divorced from the other, it is bound to prove a stumbling-block. 'Only those who believe obey' is what we say to that part of a believer's soul which obeys, and 'only those who obey believe' is what we say to that part of the soul of the obedient which believes. If the first half of the proposition stands alone, the believer is exposed to the danger of cheap grace, which is another word for damnation. If the second half stands alone, the believer is exposed to the danger of salvation through works, which is also another word for damnation.

At this point we may conveniently throw in a few observations of a pastoral character. In dealing with souls, it is essential for the pastor to bear in mind both sides of the proposition. When people complain, for instance, that they find it hard to believe, it is a sign of deliberate or unconscious disobedience. It is all too easy to put them off by offering the remedy of cheap grace. That only leaves the disease as bad as it was before, and makes the word of grace a sort of self-administered consolation, or a self-imparted absolution.

But when this happens, the poor man can no longer find any comfort in the words of priestly absolution – he has become deaf to the Word of God. And even if he absolves himself from his sins a thousand times, he has lost all capacity of faith in the true forgiveness, just because he has never really known it. Unbelief thrives on cheap grace, for it is determined to persist in disobedience. Clergy frequently come across cases like this nowadays. The outcome is usually that self-imparted absolution confirms the man in his disobedience, and makes him plead ignorance of the kindness as well as of the commandment of God. He complains that God's commandment is uncertain, and susceptible of different interpretations. At first he was aware enough of his disobedience, but with his increasing hardness of heart that awareness grows ever fainter, and in the end he becomes so enmeshed that he loses all capacity for hearing the Word, and faith is quite impossible. One can imagine him conversing thus with his pastor: 'I have lost the faith I once had.' 'You must listen to the Word as it is spoken to you in the sermon.' 'I do; but I cannot get anything out of it, it just falls on deaf ears as far as I'm concerned.' 'The trouble is, you don't really want to listen.' 'On the contrary, I do.' And here they generally break off, because the pastor is at a loss what to say next. He only remembers the first half of the proposition: 'Only those who believe obey.' But this does not help, for faith is just what this particular man finds impossible. The pastor feels himself confronted with the ultimate riddle of predestination. God grants faith to some and withholds it from others. So the pastor throws up the sponge and leaves the poor man to his fate. And yet this ought to be the turning-point of the interview. It is the complete turning-point. The pastor should give up arguing with him, and stop taking his difficulties seriously. That will really be in the man's own interest, for he is only trying to hide himself behind them. It is now time to take the bull by the horns, and say: 'Only those who obey believe.' Thus the flow of the conversation is interrupted, and the pastor can continue: 'You are disobedient, you are trying to keep some part of your life under your own control. That is what is preventing you from listening to Christ and believing in his grace. You cannot hear Christ because you are wilfully disobedient. Somewhere in your heart you are refusing to listen to his call. Your difficulty is your sins.' Christ now enters the lists again and comes to grips with the devil, who until now has been hiding under the cloak of cheap grace. It is all-important that the pastor should be ready with both sides of the proposition: 'Only those who obey can believe, and only those who believe can obey.' In the name of Christ he must exhort the man to obedience, to action, to take the first step. He must say: 'Tear yourself away from all other attachments, and follow him.' For at this stage, the first step is what matters most. The strong point which the refractory sinner had occupied must be stormed, for in it Christ cannot be heard. The truant must be dragged from the hiding-place which he has built for himself. Only then can he recover the freedom to see, hear, and believe. Of course, though it is a work, the first step entails no merit in the sight of Christ – it can never be more than a dead work. Even so Peter has to get out of the ship before he can believe.

Briefly, the position is this. Our sinner has drugged himself with cheap and easy grace by accepting the proposition that only those who believe can obey. He persists in disobedience, and seeks consolation by absolving himself. This only serves to deaden his ears to the Word of God. We cannot breach the fortress so long as we merely repeat the proposition which affords him his self-defence. So we must make for the turning point without further ado, and exhort him to obedience – 'Only those who obey can believe.'

Will that lead him astray, and encourage him to trust in his own works? Far from it. He will the more easily realize that his faith is no genuine one at all. He will be rescued from his entanglement by being compelled to come to a definite decision. In this way his ears are opened once more for the call of Jesus to faith and discipleship.

This brings us to the story of the rich young man.

And behold, one came and said unto him, Good Master, what

good things shall I do, that I may have eternal life? And he said unto him, Why callest thou me good? Thereis none good but one, that is, God: but if thou wilt enter into life, keep the commandments. He saith unto him, Which? Jesus said, Thou shalt do no murder, Thou shalt not commit adultery, Thou shalt not steal, Thou shalt not bear false witness, Honour thy father and thy mother: and, Thou shalt love thy neighbour as thyself. The young man saith unto him, All these things have I kept from my youth up: What lack I yet? Jesus said unto him, If thou wilt be perfect, go and sell that thou hast, and give to the poor, and thou shalt have treasure in heaven: and come and follow me. But when the young man heard that saying, he went away sorrowful: for he had great possessions. (Matt. 19.16-22)

The young man's enquiry about eternal life is an enquiry about salvation, the only ultimate, serious question in the world. But it is not easy to formulate in the right terms. This is shown by the way the young man obviously intends to ask one question, but actually asks another. By so doing he succeeds in avoiding the real issue. For he addresses his question to the 'good master'. He wants to hear the opinion and receive the advice of the good master, and consult the good teacher on this specific problem. He thus succeeds in giving himself away on two points. First, he feels this is such an important question that Jesus must have something significant to say about it. Secondly, what he expects from the good master and great teacher is a weighty pronouncement, but certainly not a direction from God which would make an absolute claim on his obedience. Eternal life is for him an academic problem which is worth discussing with a 'good master'. But the very first word of Jesus' answer is a rude shock to him: 'Why callest thou me good? One there is who is good.' The question has betrayed his real feelings. He wanted to speak about eternal life to a good rabbi. He now realizes he is talking not to a good master, but to God himself, and therefore the only answer he receives from the Son of God is an unmistakable pointer to the commandment of the One God. He will not receive the answer of 'good master', a personal opinion to supplement the revealed will of God. Jesus points away from himself to God who alone is good and at once proves himself thereby to be the perfect Son of God. The questioner stands before God himself and is shown up as one who is trying to evade the revealed will of God, while all the time he knows that will already. The young man knows the commandments. But such is his situation that he cannot be satisfied with them but wants to go beyond them. Jesus sees through his question and knows it to be the question of a piety shaped by and centred in the self. Why does he pretend that he has for long been ignorant of the answer? Why does he accuse God of leaving him so long in ignorance of this fundamental problem of life? So already the young man is caught and summoned to the judgement seat of God. He is challenged to drop the academic question, and recalled to a simple obedience to the will of God as it has been revealed.

Once more the young man tries to evade the issue by posing a second question: 'Which?' The very devil lurks beneath this question. The young man knew he was caught in a trap, and this was the only way out. Of course, he knows the commandments. But who can know, out of the abundance of commandments, which apply to him in his present situation? The revelation of the commandments is ambiguous, not clear, says the young man. Once again he does not see the commandments except in relation to himself and his own problems and conflicts. He neglects the unmistakable command of God for the very interesting, but purely human concern of his own moral difficulties. His mistake lies not so much in his awareness of those difficulties as in his attempt to play them off against the commandments of God. In fact, the very purpose for which these commandments were given was to solve these difficulties. Moral difficulties were the first consequence of the Fall, and are themselves the outcome of 'Man in Revolt' against God. The Serpent in Paradise put them into the mind of the first man by asking, 'Hath God said?' Until then the divine command had been clear enough, and man was ready to observe it in childlike obedience. But that is now past, and moral doubts and difficulties have crept in. The command, suggests the Serpent, needs to be explained and interpreted. 'Hath God said?' Man must decide for himself what is good by using his conscience and his knowledge of good and evil. The commandment may be variously interpreted, and it is God's will that it should be interpreted and explained: for God has given man a free will to decide what he will do.

But this means disobedience from the start. Doubt and reflection take the place of spontaneous obedience. The grown-up man with his freedom of conscience vaunts his superiority over the child of obedience. But he has acquired the freedom to enjoy moral difficulties only at the cost of renouncing obedience. In short, it is a retreat from the reality of God to the speculations of men, from faith to doubt. The young man's question shows him up in his true colours. He is – man under sin. The answer of Jesus completes his exposure. Jesus simply quotes the commandments of God as they are revealed in Scripture, and thus reaffirms them as the commandments of God. The young man is trapped once more. He had hoped to avoid committing himself to any definite moral obligations by forcing Jesus to discuss his spiritual problems. He had hoped Jesus would offer him a solution of his moral difficulties. But instead he finds Jesus attacking not his question but himself. The only answer to his difficulties is the very commandment of God, which challenges him to have done with academic discussion and to get on with the task of obedience. Only the devil has an answer for our moral difficulties, and he says: 'Keep on posing problems, and you will escape the necessity of obedience.' But Jesus is not interested in the young man's problems; he is interested in the young man himself. He refuses to take those difficulties as seriously as the young man does. There is one thing only which Jesus takes seriously, and that is, that it is high time the young man began to hear the commandment and obey it. Where moral difficulties are taken so seriously, where they torment and enslave man, because they do not leave him open to the freeing activity of obedience, it is there that his total godlessness is revealed. All his difficulties are shown to be ungodly, frivolous, and the proof of sheer disobedience. The one thing that matters is practical obedience. That will solve his difficulties and make him (and all of us) free to become the child of God. Such is God's diagnosis of man's moral difficulties.

The young man has now been twice brought face to face with the truth of the Word of God, and there is no further chance of evading his commandment. It is clear there is no alternative but to obey it. But he is still not satisfied. 'All these things have I observed from my youth up: what lack I yet?' Doubtless he was just as convinced of his sincerity this time as he was before. But it is just here that his defiance of Jesus reaches its climax. He knows the commandment and has kept it, but now, he thinks, that cannot be all God wants of him, there must be something more, some extraordinary and unique demand, and this is what he wants to do. The revealed commandment of God is incomplete, he says, as he makes the last attempt to preserve his independence and decide for himself what is good and evil. He affirms the commandment with one hand and subjects it to a frontal attack on the other. 'All these things have I observed from my youth up.' St Mark adds at this point: 'and Jesus looking upon him loved him' (10.21). Jesus sees how hopelessly the young man has closed his mind to the living Word of God, how serious he is about it, and how heartily he rages against the living commandment and the spontaneous obedience it demands. Jesus wants to help the young man because he loves him. So now comes his last word: 'If thou wouldest be perfect, go, sell all thou hast and give to the poor, and thou shalt have treasure in heaven: and come, follow me.' There are three points to notice here. First it is Jesus himself who now gives the commandment. The same Jesus who earlier had pointed the young man away from the good master to the God who alone is good, now takes up his claim to divine authority and pronounces the last word. The young man must realize that it is the very Son of God who stands before him. As the Son of God, though the young man knew it not, Jesus had pointed him away from the Son to the Father, with whom he was in perfect union. And now once more as the Son he utters the commandment of God himself. Jesus must make that commandment unmistakably clear at the moment when he calls the young man to follow him. Here is the sum of the commandments – to live in fellowship with Christ. This Christ now confronts the young man with his call.

He can no longer escape into the unreal world of his moral difficulties. The commandment is plain and straightforward: 'Follow me.' The second point to be noticed is that even this command might be misunderstood and therefore it has to be explained. For the young man might still fall back into his original mistake, and take the commandment as an opportunity for moral adventure, a thrilling way of life, but one which might easily be abandoned for another if occasion arose. It would be just as wrong if the young man were to regard discipleship as the logical conclusion of his search for truth in which he had hitherto been engaged, as an addition, a clarification or a completion of his old life. And so to avoid all misunderstandings, Jesus has to create a situation in which there can be no retreat, an irrevocable situation. At the same time it must be made clear to him that this is in no sense a fulfilment of his past life. So he bids him embrace voluntary poverty. This is the 'existential', pastoral side of the question, and its aim is to enable the young man to reach a final understanding of the true way of obedience. It springs from Jesus' love for the young man, and it represents the only link between the old life and the new. But it must be noted that the link is not identical with the new life itself; it is not even the first step in the right direction, though as an act of obedience it is the essential preliminary. *First* the young man must go and sell all that he has and give to the poor, and *then* come and follow. Discipleship is the end, voluntary poverty the means. The third point to be noticed is this. When the young man asks, 'What lack I yet?' Jesus rejoins: 'If thou wouldest be perfect. . . .' At first sight it would seem that Jesus is thinking in terms of an addition to the young man's previous life. But it is an addition which requires the abandonment of every previous attachment. Until now perfection had always eluded his grasp. Both his understanding and his practice of the commandment had been at fault. Only now, by following Christ, can he understand and practise it aright, and only now because it is Jesus Christ who calls him. In the moment he takes up the young man's question, Jesus wrenches it from him. He had asked the way to eternal life: Jesus answers: 'I call thee, and that is all.'

The answer to the young man's problem is – Jesus Christ. He had hoped to hear the word of the good master, but he now perceives that this word is the Man to whom he had addressed his question. He stands face to face with Jesus, the Son of God: it is the ultimate encounter. It is now only a question of yes or no, of obedience or disobedience. The answer is no. He went away sorrowful, disappointed and deceived of his hopes, unable to wrench himself from his past. He had great possessions. The call to follow means here what it had meant before – adherence to the person of Jesus Christ and fellowship with him. The life of discipleship is not the hero-worship we would pay to a good master, but obedience to the Son of God.

The story of the rich young man is closely paralleled by the introduction to the parable of the Good Samaritan. 'And behold, a certain lawyer stood up and tempted him, saying, Master, what shall I do to inherit eternal life? And he said unto him, What is written in the law? How readest thou? And he answering said, Thou shalt love the Lord thy God with all thy heart, and with all thy soul, and with all thy strength, and with all thy mind; and thy neighbour as thyself. And he said unto him, Thou hast answered right: this do, and thou shalt live. But he, desiring to justify himself, said unto Jesus, And who is my neighbour?' (Luke 10.25-29).

The lawyer's question is the same as the young man's, the only difference being that we are told explicitly that he meant to tempt Jesus. He has already made up his mind about the solution to his problem – he intends to land Jesus in the impasse of moral doubts and difficulties. Jesus answers him in much the same terms as he answered the rich young man. The questioner in his heart knows the answer to his question. But in the moment he asks it, although he knows the answer, he wishes to evade the obligation to obey the commandment of God. The only answer he receives is: 'You already know your duty: do it and you will live.'

The first round is already lost, so the lawyer must try again. Like the rich young man, he tries to escape by raising his moral difficulties. 'And who is my neighbour?' How often has this

question been asked since, in good faith and genuine ignorance!
It is plausible enough and any earnest seeker of the truth could
reasonably ask it. But this is not the way the lawyer meant it.
Jesus parries the question as a temptation of the devil, and that in
fact is the whole point of the parable of the Good Samaritan. It is
the sort of question you can keep on asking without ever getting
an answer. Its source lies in the 'wrangling of men, corrupted in
mind and bereft of truth'; of men 'doting about questionings and
disputes of words'. From it 'cometh envy, strife, railings, even
surmisings' (I Tim. 6.4 f). It is the question of men who are puffed
up, men who are 'ever learning, and never able to come to knowledge of the truth'. Of men 'holding a form of godliness, but
having denied the power thereof' (II Tim. 3.5 ff). They cannot
believe, and they keep on asking this same question because they
are 'branded in their own conscience as with a hot iron' (I Tim.
4.2), because they refuse to obey the Word of God. Who is my
neighbour? Does this question admit of any answer? Is it my kins-
man, my compatriot, my brother Christian, or my enemy? There
is an element of truth and falsehood in each of these answers. The
whole question lands us into doubt and disobedience, and it is a
veritable act of rebellion against the commandment of God. Of
course, I say, I want to do his will, but he does not tell me how
to set about it. The commandment does not give me any clear
directions, and does nothing to solve my problems. The question
'What shall I do?' was the lawyer's first attempt to throw dust in
his own eyes. The answer was: 'You know the commandments,
do you not? Well then, put them into practice. You must not ask
questions – get on with the job!' And the final question 'Who is my
neighbour?' is the parting shot of despair (or else of self-confidence);
the lawyer is trying to justify his disobedience. The answer is:
'You are the neighbour. Go along and try to be obedient by
loving others.' Neighbourliness is not a quality in other people, it
is simply their claim on ourselves. Every moment and every
situation challenges us to action and to obedience. We have literally no time to sit down and ask ourselves whether so-and-so is
our neighbour or not. We must get into action and obey – we

must behave like a neighbour to him. But perhaps this shocks you. Perhaps you still think you ought to think out beforehand and know what you ought to do. To that there is only one answer. You can only know and think about it by actually doing it. You can only learn what obedience is by obeying. It is no use asking questions; for it is only through obedience that you come to learn the truth.

With our consciences distracted by sin, we are confronted by the call of Jesus to spontaneous obedience. But whereas the rich young man was called to the grace of discipleship, the lawyer, who sought to tempt him, was only sent back to the commandment.

3 SINGLE-MINDED OBEDIENCE

WHEN he was challenged by Jesus to accept a life of voluntary poverty, the rich young man knew he was faced with the simple alternative of obedience or disobedience. When Levi was called from the receipt of custom and Peter from his nets, there was no doubt that Jesus meant business. Both of them were to leave everything and follow. Again, when Peter was called to walk on the rolling sea, he had to get up and risk his life. Only one thing was required in each case – to rely on Christ's word, and cling to it as offering greater security than all the securities in the world. The forces which tried to interpose themselves between the word of Jesus and the response of obedience were as formidable then as they are to-day. Reason and conscience, responsibility and piety all stood in the way, and even the law and 'scriptural authority' itself were obstacles which pretended to defend them from going to the extremes of antinomianism and 'enthusiasms'. But the call of Jesus made short work of all these barriers, and created obedience. That call was the Word of God himself, and all that it required was single-minded obedience.

If, as we read our Bibles, we heard Jesus speaking to us in this way to-day we should probably try to argue ourselves out of it like this: 'It is true that the demand of Jesus is definite enough, but I have to remember that he never expects us to take his commands legalistically. What he really wants me to have is faith. But my faith is not necessarily tied up with riches or poverty or anything of the kind. We may be both poor and rich in the spirit. It is not important that I should have no possessions, but if I do I must keep them as though I had them not, in other words I must cultivate a spirit of inward detachment, so that my heart is not in my possessions.' Jesus may have said: 'Sell thy goods', but he meant: 'Do not let it be a matter of consequence to you that you have outward prosperity; rather keep your goods quietly, having

them as if you had them not. Let not your heart be in your goods.'
– We are excusing ourselves from single-minded obedience to the
word of Jesus on the pretext of legalism and a supposed preference
for an obedience 'in faith'. The difference between ourselves and
the rich young man is that he was not allowed to solace his regrets
by saying: 'Never mind what Jesus says, I can still hold on to my
riches, but in a spirit of inner detachment. Despite my inadequacy
I can take comfort in the thought that God has forgiven me my sins
and can have fellowship with Christ in faith.' But no, he went
away sorrowful. Because he would not obey, he could not believe.
In this the young man was quite honest. He went away from Jesus
and indeed this honesty had more promise than any apparent
communion with Jesus based on disobedience. As Jesus realized,
the trouble with the young man was that he was not capable of
such an inward detachment from riches. As an earnest seeker for
perfection he had probably tried it a thousand times before and
failed, as he showed by refusing to obey the word of Jesus when
the moment of decision came. It is just here that the young man
was entirely honest. But we in our sophistry differ altogether
from the hearers of Jesus' word of whom the Bible speaks. If
Jesus said to someone: 'Leave all else behind and follow me;
resign your profession, quit your family, your people, and the
home of your fathers,' then he knew that to this call there was
only one answer – the answer of single-minded obedience, and
that it is only to this obedience that the promise of fellowship
with Jesus is given. But we should probably argue thus: 'Of course
we are meant to take the call of Jesus with "absolute seriousness",
but after all the true way of obedience would be to continue all
the more in our present occupations, to stay with our families, and
serve him there in a spirit of true inward detachment.' If Jesus
challenged us with the command: 'Get out of it', we should take
him to mean: 'Stay where you are, but cultivate that inward
detachment.' Again, if he were to say to us: 'Be not anxious', we
should take him to mean: 'Of course it is not wrong for us to be
anxious: we must work and provide for ourselves and our de-
pendants. If we did not we should be shirking our responsibilities.

But all the time we ought to be inwardly free from all anxiety.' Perhaps Jesus would say to us: 'Whosoever smiteth thee on the right cheek, turn to him the other also.' We should then suppose him to mean: 'The way really to love your enemy is to fight him hard and hit him back.' Jesus might say: 'Seek ye first the kingdom of God', and we should interpret it thus: 'Of course we should have to seek all sorts of other things first; how could we otherwise exist? What he really means is the final preparedness to stake all on the kingdom of God.' All along the line we are trying to evade the obligation of single-minded, literal obedience.

How is such absurdity possible? What has happened that the word of Jesus can be thus degraded by this trifling, and thus left open to the mockery of the world? When orders are issued in other spheres of life there is no doubt whatever of their meaning. If a father sends his child to bed, the boy knows at once what he has to do. But suppose he has picked up a smattering of pseudo-theology. In that case he would argue more or less like this: 'Father tells me to go to bed, but he really means that I am tired, and he does not want me to be tired. I can overcome my tiredness just as well if I go out and play. Therefore though father tells me to go to bed, he really means: "Go out and play." ' If a child tried such arguments on his father or a citizen on his government, they would both meet with a kind of language they could not fail to understand – in short they would be punished. Are we to treat the commandment of Jesus differently from other orders and exchange single-minded obedience for downright disobedience? How could that be possible!

It is possible because there is an element of truth underlying all this sophistry. When Jesus calls the young man to enter into the situation where faith is possible, he does it only with the aim of making the man have faith in him, that is to say, he calls him into fellowship with himself. In the last resort what matters is not what the man *does*, but only his faith in Jesus as the Son of God and Mediator. At all events poverty or riches, marriage or celibacy, a profession or the lack of it, have in the last resort nothing to do with it – everything depends on faith alone. So far then we are quite right; it is possible to have wealth and the possession of this world's goods and to believe in Christ – so that a man may have these goods as one who has them not. But this is an *ultimate* possibility of the Christian life, only within our capacity in so far as we await with earnest expectation the immediate return of Christ. It is by no means the first and the simplest possibility. The paradoxical understanding of the commandments has its Christian justification, but it must never lead to the abandoning of the single-minded understanding of the commandments. This is only possible and right for somebody who has already at some point or other in his life put into action his single-minded understanding, somebody who thus lives with Christ as his disciple and in anticipation of the end. This is the infinitely more difficult, and humanly speaking 'impossible possibility', to interpret the call of Jesus in this paradoxical way. And it is just this paradoxical element which exposes his call to the constant danger of being transformed into its very opposite, and used as an excuse for shirking the necessity of concrete obedience. Anybody who does not feel that he would be much happier were he only permitted to understand and obey the commandments of Jesus in a straightforward literal way, and e.g. surrender all his possessions at his bidding rather than cling to them, has no right to this paradoxical interpretation of Jesus' words. We have to hold the two together in mind all the time.

The actual call of Jesus and the response of single-minded obedience have an irrevocable significance. By means of them Jesus calls people into an actual situation where faith is possible. For that reason his call is an actual call and he wishes it so to be understood, because he knows that it is only through actual obedience that a man can become liberated to believe.

The elimination of single-minded obedience on principle is but another instance of the perversion of the costly grace of the call of Jesus into the cheap grace of self-justification. By this means a false law is set up which deafens men to the concrete call of Christ. This false law is the law of the world, of which the law of grace is at once the complement and the antithesis. The 'world' here is not the world overcome in Christ, and daily to be overcome anew in fellowship with him, but the world hardened into a rigid, impenetrable legalistic principle. When that happens grace has ceased to be the gift of the living God, in which we are rescued from the world and put under the obedience of Christ; it is rather a general law, a divine principle, which only needs to be applied to particular cases. Struggling against the legalism of simple obedience, we end by setting up the most dangerous law of all, the law of the world and the law of grace. In our effort to combat legalism we land ourselves in the worst kind of legalism. The only way of overcoming this legalism is by real obedience to Christ when he calls us to follow him; for in Jesus the law is at once fulfilled and cancelled.

By eliminating simple obedience on principle, we drift into an unevangelical interpretation of the Bible. We take it for granted as we open the Bible that we have a key to its interpretation. But then the key we use would not be the living Christ, who is both Judge and Saviour, and our use of this key no longer depends on the will of the living Holy Spirit alone. The key we use is a general doctrine of grace which we can apply as we will. The problem of discipleship then becomes a problem of exegesis as well. If our exegesis is truly evangelical, we shall realize that we cannot identify ourselves *altogether* with those whom Jesus called, for they themselves are part and parcel of the Word of God in the Scriptures, and therefore part of the message. We hear in the sermon not only the answer which Jesus gave to the young man's question, which would also be our question, but both question and answer are, as the Word of the Scriptures, contents of the message. It would be a false exegesis if we tried to behave in our discipleship as though we were the immediate contemporaries of the men whom Jesus called. But the Christ whom the Scriptures proclaim is in every word he utters one who grants faith to those only who obey him. It is neither possible nor right for us to try to get behind the Word of the Scriptures to the events as they actually occurred. Rather the whole Word of the Scriptures summons us to follow Jesus. We must not do violence to the Scriptures by interpreting them in terms of an abstract principle, even if that principle be a doctrine of grace. Otherwise we shall end up in legalism.

We must therefore maintain that the paradoxical interpretation of the commandments of Jesus always includes the literal interpretation, for the very reason that our aim is not to set up a law, but to proclaim Christ. There remains just a word to be said about the suspicion that this simple obedience involves a doctrine of human merit, of a *facere quod in se est*, of insistence on preliminary conditions before faith becomes possible. Obedience to the call of Jesus never lies within our own power. If for instance we give away all our possessions, that act is not in itself the obedience he demands. In fact such a step might be the precise opposite of obedience to Jesus, for we might then be choosing a way of life for ourselves, some Christian ideal, or some ideal of Franciscan poverty. Indeed in the very act of giving away his goods a man can give allegiance to himself and to an ideal and not to the command of Jesus. He is not set free from his own self but still more enslaved to himself. The step into the situation where faith is possible is not an offer which we can make to Jesus, but always his gracious offer to us. Only when the step is taken in this spirit is it admissible. But in that case we cannot speak of a freedom of choice on our part.

> And Jesus said unto his disciples, Verily I say unto you, It is hard for a rich man to enter into the kingdom of heaven. And again I say unto you, It is easier for a camel to go through a needle's eye, than for a rich man to enter the kingdom of God. And when the disciples heard it, they were astonished exceedingly, saying, Who then can be saved? And Jesus looking upon them said unto them, With men this is impossible, but with God all things are possible. (Matt. 19.23-26)

The shocked question of the disciples 'Who then can be saved?' seems to indicate that they regarded the case of the rich young man not as in any way exceptional, but as typical. For they do not ask: 'Which rich man?' but quite generally, '*Who* then can be saved?' For every man, even the disciples themselves, belongs to those rich ones for whom it is so difficult to enter the kingdom of heaven. The answer Jesus gives showed the disciples that they had understood him well. Salvation through following Jesus is not something we men can achieve for ourselves – but with God all things are possible.

4 DISCIPLESHIP AND THE CROSS

And he began to teach them, that the Son of man must suffer many things, and be rejected by the elders, and the chief priests, and the scribes, and be killed, and after three days rise again. And he spake the saying openly. And Peter took him, and began to rebuke him. But he turning about, and seeing his disciples, rebuked Peter and saith, Get thee behind me, Satan: for thou mindest not the things of God, but the things of men. And he called unto him the multitude with his disciples, and said unto them, If any man would come after me, let him deny himself, and take up his cross, and follow me. For whosoever would save his life shall lose it; and whosoever shall lose his life for my sake and the gospel's shall save it. For what doth it profit a man, to gain the whole world, and to forfeit his life? For what should a man give in exchange for his life? For whosoever shall be ashamed of me and of my words in this adulterous and sinful generation, the Son of man also shall be ashamed of him, when he cometh in the glory of his Father with the holy angels. (Mark 8.31-38)

HERE the call to follow is closely connected with Jesus' prediction of his passion. Jesus Christ must suffer and be rejected. This 'must' is inherent in the promise of God – the Scriptures must be fulfilled. There is a distinction here between suffering and rejection. Had he only suffered, Jesus might still have been applauded as the Messiah. All the sympathy and admiration of the world might have been focused on his passion. It could have been viewed as a tragedy with its own intrinsic value, dignity and honour. But in the passion Jesus is a rejected Messiah. His rejection robs the passion of its halo of glory. It must be a passion without honour. Suffering and rejection sum up the whole cross of Jesus. To die on the cross means to die despised and rejected of men. Suffering and rejection are laid upon Jesus as a divine necessity, and every attempt to prevent it is the work of the devil, especially when it comes from his own disciples; for it is in fact an attempt to prevent Christ from being Christ. It is Peter, the Rock of the Church, who commits that sin, immediately after he has confessed Jesus as the Messiah and has been appointed to the primacy. That shows how the very notion of a suffering Messiah was a scandal to the Church, even in its earliest days. That is not the kind of Lord it wants, and as the Church of Christ it does not like to have the law of suffering imposed upon it by its Lord. Peter's protest displays his own unwillingness to suffer, and that means that Satan has gained entry into the Church, and is trying to tear it away from the cross of its Lord.

Jesus must therefore make it clear beyond all doubt that the 'must' of suffering applies to his disciples no less than to himself. Just as Christ is Christ only in virtue of his suffering and rejection, so the disciple is a disciple only in so far as he shares his Lord's suffering and rejection and crucifixion. Discipleship means adherence to the person of Jesus, and therefore submission to the law of Christ which is the law of the cross.

Surprisingly enough, when Jesus begins to unfold this inescapable truth to his disciples, he once more sets them free to choose or reject him. 'If any man would come after me,' he says. For it is not a matter of course, not even among the disciples. Nobody can be forced, nobody can even be expected to come. He says rather '*If* any man' is prepared to spurn all other offers which come his way in order to follow him. Once again, everything is left for the individual to decide. When the disciples are half-way along the road of discipleship, they come to another cross-roads. Once more they are left free to choose for themselves, nothing is expected of them, nothing forced upon them. So crucial is the demand of the present hour that the disciples must be left free to make their own choice before they are told of the law of discipleship.

'If any man would come after me, let him deny himself.' The disciple must say to himself the same words Peter said of Christ when he denied him: 'I know not this man.' Self-denial is never just a series of isolated acts of mortification or asceticism. It is not suicide, for there is an element of self-will even in that. To deny oneself is to be aware only of Christ and no more of self, to see only him who goes before and no more the road which is too hard for us. Once more, all that self-denial can say is: 'He leads the way, keep close to him.'

'. . . and take up his cross.' Jesus has graciously prepared the way for this word by speaking first of self-denial. Only when we have become completely oblivious of self are we ready to bear the cross for his sake. If in the end we know only him, if we have ceased to notice the pain of our own cross, we are indeed looking only unto him. If Jesus had not so graciously prepared us for this word, we should have found it unbearable. But by preparing us for it he has enabled us to receive even a word as hard as this as a word of grace. It comes to us in the joy of discipleship and confirms us in it.

To endure the cross is not a tragedy; it is the suffering which is the fruit of an exclusive allegiance to Jesus Christ. When it comes, it is not an accident, but a necessity. It is not the sort of suffering which is inseparable from this mortal life, but the suffering which is an essential part of the specifically Christian life. It is not suffering *per se* but suffering-and-rejection, and not rejection for any cause or conviction of our own, but rejection for the sake of Christ. If our Christianity has ceased to be serious about discipleship, if we have watered down the gospel into emotional uplift which makes no costly demands and which fails to distinguish between natural and Christian existence, then we cannot help regarding the cross as an ordinary everyday calamity, as one of the trials and tribulations of life. We have then forgotten that the cross means rejection and shame as well as suffering. The Psalmist was lamenting that he was despised and rejected of men, and that is an essential quality of the suffering of the cross. But this notion has ceased to be intelligible to a Christianity which can no longer see any difference between an ordinary human life and a life committed to Christ. The cross means sharing the suffering of Christ to the last and to the fullest. Only a man thus totally committed in discipleship can experience the meaning of the cross. The cross is there, right from the beginning, he has only got to pick it up; there is no need for him to go out and look for a cross for himself, no need for him deliberately to run after suffering. Jesus says that every Christian has his own cross waiting for him, a cross destined and appointed by God. Each must endure his allotted share of suffering and rejection. But each has a different share: some God deems worthy of the highest form of suffering, and gives them the grace of martyrdom, while others he does not allow to be tempted above that they are able to bear. But it is the one and the same cross in every case.

The cross is laid on every Christian. The first Christ-suffering which every man must experience is the call to abandon the attachments of this world. It is that dying of the old man which is the result of his encounter with Christ. As we embark upon discipleship we surrender ourselves to Christ in union with his death – we give over our lives to death. Thus it begins; the cross is not the terrible end to an otherwise god-fearing and happy life, but it meets us at the beginning of our communion with Christ. When Christ calls a man, he bids him come and die. It may be a death like that of the first disciples who had to leave home and work to follow him, or it may be a death like Luther's, who had to leave the monastery and go out into the world. But it is the same death every time – death in Jesus Christ, the death of the old man at his call. Jesus' summons to the rich young man was calling him to die, because only the man who is dead to his own will can follow Christ. In fact every command of Jesus is a call to die, with all our affections and lusts. But we do not want to die, and therefore Jesus Christ and his call are necessarily our death as well as our life. The call to discipleship, the baptism in the name of Jesus Christ means both death and life. The call of Christ, his baptism, sets the Christian in the middle of the daily arena against sin and the devil. Every day he encounters new temptations, and every day he must suffer anew for Jesus Christ's sake. The wounds and scars he receives in the fray are living tokens of this participation in the cross of his Lord. But there is another kind of suffering and shame which the Christian is not spared. While it is true that only the sufferings of Christ are a means of atonement, yet since he has suffered for and borne the sins of the whole world and shares with

79

his disciples the fruits of his passion, the Christian also has to undergo temptation, he too has to bear the sins of others; he too must bear their shame and be driven like a scapegoat from the gate of the city. But he would certainly break down under this burden, but for the support of him who bore the sins of all. The passion of Christ strengthens him to overcome the sins of others by forgiving them. He becomes the bearer of other men's burdens – 'Bear ye one another's burdens, and so fulfil the law of Christ' (Gal. 6.2). As Christ bears our burdens, so ought we to bear the burdens of our fellow-men. The law of Christ, which it is our duty to fulfil, is the bearing of the cross. My brother's burden which I must bear is not only his outward lot, his natural characteristics and gifts, but quite literally his sin. And the only way to bear that sin is by forgiving it in the power of the cross of Christ in which I now share. Thus the call to follow Christ always means a call to share the work of forgiving men their sins. Forgiveness is the Christlike suffering which it is the Christian's duty to bear.

But how is the disciple to know what kind of cross is meant for him? He will find out as soon as he begins to follow his Lord and to share his life.

Suffering, then, is the badge of true discipleship. The disciple is not above his master. Following Christ means *passio passiva*, suffering because we have to suffer. That is why Luther reckoned suffering among the marks of the true Church, and one of the memoranda drawn up in preparation for the Augsburg Confession similarly defines the Church as the community of those 'who are persecuted and martyred for the gospel's sake'. If we refuse to take up our cross and submit to suffering and rejection at the hands of men, we forfeit our fellowship with Christ and have ceased to follow him. But if we lose our lives in his service and carry our cross, we shall find our lives again in the fellowship of the cross with Christ. The opposite of discipleship is to be ashamed of Christ and his cross and all the offence which the cross brings in its train.

Discipleship means allegiance to the suffering Christ, and it is therefore not at all surprising that Christians should be called upon to suffer. In fact it is a joy and a token of his grace. The acts of the early Christian martyrs are full of evidence which shows how Christ transfigures for his own the hour of their mortal agony by granting them the unspeakable assurance of his presence. In the hour of the cruellest torture they bear for his sake, they are made partakers in the perfect joy and bliss of fellowship with him. To bear the cross proves to be the only way of triumphing over suffering. This is true for all who follow Christ, because it was true for him.

> And he went forward a little, and fell on his face, and prayed, saying, O my Father, if it be possible, let this cup pass away from me: nevertheless, not as I will, but as thou wilt. . . . Again a second time he went away, and prayed, saying, O my Father, if this cannot pass away, except I drink it, thy will be done. (Matt. 26.39, 42)

Jesus prays to his Father that the cup may pass from him, and his Father hears his prayer; for the cup of suffering will indeed pass from him – *but only by his drinking it.* That is the assurance he receives as he kneels for the second time in the garden of Gethsemane that suffering will indeed pass as he accepts it. That is the only path to victory. The cross is his triumph over suffering.

Suffering means being cut off from God. Therefore those who live in communion with him cannot really suffer. This Old Testament doctrine was expressly reaffirmed by Jesus. That is why he takes upon himself the suffering of the whole world, and in doing so proves victorious over it. He bears the whole burden of man's separation from God, and in the very act of drinking the cup he causes it to pass over him. He sets out to overcome the suffering of the world, and so he must drink it to the dregs. Hence while it is still true that suffering means being cut off from God, yet within the fellowship of Christ's suffering, suffering is overcome by suffering, and becomes the way to communion with God.

Suffering has to be endured in order that it may pass away. Either the world must bear the whole burden and collapse beneath it, or it must fall on Christ to be overcome in him. He therefore suffers vicariously for the world. His is the only suffering which has redemptive efficacy. But the Church knows that the world is still seeking for someone to bear its sufferings, and so, as it follows Christ, suffering becomes the Church's lot too and bearing it, it is borne up by Christ. As it follows him beneath the cross, the Church stands before God as the representative of the world.

For God is a God who *bears*. The Son of God bore our flesh, he bore the cross, he bore our sins, thus making atonement for us. In the same way his followers are also called upon to bear, and that is precisely what it means to be a Christian. Just as Christ maintained his communion with the Father by his endurance, so his followers are to maintain their communion with Christ by their endurance. We can of course shake off the burden which is laid upon us, but only find that we have a still heavier burden to carry – a yoke of our own choosing, the yoke of our self. But Jesus invites all who travail and are heavy laden to throw off their own yoke and take his yoke upon them – and his yoke is easy, and his burden is light. The yoke and the burden of Christ are his cross. To go one's way under the sign of the cross is not misery and desperation, but peace and refreshment for the soul, it is the highest joy. Then we do not walk under our self-made laws and burdens, but under the yoke of him who knows us and who walks under the yoke with us. Under his yoke we are certain of his nearness and communion. It is he whom the disciple finds as he lifts up his cross.

'Discipleship is not limited to what you can comprehend – it must transcend all comprehension. Plunge into the deep waters beyond your own comprehension, and I will help you to comprehend even as I do. Bewilderment is the true comprehension. Not to know where you are going is the true knowledge. My comprehension transcends yours. Thus Abraham went forth from his father and not knowing whither he went. He trusted himself to my knowledge, and cared not for his own, and thus he took the right road and came to his journey's end. Behold, that is the way of the cross. You cannot find it yourself, so you must let me lead you as though you were a blind man. Wherefore it is not you, no man, no living creature, but I myself, who instruct you by my word and Spirit in the way you should go. Not the work which you choose, not the suffering you devise, but the road which is clean contrary to all that you choose or contrive or desire – that is the road you must take. To that I call you and in that you must be my disciple. If you do that, there is the acceptable time and there your master is come' (Luther).

If any man cometh unto me, and hateth not his own father, and mother, and wife, and children, and brethren, and sisters, yea, and his own life also, he cannot be my disciple. (Luke 14.26)

THROUGH the call of Jesus men become individuals. Willy-nilly, they are compelled to decide, and that decision can only be made by themselves. It is no choice of their own that makes them individuals: it is Christ who makes them individuals by calling them. Every man is called separately, and must follow alone. But men are frightened of solitude, and they try to protect themselves from it by merging themselves in the society of their fellow-men and in their material environment. They become suddenly aware of their responsibilities and duties, and are loath to part with them. But all this is only a cloak to protect them from having to make a decision. They are unwilling to stand alone before Jesus and to be compelled to decide with their eyes fixed on him alone. Yet neither father nor mother, neither wife nor child, neither nationality nor tradition, can protect a man at the moment of his call. It is Christ's will that he should be thus isolated, and that he should fix his eyes solely upon him.

At the very moment of their call, men find that they have already broken with all the natural ties of life. This is not their own doing, but his who calls them. For Christ has delivered them from immediacy with the world, and brought them into immediacy with himself. We cannot follow Christ unless we are prepared to accept and affirm that breach as a *fait accompli*. It is no arbitrary choice on the disciple's part, but Christ himself, who compels him thus to break with his past.

Why is this necessary? Why are we not allowed to grow slowly, gradually, uninterruptedly in progressive sanctification out of the natural order into the fellowship of Christ? What is this power which so angrily comes between a man and the natural life in which it had pleased God to place him? Surely such a breach with the past is a legalistic technique and surly contempt for the good gifts of God, a technique far removed from the 'liberty of the Christian man'? We must face up to the truth that the call of Christ *does* set up a barrier between man and his natural life. But this barrier is no surly contempt for life, no legalistic piety, it is the life which is life indeed, the gospel, the person of Jesus Christ. By virtue of his incarnation he has come between man and his natural life. There can be no turning back, for Christ bars the way. By calling us he has cut us off from all immediacy with the things of this world. He wants to be the centre, through him alone all things shall come to pass. He stands between us and God, and for that very reason he stands between us and all other men and things. *He is the Mediator*, not only between God and man, but between man and man, between man and reality. Since the whole world was created through him and unto him (John 1.3; I Cor. 8.6; Heb. 1.2), he is the sole Mediator in the world. Since his coming man has no immediate relationship of his own any more to anything, neither to God nor to the world; Christ wants to be the mediator. Of course, there are plenty of gods who offer men direct access, and the world naturally uses every means in its power to retain its direct hold on men, but that is the very reason why it is so bitterly opposed to Christ, the Mediator.

This breach with the immediacies of the world is identical with the acknowledgement of Christ as the Son of God the Mediator. It is never a deliberate act whereby we renounce all contact with the world for the sake of some ideal or other, as though for instance we were exchanging a lower ideal for a higher one. That would be enthusiasm and wilfulness, and again an attempt at direct relationship with the world. Only the recognition of the *fait accompli* of Christ as the Mediator can separate the disciple from the world of men and things. It is the call of Jesus, regarded not as an ideal, but as the word of a Mediator, which effects in us this complete breach with the world. If it were only a question of weighing one ideal against another, we should naturally hanker after a compromise. In that case the Christian ideal might come out on top, but its claim could never be absolute. If we were only concerned with ideals, if we gave due regard to our natural responsibilities, we should never be justified in giving the Christian ideal a priority over the natural ordinances of life. On the contrary, a case could be made for exactly the opposite evaluation, even from the standpoint of a Christian idealism, or a Christian ethic of duty or conscience. But we are concerned not with ideals, duties or values, but with the recognition and acceptance of a *fait accompli*, namely of the person of the Mediator himself who has come between us and the world. There can only be a complete breach with the immediacies of life: the call of Christ brings us as individuals face to face with the Mediator.

The call of Jesus teaches us that our relation to the world has been built on an illusion. All the time we thought we had enjoyed a direct relation with men and things. This is what had hindered us from faith and obedience. Now we learn that in the most intimate relationships of life, in our kinship with father and mother, brothers and sisters, in married love, and in our duty to the community, direct relationships are impossible. Since the coming of Christ, his followers have no more immediate realities of their own, not in their family relationships nor in the ties with their nation nor in the relationships formed in the process of living. Between father and son, husband and wife, the individual and the nation, stands Christ the Mediator, whether they are able to recognize him or not. We cannot establish direct contact outside ourselves except through him, through his word, and through our following of him. To think otherwise is to deceive ourselves.

But since we are bound to abhor any deception which hides the truth from our sight, we must of necessity repudiate any direct relationship with the things of this world – and that for the sake of Christ. Wherever a group, be it large or small, prevents us from standing alone before Christ, wherever such a group raises a claim of immediacy it must be hated for the sake of Christ. For every immediacy, whether we realize it or not, means hatred of Christ, and this is especially true where such relationships claim the sanction of Christian principles.

It is theological error of the first magnitude to exploit the doctrine of Christ the Mediator so as to justify direct relationships with the things of this world. It is sometimes argued that if Christ is the Mediator he has borne all the sin which underlies our direct relationships with the world and that he has justified us in them. Jesus has reconciled us to God; we can then, it is supposed, return to the world and enjoy our direct relation with it with a good conscience – although that world is the very world which crucified Christ! This is to equate the love of God with the love of the world. The breach with the things of the world is now branded as a legalistic misinterpretation of the grace of God, the purpose of which, we fondly suppose, is to spare us the necessity of this very breach. The saying of Christ about hating our immediate relationships is thus turned into a cheerful affirmation of the 'God-given realities of this world'. Once again the justification of the sinner has become the justification of sin.

For the Christian the only God-given realities are those he receives from Christ. What is not given us through the incarnate Son is not given us by God. What has not been given me for Christ's sake, does not come from God. When we offer thanks for the gifts of creation we must do it through Jesus Christ, and when we pray for the preservation of this life by the grace of God, we must make our prayer for Christ's sake. Anything I cannot thank God for for the sake of Christ, I may not thank God for at all; to do so would be sin. The path, too, to the 'god-given reality' of my fellow-man or woman with whom I have to live leads through Christ, or it is a blind alley. We are separated from one another by an unbridgeable gulf of otherness and strangeness which resists all our attempts to overcome it by means of natural association or emotional or spiritual union. There is no way from one person to another. However loving and sympathetic we try to be, however sound our psychology, however frank and open our behaviour, we cannot penetrate the incognito of the other man, for there are no direct relationships, not even between soul and soul. Christ stands between us, and we can only get into touch with our neighbours through him. That is why intercession is the most promising way to reach our neighbours, and corporate prayer, offered in the name of Christ, the purest form of fellowship.

We cannot rightly acknowledge the gifts of God unless we acknowledge the Mediator for whose sake alone they are given to us. There can be no genuine thanksgiving for the blessings of nation, family, history and nature without that heart-felt penitence which gives the glory to Christ alone above all else. There can be no real attachment to the given creation, no genuine responsibility in the world, unless we recognize the breach which already separates us from it. There can be no genuine love of the world except the love wherewith God loved it in Jesus Christ. 'Love not the world' (I John 2.15). Yes, but we must also remember that 'God so loved the world, that he gave his only begotten Son, that whosoever believeth in him should not perish, but have eternal life' (John 3.16).

This breach with all our immediate relationships is inescapable. It may take the form of an external breach with family or nation; in that case we shall be called upon to bear visibly the reproach of Christ, the *odium generis humani*. Or it may be a hidden and a secret breach. But even then we must always be ready to come out into the open. In the last resort it makes no difference whether the breach be secret or open. Abraham is an example of both. He had to leave his friends and his father's house because Christ came between him and his own. On this occasion the breach was evident. Abraham became a stranger and a sojourner in order to gain the promised land. This was his first call. Later on he was called by God to offer his own son Isaac as a sacrifice. Christ had come between the father of faith and the child of promise. This time the direct relationship not only of flesh and blood, but also of the spirit, must be broken. Abraham must learn that the promise does not depend on Isaac, but on God alone. No one else hears this call of God, not even the servants who accompanied Abraham to Mount Moriah. Once again, as when he left his father's house, Abraham becomes an individual, a lonely and solitary figure. He accepts the call as it comes; he will not shirk it or 'spiritualize' it. He takes God at his word and is ready to obey. Against every direct claim upon him, whether natural, ethical or religious, he will be obedient to the Word of God. By his willingness to sacrifice Isaac, he shows that he is prepared to come out into the open with the breach which he had already made secretly, and to do so for the sake of the Mediator. And at that very moment all that he had surrendered was given back to him. He receives back his son. God shows him a better sacrifice which will take the place of Isaac. The tables are completely turned, Abraham receives Isaac back, but henceforth he will have his son in quite a new way – through the Mediator and for the Mediator's sake. Since he had shown himself ready to obey God literally, he is now allowed to possess Isaac as though he had him not – to possess him through Jesus Christ. No one else knows what has happened. Abraham comes down from the mountain with Isaac just as he went up, but the whole situation has changed. Christ has stepped between father and son. Abraham had left all and followed Christ, and as he follows him he is allowed to go back and live in the world as he had done before. Outwardly the picture is unchanged, but the old is passed away, and behold all things are new. Everything has had to pass through Christ.

This is the second way of becoming an individual – to be a follower of Christ in the midst of society, among our own kith and kin and in the enjoyment of all our worldly wealth. But note that it is *Abraham* who is called to this manner of life, Abraham who had already known what it was to make a visible breach with the past, Abraham who in the New Testament became the example of faith. We are easily tempted to generalize the possibility that was granted to Abraham, to understand it as a spiritual principle and without hesitation to apply it to ourselves. We would like to think that we had the same call to a Christian life, as a specially called follower of Christ who yet retained the enjoyment of his worldly possessions. Yet the outward breach is most certainly easier than the hidden one. Unless we have learnt this from the Bible and from our experience, we are indeed deceiving ourselves. We shall fall back on our direct relationships and forfeit our fellowship with Christ.

It is not for us to choose which way we shall follow. That depends on the will of Christ. But this at least is certain: in one way or the other we shall have to leave the immediacy of the world and become individuals, whether secretly or openly.

But the same Mediator who makes us individuals is also the founder of a new fellowship. He stands in the centre between my neighbour and myself. He divides, but he also unites. Thus although the direct way to our neighbour is barred, we now find the new and only real way to him – the way which passes through the Mediator.

Peter began to say unto him, Lo, we have left all, and have followed thee. Jesus said, Verily I say unto you, there is no man that hath left house, or brethren, or sisters, or mother, or father, or children, or lands, for my sake, and for the gospel's sake, but he shall receive a hundredfold now in this time, houses, and brethren, and sisters, and mothers, and children, and lands, with persecutions; and in the world to come, eternal life. But many that are first shall be last, and the last first. (Mark 10.28-31)

Jesus is here speaking to men who have become individuals for his sake, who have left all at his call, and can say of themselves: 'Lo, we have left all, and have followed thee.' They receive the promise of a new fellowship. According to the word of Jesus, they will receive in this time a hundredfold of what they have left. Jesus is referring to his Church, which finds itself in him. He who leaves his father for Jesus' sake does most assuredly find father and mother, brothers and sisters again, and even lands and houses. Though we all have to enter upon discipleship alone, we do not remain alone. If we take him at his word and dare to become individuals, our reward is the fellowship of the Church. Here is a visible brotherhood to compensate a hundredfold for all we have lost. A hundredfold? Yes, for we now have everything through the Mediator, but with this proviso – 'with persecutions'. A hundredfold with persecutions – such is the grace which is granted to the Church which follows its Lord beneath the cross. Such also is the promise which is held out to Christ's followers – they will be members of the community of the cross, the People of the Mediator, the People under the cross.

> And they were in the way, going up to Jerusalem; and Jesus was going before them: and they were amazed; and they that followed were afraid. And he took again the twelve, and began to tell them the things that were to happen unto him. (Mark 10.32)

As if to bring home to them how serious was his call, to show them how impossible it was to follow in their own strength, and to emphasize that adherence to him means persecutions, Jesus goes on before to Jerusalem and to the cross, and they are filled with fear and amazement at the road he calls them to follow.

Part Two

THE SERMON ON THE MOUNT

ST MATTHEW 5   Of the 'Extraordinariness' of the
                Christian Life
                CHAPTERS 6-13

ST MATTHEW 6   Of the Hidden Character of the
                Christian Life
                CHAPTERS 14-17

ST MATTHEW 7   The Separation of the Disciple Com-
                munity
                CHAPTERS 18-20

6   THE BEATITUDES

Matt. 5.1-12

LET us picture the scene: Jesus on the mountain, the multitudes, and the disciples. The *people* see Jesus with his disciples, who have gathered around him. Until quite recently these men had been completely identified with the multitude, they were just like the rest. Then came the call of Jesus, and at once they left all and followed him. Since then they have belonged to him, body and soul. Now they go with him, live with him, and follow him wherever he leads them. Something unique had occurred to them. That disconcerting and offensive fact stares the people in the face. The *disciples* see the people, from whose midst they themselves have come. These people are the lost sheep of the house of Israel, the elect people of God, the 'national Church'. When the call of Jesus had selected them from among the people, the disciples had done what for the lost sheep of the house of Israel was the only natural and necessary thing to do – they had followed the voice of the Good Shepherd, because they knew his voice. Thus their very action in enlisting as disciples proves that they are members of this people; they will live among them, going into their midst, and preaching the call of Jesus and the glory of discipleship. But what will the end be? *Jesus* sees his disciples. They have publicly left the crowd to join him. He has called them, every one, and they have renounced everything at his call. Now they are living in want and privation, the poorest of the poor, the sorest afflicted, and the hungriest of the hungry. They have only him, and with him they have nothing, literally nothing in the world, but everything with and through God. It is but a little flock he has found, and it is a great flock he is seeking as he looks at the people. Disciples and people, they belong together. The disciples will be his messengers and here and there they will find men to hear and believe their message. Yet there will be enmity between them right to the bitter end. All the wrath of God's people against him and his Word will fall on his disciples; his rejection will be theirs. The cross casts its shadow before. Christ, the disciples, and the people – the stage is already set for the passion of Jesus and his Church.[1]

Therefore Jesus calls his disciples blessed (cf. Luke 6.20 ff). He spoke to men who had already responded to the power of his call, and it is that call which has made them poor, afflicted and hungry. He calls them blessed, not because of their privation, or the renunciation they have made, for these are not blessed in themselves. Only the call and the promise, for the sake of which they are ready to suffer poverty and renunciation, can justify the beatitudes. Admittedly, Jesus sometimes speaks of privation and sometimes of deliberate renunciation as if they implied particular virtues in his disciples, but that is neither here nor there. External privation and personal renunciation both have the same ground – the call and the promise of Jesus. Neither possesses any intrinsic claim to recognition.[2]

Jesus calls his disciples blessed in the hearing of the crowd, and the crowd is called upon as a startled witness. The heritage which God had promised to Israel as a whole is here attributed to the little flock of disciples whom Jesus had chosen. 'Theirs is the kingdom of heaven.' But disciples and people are one, for they

[1] The warrant for this exposition lies in the phrase ἀνοίξας τὸ στόμα. Even in the early Church this point was emphasized. Before Jesus speaks there is a pause—all is silent for a moment or two.

[2] There is no justification whatever for setting Luke's version of the beatitudes over against Matthew's. Matthew is not spiritualizing the beatitudes, and Luke giving them in their original form, nor is Luke giving a political twist to an original form of the beatitude which applied only to a poverty of disposition. Privation is not the ground of the beatitude in Luke, nor renunciation in Matthew. On the contrary, both gospels recognize that neither privation nor renunciation, spiritual or political, is justified, except by the call and promise of Jesus, who alone makes blessed those whom he calls, and who is in his person the sole ground of their beatitude. Since the days of the Clementines, Catholic exegesis has applied this beatitude to the virtue of poverty, the *paupertas voluntaria* of the monks, or any kind of poverty undertaken voluntarily for the sake of Christ. But in both cases the error lies in looking for some kind of human behaviour as the ground for the beatitude instead of the call and promise of Jesus alone.

are all members of the Church which is called of God. Hence the aim of this beatitude is to bring *all* who hear it to decision and salvation. All are called to be what in the reality of God they are already. The disciples are called blessed because they have obeyed the call of Jesus, and the people as a whole because they are heirs of the promise. But will they now claim their heritage by believing in Jesus Christ and his word? Or will they fall into apostasy by refusing to accept him? That is the question which still remains to be answered.

'*Blessed are the poor in spirit, for theirs is the kingdom of heaven.*' Privation is the lot of the disciples in every sphere of their lives. They are the 'poor' *tout court* (Luke 6.20). They have no security, no possessions to call their own, not even a foot of earth to call their home, no earthly society to claim their absolute allegiance. Nay more, they have no spiritual power, experience or knowledge to afford them consolation or security. For his sake they have lost all. In following him they lost even their own selves, and everything that could make them rich. Now they are poor – so inexperienced, so stupid, that they have no other hope but him who called them. Jesus knows all about the others too, the representatives and preachers of the national religion, who enjoy greatness and renown, whose feet are firmly planted on the earth, who are deeply rooted in the culture and piety of the people and moulded by the spirit of the age. Yet it is not they, but the disciples who are called blessed – *theirs* is the kingdom of heaven. That kingdom dawns on *them*, the little band who for the sake of Jesus live a life of absolute renunciation and poverty. And in that very poverty they are heirs of the kingdom. They have their treasure in secret, they find it on the cross. And they have the promise that they will one day visibly enjoy the glory of the kingdom, which in principle is already realized in the utter poverty of the cross.

This beatitude is poles removed from the caricatures of it which appear in political and social manifestos. The Antichrist also calls the poor blessed, but not for the sake of the cross, which embraces all poverty and transforms it into a source of blessing. He fights the cross with political and sociological ideology. He may call it Christian, but that only makes him a still more dangerous enemy.

'*Blessed are they that mourn, for they shall be comforted.*' With each beatitude the gulf is widened between the disciples and the people, their call to come forth from the people becomes increasingly manifest. By 'mourning' Jesus, of course, means doing without what the world calls peace and prosperity: He means refusing to be in tune with the world or to accommodate oneself to its standards. Such men mourn for the world, for its guilt, its fate and its fortune. While the world keeps holiday they stand aside, and while the world sings, 'Gather ye rose-buds while ye may', they mourn. They see that for all the jollity on board, the ship is beginning to sink. The world dreams of progress, of power and of the future, but the disciples meditate on the end, the last judgement, and the coming of the kingdom. To such heights the world cannot rise. And so the disciples are strangers in the world, unwelcome guests and disturbers of the peace. No wonder the world rejects them! Why does the Christian Church so often have to look on from outside when the nation is celebrating? Have churchmen no understanding and sympathy for their fellow-men? Have they become victims of misanthropy? Nobody loves his fellow-men better than a disciple, nobody understands his fellow-men better than the Christian fellowship, and that very love impels them to stand aside and mourn. It was a happy and suggestive thought of Luther, to translate the Greek word here by the German *Leidtragen* (sorrow-bearing). For the emphasis lies on the *bearing* of sorrow. The disciple-community does not shake off sorrow as though it were no concern of its own, but willingly bears it. And in this way they show how close are the bonds which bind them to the rest of humanity. But at the same time they do not go out of their way to look for suffering, or try to contract out of it by adopting an attitude of contempt and disdain. They simply bear the suffering which comes their way as they try to follow Jesus Christ, and bear it for *his* sake. Sorrow cannot tire them or wear them down, it cannot embitter them or cause them to break down under the strain; far from it, for they bear their sorrow in the strength of him who bears them up, who bore the whole suffering of the world upon the cross. They stand as the bearers of sorrow in the fellowship of the Crucified: they stand as strangers in the world in the power of him who was such a stranger to the world that it crucified him. This is their comfort, or better still, this *Man* is their comfort, the Comforter (cf. Luke 2.25). The community of strangers find their comfort in the cross, they are comforted by being cast upon the place where the Comforter of Israel awaits them. Thus do they find their true home with their crucified Lord, both here and in eternity.

'*Blessed are the meek: for they shall inherit the earth.*' This community of strangers possesses no inherent right of its own to protect its members in the world, nor do they claim such rights, for they are meek, they renounce every right of their own and live for the sake of Jesus Christ. When reproached, they hold their peace; when treated with violence they endure it patiently; when men drive them from their presence, they yield their ground. They will not go to law to defend their rights, or make a scene when they suffer injustice, nor do they insist on their legal rights. They are determined to leave their rights to God alone – *non cupidi vindictae*, as the ancient Church paraphrased it. Their right is in the will of their lord – that and no more. They show by every word and gesture that they do not belong to this earth. Leave heaven to them, says the world in its pity, that is where they belong.[1] But Jesus says: 'They shall inherit the earth.' To these, the powerless and the disenfranchised, the very earth belongs. Those who now possess it by violence and injustice shall lose it, and those who here have utterly renounced it, who were meek to the point of the cross, shall rule the new earth. We must not interpret this as a reference to God's exercise of juridical punishment within the world, as Calvin did: what it means is that when the kingdom of heaven descends, the face of the earth will be renewed, and it will belong to the flock of Jesus. God does not forsake the earth: he

---

[1] The Emperor Julian wrote mockingly in a letter (No. 43) that he only confiscated the property of Christians so as to make them poor enough to enter the kingdom of heaven.

99

made it, he sent his Son to it, and on it he built his Church. Thus a beginning has already been made in this present age. A sign has been given. The powerless have here and now received a plot of earth, for they have the Church and its fellowship, its goods, its brothers and sisters, in the midst of persecutions even to the length of the cross. The renewal of the earth begins at Golgotha, where the meek One died, and from thence it will spread. When the kingdom finally comes, the meek shall possess the earth.

'*Blessed are they that hunger and thirst after righteousness: for they shall be filled.*' Not only do the followers of Jesus renounce their rights, they *renounce their own righteousness* too. They get no praise for their achievements or sacrifices. They cannot have righteousness except by hungering and thirsting for it (this applies equally to their own righteousness and to the righteousness of God on earth), always they look forward to the future righteousness of God, but they cannot establish it for themselves. Those who follow Jesus grow hungry and thirsty on the way. They are longing for the forgiveness of all sin, for complete renewal, for the renewal too of the earth and the full establishment of God's law. They are still involved in the world's curse, and affected by its sin. He whom they follow must die accursed on the cross, with a desperate cry for righteousness on his lips: 'My God, my God, why hast thou forsaken me?' But the disciple is not above his master, he follows in his steps. Happy are they who have the promise that they shall be filled, for the righteousness they receive will be no empty promise, but real satisfaction. They will eat the Bread of Life in the Messianic Feast. They are blessed because they already enjoy this bread here and now, for in their hunger they are sustained by the bread of life, the bliss of sinners.

'*Blessed are the merciful, for they shall obtain mercy.*' These men without possessions or power, these strangers on earth, these sinners, these followers of Jesus, have in their life with him *renounced their own dignity*, for they are merciful. As if their own needs and their own distress were not enough, they take upon themselves the distress and humiliation and sin of others. They have an irresistible love for the down-trodden, the sick, the wretched, the wronged, the outcast and all who are tortured with anxiety. They go out and seek all who are enmeshed in the toils of sin and guilt. No distress is too great, no sin too appalling for their pity. If any man falls into disgrace, the merciful will sacrifice their own honour to shield him, and take his shame upon themselves. They will be found consorting with publicans and sinners, careless of the shame they incur thereby. In order that they may be merciful they cast away the most priceless treasure of human life, their personal dignity and honour. For the only honour and dignity they know is their Lord's own mercy, to which alone they owe their very lives. He was not ashamed of his disciples, he became the brother of mankind, and bore their shame unto the death of the cross. That is how Jesus, the crucified, was merciful. His followers owe their lives entirely to that mercy. It makes them forget their own honour and dignity, and seek the society of sinners. They are glad to incur reproach, for they know that then they are blessed. One day God himself will come down and take upon himself their sin and shame. He will cover them with his own honour and remove their disgrace. It will be his glory to bear the shame of sinners and to clothe them with his honour. Blessed are the merciful, for they have the Merciful for their Lord.

'*Blessed are the pure in heart: for they shall see God.*' Who is pure in heart? Only those who have surrendered their hearts completely to Jesus that he may reign in them alone. Only those whose hearts are undefiled by their own evil – and by their own virtues too. The pure in heart have a child-like simplicity like Adam before the fall, innocent alike of good and evil: their hearts are not ruled by their conscience, but by the will of Jesus. If men renounce their own good, if in penitence they have renounced their own hearts, if they rely solely upon Jesus, then his word purifies their hearts. Purity of heart is here contrasted with all outward purity, even the purity of high intentions. The pure heart is pure alike of good and evil, it belongs exclusively to Christ and looks only to him who goes on before. Only they will see God, who in this life have looked solely unto Jesus Christ, the Son of God. For then their hearts are free from all defiling phantasies and are not dis-

tracted by conflicting desires and intentions. They are wholly
absorbed by the contemplation of God. They shall see God, whose
hearts have become a reflection of the image of Jesus Christ.

'*Blessed are the peacemakers: for they shall be called the children of
God.*' The followers of Jesus have been called to peace. When he
called them they found their peace, for he is their peace. But now
they are told that they must not only *have* peace but *make* it.[1] And
to that end they renounce all violence and tumult. In the cause of
Christ nothing is to be gained by such methods. His kingdom is
one of peace, and the mutual greeting of his flock is a greeting of
peace. His disciples keep the peace by choosing to endure suffering
themselves rather than inflict it on others. They maintain fellowship where others would break it off. They renounce all self-
assertion, and quietly suffer in the face of hatred and wrong. In so
doing they overcome evil with good, and establish the peace of
God in the midst of a world of war and hate. But nowhere will
that peace be more manifest than where they meet the wicked in
peace and are ready to suffer at their hands. The peacemakers will
carry the cross with their Lord, for it was on the cross that peace
was made. Now that they are partners in Christ's work of reconciliation, they are called the sons of God as he is the Son of God.

'*Blessed are they that have been persecuted for righteousness' sake:
for theirs is the kingdom of heaven.*' This does not refer to the
righteousness of God, but to suffering in a just cause,[2] suffering
for their own just judgements and actions. For it is by these that
they who renounce possessions, fortune, rights, righteousness,
honour, and force for the sake of following Christ, will be distinguished from the world. The world will be offended at them,
and so the disciples will be persecuted for righteousness' sake. Not
recognition, but rejection, is the reward they get from the world
for their message and works. It is important that Jesus gives his
blessing not merely to suffering incurred directly for the confession

---

[1] There is a *double entendre* in the Greek εἰρηνοποιοί. Even Luther's *Friedfertig*, as
he himself explained, is not to be taken exclusively in a passive sense. The English
translation 'peacemakers', is onesided, and has encouraged a Pelagian and activistic
interpretation of this beatitude.

[2] Note the absence of the definite article.

of his name, but to suffering in any just cause. They receive the same promise as the poor, for in persecution they are their equals in poverty.

Having reached the end of the beatitudes, we naturally ask if there is any place on this earth for the community which they describe. Clearly, there is one place, and only one, and that is where the poorest, meekest, and most sorely tried of all men is to be found – on the cross at Golgotha. The fellowship of the beatitudes is the fellowship of the Crucified. With him it has lost all, and with him it has found all. From the cross there comes the call 'blessed, blessed'. The last beatitude is addressed directly to the disciples, for only they can understand it, 'Blessed are *ye* when men shall reproach you, and persecute you, and say all manner of evil against you falsely for my sake. Rejoice and be exceeding glad, for great is your reward in heaven: for so persecuted they the prophets which were before you.' 'For my sake' the disciples are reproached, but because it is for his sake, the reproach falls on him. It is he who bears the guilt. The curse, the deadly persecution and evil slander confirm the blessed state of the disciples in their fellowship with Jesus. It could not be otherwise, for these meek strangers are bound to provoke the world to insult, violence and slander. Too menacing, too loud are the voices of these poor meek men, too patient and too silent their suffering. Too powerful are the testimony of their poverty and their endurance of the wrongs of the world. This is fatal, and so, while Jesus calls them blessed, the world cries: 'Away with them, away with them!' Yes, but whither? To the kingdom of heaven. 'Rejoice and be exceeding glad: for great is your reward in heaven.' There shall the poor be seen in the halls of joy. With his own hand God wipes away the tears from the eyes of those who had mourned upon earth. He feeds the hungry at his Banquet. There stand the scarred bodies of the martyrs, now glorified and clothed in the white robes of eternal righteousness instead of the rags of sin and repentance. The echoes of this joy reach the little flock below as it stands beneath the cross, and they hear Jesus saying: 'Blessed are ye!'

> Ye are the salt of the earth: but if the salt have lost its savour,
> wherewith shall it be salted? it is thenceforth good for nothing,
> but to be cast out and trodden under foot of men. Ye are the
> light of the world. A city set on a hill cannot be hid. Neither
> do men light a lamp, and put it under the bushel, but on the
> stand; and it shineth unto all that are in the house. Even so let
> your light shine before men, that they may see your good works,
> and glorify your Father which is in heaven. (Matt. 5.13-16)

THESE words are addressed to the same audience as the beatitudes
– to those who are summoned to follow the Crucified in the life
of grace. Up to now we must have had the impression that the
blessed ones were too good for this world, and only fit to live in
heaven. But now Jesus calls them the salt of the earth – salt, the
most indispensable necessity of life. The disciples, that is to say,
are the highest good, the supreme value which the earth possesses,
for without them it cannot live. They are the salt that sustains the
earth, for their sake the world exists, yes, for the sake of these, the
poor, ignoble and weak, whom the world rejects. In casting out
the disciples the earth is destroying its very life. And yet, wonder
of wonders, it is for the sake of the outcasts that the earth is
allowed to continue. The 'divine salt', as Homer called it, maintains itself by fulfilling its proper function. It penetrates the whole
earth, and by it the earth subsists. The disciples, then, must not
only think of heaven; they have an earthly task as well. Now that
they are bound exclusively to Jesus they are told to look at the
earth whose salt they are. It is to be noted that Jesus calls not
himself, but his disciples the salt of the earth, for he entrusts his
work on earth to them. His own work rests with the people of
Israel, but the whole earth is committed to the disciples. But only
as long as it remains salt and retains its cleansing and savouring
properties can the salt preserve the earth. For its own sake, as well
as for the sake of the earth, the salt must remain salt, the disciple

community must be faithful to the mission which the call of Christ has given it. That will be its proper function on earth and will give it its preservative power. Salt is said to be imperishable; it can never lose its cleansing properties. That is why salt was required in the ritual of the Old Testament sacrifices, and why in the baptismal rite of the Roman Church salt is placed in the infant's mouth (see Ex. 30.35; Ezek. 16.4). In the imperishability of salt we have a guarantee of the permanence of the divine community.

'*Ye are* the salt.' Jesus does not say: 'You *must* be the salt.' It is not for the disciples to decide whether they will be the salt of the earth, for they are so whether they like it or not, they have been made salt by the call they have received. Again, it is :'Ye *are* the salt', not 'Ye *have* the salt.' By identifying the salt with the apostolic proclamation the Reformers robbed the saying of all its sting. No, the word speaks of their whole existence in so far as it is grounded anew in the call of Christ, that same existence which was the burden of the beatitudes. The call of Christ makes those who respond to it the salt of the earth in their total existence.

Of course there is another possibility – the salt may lose its savour and cease to be salt at all. It just stops working. Then it is indeed good for nothing but to be thrown away. That is the peculiar quality of salt. Everything else needs to be seasoned with salt, but once the salt itself has lost its savour, it can never be salted again. Everything else can be saved by salt, however bad it has gone – only salt which loses its savour has no hope of recovery. That is the other side of the picture. That is the judgement which always hangs over the disciple community, whose mission is to save the world, but which, if it ceases to live up to that mission, is itself irretrievably lost. The call of Jesus Christ means either that we are the salt of the earth, or else we are annihilated; either we follow the call or we are crushed beneath it. There is no question of a second chance.

The call of Jesus makes the disciple community not only the salt but also the light of the world: their activity is visible, as well as imperceptible. 'Ye *are* the light.' Once again it is not: 'You are to be the light', they are already the light because Christ has called them, they are a light which is seen of men, they cannot be otherwise, and if they were it would be a sign that they had not been called. How impossible, how utterly absurd it would be for the disciples – *these* disciples, such men as these! – to try and *become* the light of the world! No, they are already the light, and the call has made them so. Nor does Jesus say: 'You *have* the light.' The light is not an instrument which has been put into their hands, such as their preaching. It is the disciples themselves. The same Jesus who, speaking of himself, said, 'I am the light', says to his followers: 'You are the light in your whole existence, provided you remain faithful to your calling. And since you are that light, you can no longer remain hidden, even if you want to.' It is the property of light to shine. A city set on a hill cannot be hid; it can be seen for miles away, whether it is a fortified burgh, a stronghold or a tottering ruin. This city set on the hill (the Israelite would instinctively think of 'Jerusalem on high') is the disciple community. But this is not to say that the disciples have now to make their first decision. The only necessary decision has already been taken. Now they must be what they really are – otherwise they are not followers of Jesus. The followers are a visible community; their discipleship visible in action which lifts them out of the world – otherwise it would not be discipleship. And of course the following is as visible to the world as a light in the darkness or a mountain rising from a plain.

Flight into the invisible is a denial of the call. A community of Jesus which seeks to hide itself has ceased to follow him. 'Neither do men light a lamp and put it under a bushel, but on the stand.' Once again we are confronted with an alternative; the light may be covered of its own choice; it may be extinguished under a bushel, and the call may be denied. The bushel may be the fear of men, or perhaps deliberate conformity to the world for some ulterior motive, a missionary purpose for example, or a sentimental humanitarianism. But the motive may be more sinister than that; it may be 'Reformation theology' which boldly claims the name of *theologia crucis*, and pretends to prefer to Pharisaic ostentation a modest invisibility, which in practice means conformity to the world. When that happens, the hall-mark of the Church becomes *justitia civilis* instead of extraordinary visibility. The very failure of the light to shine becomes the touchstone of our Christianity. But Jesus says: 'Let your light so shine before men.' For when all is said and done, it is the light of the call of Jesus Christ which shines here. But what manner of light is it which these followers of Jesus, these disciples of the beatitudes, are to kindle on earth? What sort of light is to shine from the place where only the disciples have a right to be? How are we to reconcile the obscurity of the cross of Christ with the light that shines? Ought not the Christian life to be as obscure as the cross itself? Is not the light exactly what they ought to avoid? It is a wicked sophistry to justify the worldliness of the Church by the cross of Jesus. Is it not plain to the simplest hearer that the cross is the very place where something extraordinary has been made visible? Or is the cross no more than an example of *justitia civilis*? Does it stand for nothing more than worldliness? Did not the cross become extraordinarily visible amongst all the darkness to the terrified spectators? Are the rejection and the suffering of Christ, his death before the gates of the city on the hill of shame, not visible enough? Are they what is meant by 'invisibility'?

It is in *this* light that the good works of the disciples are meant to be seen. Men are not to see the disciples but their good works, says Jesus. And these works are none other than those which the Lord Jesus himself has created in them by calling them to be the light of the world under the shadow of his cross. The good works are poverty, peregrination, meekness, peaceableness, and finally persecution and rejection. All these good works are a bearing of the cross of Jesus Christ. The cross is the strange light which alone illuminates these good works of the disciples. Jesus does not say that men will see God; they will see the good works and glorify God for them. The cross and the works of the cross, the poverty and renunciation of the blessed in the beatitudes, these are the things which will become visible. Neither the cross, nor their membership in such a community betoken any merit of their own – the praise is due to God alone. If the good works were a galaxy of human virtues, we should then have to glorify the disciples, not God. But there is nothing for us to glorify in the disciple who bears the cross, or in the community whose light so shines because it stands visibly on the hill – only the Father which is in heaven can be praised for the 'good works'. It is by *seeing* the cross and the community beneath it that men come to believe in God. But that is the light of the Resurrection.

8   THE RIGHTEOUSNESS OF CHRIST

> Think not that I came to destroy the law or the prophets: I
> came not to destroy, but to fulfil. For verily I say unto you,
> Till heaven and earth pass away, one jot or one tittle shall in no
> wise pass away from the law, till all things be accomplished.
> Whosoever therefore shall break one of these least command-
> ments, and shall teach men so, shall be called least in the kingdom
> of heaven: but whosoever shall do and teach them, he shall be
> called great in the kingdom of heaven. For I say unto you, that
> except your righteousness shall exceed the righteousness of the
> scribes and Pharisees, ye shall in no wise enter into the kingdom
> of heaven. (Matt. 5.17-20)

IT is not at all surprising that the disciples imagined that the law
had been abrogated, when Jesus made promises like this. For these
promises reversed all popular notions of right and wrong, and
pronounced a blessing on all that was accounted worthless. Jesus
spoke to his disciples and described them as men who now possessed all things through the sovereign grace of God, as heirs-
apparent of the kingdom of heaven. They enjoy perfect communion with Christ, who had made all things new. They are the
salt, the light, the city set on the hill. The old life is dead and done
with. How tempting then to suppose that Jesus would give the
old order its *coup de grâce* by repealing the law of the old covenant,
and pronounce his followers free to enjoy the liberty of the Son
of God! After all Jesus had said, the disciples might well have
thought like Marcion, who accused the Jews of tampering with
the text, and altered it to: 'Think ye that I am come to fulfil the
law and the prophets? I am not come to fulfil, but to destroy.'
Many others since Marcion have read and expounded this saying
of Jesus as if that were what he said. But Jesus says: 'You must not
imagine that I have come to destroy the law or the prophets. . . .'
And so saying he vindicates the authority of the law of the old
covenant.

How is this to be understood? We know that Jesus is speaking to his own followers, to men who owe an exclusive allegiance to himself. He had allowed no law to act as a barrier to his fellowship with his disciples; we saw that when we were dealing with Luke 9.57 ff. Discipleship means adherence to Jesus Christ alone, and immediately. But now comes the surprise – the disciples are bound to the Old Testament law. This has a double significance. First, it means that adherence to the law is something quite different from the following of Christ, and, secondly, it means that any adherence to his person that disregards the law is equally removed from the following of him. It is, however, Jesus himself who points to the law those to whom he has granted his whole promise and his whole fellowship. Because it is their Lord who does this, they are bound to acknowledge the law. The question inevitably arises, Which is our final authority, Christ or the law? To which are we bound? Christ had said that no law was to be allowed to come between him and his disciples. Now he tells us that to abandon the law would be to separate ourselves from him. What exactly does he mean?

The law Jesus refers to is the law of the old covenant, not a new law, but the same law which he quoted to the rich young man and the lawyer when they wanted to know the revealed will of God. It becomes a new law only because it is Christ who binds his followers to it. For Christians, therefore, the law is not a 'better law' than that of the Pharisees, but one and the same; every letter of it, every jot and tittle, must remain in force and be observed until the end of the world. But there is a 'better righteousness' which is expected of Christians. Without it none can enter into the kingdom of heaven, for it is the indispensable condition of discipleship. None can have this better righteousness but those to whom Christ is speaking here, those whom he has called. The call of Christ, in fact Christ himself, is the *sine qua non* of this better righteousness.

Now we can see why up to now Jesus has said nothing about himself in the Sermon on the Mount. Between the disciples and the better righteousness demanded of them stands the Person of

Christ, who came to fulfil the law of the old covenant. This is the fundamental presupposition of the whole Sermon on the Mount. Jesus manifests his perfect union with the will of God as revealed in the Old Testament law and prophets. He has in fact nothing to add to the commandments of God, except this, that he keeps them. He fulfils the law, and he tells us so himself, therefore it must be true. He fulfils the law down to the last iota. But that means that he must die, he alone understands the true nature of the law as God's law: the law is not itself God, nor is God the law. It was the error of Israel to put the law in God's place, to make the law their God and their God a law. The disciples were confronted with the opposite danger of denying the law its divinity altogether and divorcing God from his law. Both errors lead to the same result. By confounding God and the law, the Jews were trying to use the law to exploit the Law-giver: He was swallowed up in the law, and therefore no longer its Lord. By imagining that God and the law could be divorced from one another, the disciples were trying to exploit God by their possession of salvation. In both cases, the gift was confounded with the Giver: God was denied equally, whether it was with the help of the law, or with the promise of salvation.

Confronted with these twin errors, Jesus vindicates the divine authority of the law. God is its giver and its Lord, and only in personal communion with God is the law fulfilled. There is no fulfilment of the law apart from communion with God, and no communion with God apart from fulfilment of the law. To forget the first condition was the mistake of the Jews, and to forget the second the temptation of the disciples.

Jesus, the Son of God, who alone lives in perfect communion with him, vindicates the law of the old covenant by coming to fulfil it. He was the only Man who ever fulfilled the law, and therefore he alone can teach the law and its fulfilment aright. The disciples would naturally grasp that as soon as he told them, for they knew who he was. But the Jews could not grasp it as long as they refused to believe in him. It was thus only to be expected that they would reject his teaching on the law: to them it was blasphemy against God, because it was blasphemy against his law. Jesus, the champion of the true law, must suffer at the hands of the champions of the false law. He dies on the cross as a blasphemer, a transgressor of the law, because he has vindicated the true against the false.

The only way for him to fulfil the law is by dying a sinner's death on the cross. There he embodies in his person the perfect fulfilment of the law.

That is to say, Jesus Christ and he alone fulfils the law, because he alone lives in perfect communion with God. It is Jesus himself who comes between the disciples and the law, not the law which comes between Jesus and the disciples. They find their way to the law through the cross of Christ. Thus by pointing his disciples to the law which he alone fulfils, he forges a further bond between himself and them. He must needs reject the notion that men can cleave to him and be free from the law, for that spells enthusiasm, and so far from leading to adherence to Jesus, means libertarianism. But this allays the disciples' anxiety that adherence to the law would sever them from Jesus. Such an anxiety could only spring from that self-same error which cut off the Jews from God. Instead the disciples now learn that genuine adherence to Christ also means adherence to the law of God.

But if Jesus comes between the disciples and the law, he does so not to release them from the duties it imposes, but to validate his demand that they should fulfil it. Just because they are bound to him, they must obey the law as he does. The fact that Jesus has fulfilled the law down to the very last letter does not release them from the same obedience. The law is fulfilled, that is all. But it is precisely this which makes it properly valid for the first time. That is why he who obeys and teaches the law will be great in the kingdom of heaven. '*Do* and teach': we are reminded that it is possible to teach the law without fulfilling it, to teach it in such a way that it cannot be fulfilled. That sort of teaching has no warrant from Jesus. The law will be obeyed as certainly as he obeyed it himself. If men cleave to him who fulfilled the law and follow him, they will find themselves both teaching and fulfilling the law. Only the doer of the law can remain in communion with Jesus.

It is not the law which distinguishes the disciples from the Jews, but the 'better righteousness'. The righteousness of the disciples, we are told, exceeds that of the scribes. That is because it is something extraordinary and unusual. This is the first time we meet the word περισσεύειν, which is so important in verse 47. We must ask, how exactly does the righteousness of the Pharisees differ from that of the disciples? Certainly the Pharisees never imagined that the law must be taught but not obeyed: they knew their Bibles better than that! No, it was rather their ambition to be doers of the law. Their idea of righteousness was a direct, literal and practical fulfilment of the commandment, their ideal was to model their behaviour exactly on the demands of the law. Of course they knew that they could never realize that ideal, there was bound to be an excess which needed forgiveness of sins to cover it. Their obedience was never more than imperfect. With the disciple also righteousness could only take the form of obedience to the law. No one who failed to do the law could be accounted righteous. But the disciple had the advantage over the Pharisee in that his doing of the law is in fact perfect. How is such a thing possible? Because between the disciples and the law stands one who has perfectly fulfilled it, one with whom they live in communion. They are faced not with a law which has never yet been fulfilled, but with one whose demands have already been satisfied. The righteousness it demands is already there, the righteousness of Jesus which submits to the cross because that is what the law demands. This righteousness is therefore not a duty owed, but a perfect and truly personal communion with God, and Jesus not only possesses this righteousness, but is himself the personal embodiment of it. He *is* the righteousness of the disciples. By calling them he has admitted them to partnership with himself, and made them partakers of his righteousness in its fulness. That is what Jesus means when he prefaces his teaching on the 'better righteousness' with reference to his own fulfilment of the law. Of course the righteousness of the disciples can never be a personal achievement; it is always a gift, which they received when they were called to follow him. In fact their righteousness consists precisely in their following him, and in the beatitudes the reward of the kingdom of heaven has been promised to it. It is a righteousness under the cross, it belongs only to the poor, the tempted, the hungry, the meek, the peacemakers, the persecuted – who endure their lot for the sake of Jesus; it is the visible righteousness of those who for the sake of Jesus are the light of the world and the city set on the hill. This is where the righteousness of the disciple exceeds that of the Pharisees; it is grounded solely upon the call to fellowship with him who alone fulfils the law. Their righteousness is righteousness indeed, for from henceforth they do the will of God and fulfil the law themselves. Again, it is not enough to teach the law of Christ, it must be *done*, otherwise it is no better than the old law. In what follows the disciples are told how to practise this righteousness of Christ. In a word, it means following him. It is the real and active faith in the righteousness of Christ. It is the new law, the law of Christ.

9 THE BROTHER

> Ye have heard that it was said to them of old time, Thou shalt not kill; and whosoever shall kill shall be in danger of the judgement: but I say unto you, that every one who is angry with his brother shall be in danger of the judgement; and whosoever shall say to his brother, Raca, shall be in danger of the council; and whosoever shall say, Thou fool, shall be in danger of the hell of fire. If therefore thou art offering thy gift at the altar, and there rememberest that thy brother hath aught against thee, leave there thy gift before the altar, and go thy way, first be reconciled to thy brother, and then come and offer thy gift. Agree with thine adversary quickly, whiles thou art with him in the way; lest haply the adversary deliver thee to the judge, and the judge deliver thee to the officer, and thou be cast into prison. Verily I say unto thee, Thou shalt by no means come out thence, till thou have paid the last farthing. (Matt. 5.21-26)

'BUT I say unto you' – Jesus sums up the whole purport of the law. All he has said so far makes it impossible to regard him here as a revolutionary, or as a rabbi pitting one opinion against another. On the contrary, Jesus is simply picking up the argument where he left off, and affirming his agreement with the law of the Mosaic covenant. But – and this is where he is at one with the law of God – he makes it perfectly clear that he, the Son of God, is the Author and Giver of the law. Only those who apprehend the law as the word of Christ are in a position to fulfil it. The heresy of the Pharisees must be excluded at all costs. Only by knowing Christ as the Giver and Fulfiller of the law can we attain to a true knowledge of the law. Christ has laid his hand on the law, and by claiming it for his own, he brings it to fruition. But while he is in perfect agreement with the law as such, he declares war on all false interpretations of it, and by honouring it he gives himself into the hands of its false devotees.

The first law which Jesus commends to his disciples is the one which forbids murder and entrusts their brother's welfare to their keeping. The brother's life is a divine ordinance, and God alone

has power over life and death. There is no place for the murderer
among the people of God. The judgement he passes on others
falls on the murderer himself. In this context 'brother' means
more than 'fellow-Christian': for the follower of Jesus there can
be no limit as to who is his neighbour, except as his Lord decides.
He is forbidden to commit murder under pain of divine judgement. For him the brother's life is a boundary which he dare not
pass. Even anger is enough to overstep the mark, still more the
casual angry word (*Raca*), and most of all the deliberate insult of
our brother ('Thou fool').

Anger is always an attack on the brother's life, for it refuses to
let him live and aims at his destruction. Jesus will not accept the
common distinction between righteous indignation and unjustifiable anger.[1] The disciple must be entirely innocent of anger,
because anger is an offence against both God and his neighbour.
Every idle word which we think so little of betrays our lack of
respect for our neighbour, and shows that we place ourselves on
a pinnacle above him and value our own lives higher than his.
The angry word is a blow struck at our brother, a stab at his
heart: it seeks to hit, to hurt and to destroy. A deliberate insult is
even worse, for we are then openly disgracing our brother in the
eyes of the world, and causing others to despise him. With our
hearts burning with hatred, we seek to annihilate his moral and
material existence. We are passing judgement on him, and that
is murder. And the murderer will himself be judged.

When a man gets angry with his brother and swears at him,
when he publicly insults or slanders him, he is guilty of murder
and forfeits his relation to God. He erects a barrier not only
between himself and his brother, but also between himself and
God. He no longer has access to him: his sacrifice, worship and
prayer are not acceptable in his sight. For the Christian, worship
cannot be divorced from the service of the brethren, as it was with
the rabbis. If we despise our brother our worship is unreal, and it
forfeits every divine promise. When we come before God with

---

[1] The addition εἰκῇ in the majority of MSS. (though not in ℵ and B) is the
first attempt to mitigate the harshness of this saying.

hearts full of contempt and unreconciled with our neighbours, we are, both individually and as a congregation, worshipping an idol. So long as we refuse to love and serve our brother and make him an object of contempt and let him harbour a grudge against me or the congregation, our worship and sacrifice will be un-acceptable to God. Not just the fact that I am angry, but the fact that there is somebody who has been hurt, damaged and disgraced by me, who 'has a cause against me', erects a barrier between me and God. Let us therefore as a Church examine ourselves, and see whether we have not often enough wronged our fellow-men. Let us see whether we have tried to win popularity by falling in with the world's hatred, its contempt and its contumely. For if we do that we are murderers. Let the fellowship of Christ so examine itself to-day and ask whether, at the hour of prayer and worship, any accusing voices intervene and make its prayer vain. Let the fellowship of Christ examine itself and see whether it has given any token of the love of Christ to the victims of the world's contumely and contempt, any token of that love of Christ which seeks to preserve, support and protect life. Otherwise however liturgically correct our services are, and however devout our prayer, however brave our testimony, they will profit us nothing, nay rather, they must needs testify against us that we have as a Church ceased to follow our Lord. God will not be separated from our brother: he wants no honour for himself so long as our brother is dishonoured. God is the Father, the Father of our Lord Jesus Christ, who became the Brother of us all. Here is the final reason why God will not be separated from our brother. His only-begotten Son bore the shame and insults for his Father's glory. But the Father would not be separated from his Son, nor will he now turn his face from those whose likeness the Son took upon him, and for whose sake he bore the shame. The Incarnation is the ultimate reason why the service of God cannot be divorced from the service of man. He who says he loves God and hates his brother is a liar.

There is therefore only one way of following Jesus and of worshipping God, and that is to be reconciled with our brethren.

If we come to hear the Word of God and receive the sacrament without first being reconciled with our neighbours, we shall come to our own damnation. In the sight of God we are murderers. Therefore 'go thy way, first be reconciled with thy brother, and then come and offer thy gift'. This is a hard way, but it is the way Jesus requires if we are to follow him. It is a way which brings much personal humiliation and insult, but it is indeed the way to him, our crucified Brother, and therefore a way of grace abounding. In Jesus the service of God and the service of the least of the brethren were one. He went his way and became reconciled with his brother and offered himself as the one true sacrifice to his Father.

We are still living in the age of grace, for each of us still has a brother, we are still 'with him in the way'. The court of judgement lies ahead, and there is still a chance for us to be reconciled with our brother and pay our debt to him. The hour is coming when we shall meet the judge face to face, and then it will be too late. We shall then receive our sentence and be made to pay the last farthing. But do we realize that at this point our brother comes to us in the guise not of law, but of grace? It is grace that we are allowed to please our brother, and pay our debt to him, it is grace that we are allowed to become reconciled with him. In our brother we find grace before the seat of judgement.

Only he can speak thus to us, who as our Brother has himself become our grace, our atonement, our deliverance from judgement. The humanity of the Son of God grants us the gift of a brother. May the disciples of Jesus think upon this grace aright!

To serve our brother, to please him, to allow him his due and to let him live, is the way of self-denial, the way of the cross. Greater love hath no man than this, that a man lay down his life for his friends. That is the love of the Crucified. Only in the cross of Christ do we find the fulfilment of the law.

10 WOMAN

> Ye have heard that it was said, Thou shalt not commit adultery:
> but I say unto you, that every one that looketh on a woman to
> lust after her hath committed adultery with her already in his
> heart. And if thy right eye causeth thee to stumble, pluck it out,
> and cast it from thee: for it is profitable for thee that one of thy
> members should perish, and not thy whole body be cast into
> hell. And if thy right hand causeth thee to stumble, cut it off,
> and cast it from thee: for it is profitable for thee that one of thy
> members should perish, and not thy whole body go into hell.
> It was said also, Whosoever shall put away his wife, saving for
> the cause of fornication, maketh her an adulteress: and who-
> soever shall marry her when she is put away committeth adultery.
> (Matt. 5.27-32)

ADHERENCE to Jesus allows no free rein to desire unless it be
accompanied by love. To follow Jesus means self-renunciation
and absolute adherence to him, and therefore a will dominated by
lust can never be allowed to do what it likes. Even momentary
desire is a barrier to the following of Jesus, and brings the whole
body into hell, making us sell our heavenly birthright for a mess
of pottage, and showing that we lack faith in him who will reward
mortification with joy a hundredfold. Instead of trusting to the
unseen, we prefer the tangible fruits of desire, and so we fall from
the path of discipleship and lose touch with Jesus. Lust is impure
because it is unbelief, and therefore it is to be shunned. No sacrifice
is too great if it enables us to conquer a lust which cuts us off from
Jesus. Both eye and hand are less than Christ, and when they are
used as the instruments of lust and hinder the whole body from
the purity of discipleship, they must be sacrificed for the sake of
him. The gains of lust are trivial compared with the loss it brings
– you forfeit your body eternally for the momentary pleasure of
eye or hand. When you have made your eye the instrument of
impurity, you cannot see God with it. Surely, at this point we
must make up our minds once and for all whether Jesus means his

precepts to be taken literally or only figuratively, for here it is a matter of life or death. But the question is answered by the reaction of the disciples. Our natural inclination is to avoid a definite decision over this apparently crucial question. But the question is itself both wrong and wicked, and it does not admit of an answer. If we decided not to take it literally, we should be evading the seriousness of the commandment, and if on the other hand we decided it was to be taken literally, we should at once reveal the absurdity of the Christian position, and thereby invalidate the commandment. The fact that we receive no answer to the question only makes the commandment even more inescapable. We cannot evade the issue either way; we are placed in a position where there is no alternative but to obey. Jesus does not impose intolerable restrictions on his disciples, he does not forbid them to look at anything, but bids them look on him. If they do that he knows that their gaze will always be pure, even when they look upon a woman. So far from imposing on them an intolerable yoke of legalism, he succours them with the grace of the gospel.

Jesus does not enjoin his disciples to marry, but he does sanctify marriage according to the law by affirming its indissolubility and by prohibiting the innocent party from remarrying when the guilty partner has broken the marriage by adultery. This prohibition liberates marriage from selfish, evil desire, and consecrates it to the service of love, which is possible only in a life of discipleship. Jesus does not depreciate the body and its natural instincts, but he does condemn the unbelief which is so often latent in its desires. So far then from abolishing marriage, he sets it on a firmer basis and sanctifies it through faith. The disciple's exclusive adherence to Christ therefore extends even to his married life. Christian marriage is marked by discipline and self-denial. Christ is the Lord even of marriage. There is of course a difference between the Christian and the bourgeois conception of marriage, but Christianity does not therefore depreciate marriage, it sanctifies it.

It would appear that by affirming the indissolubility of marriage Jesus contradicts the law of the Old Testament. But there is another passage (Matt. 19.8) which shows that in fact he is at one with the law of Moses. There he says that divorce was permitted to the Israelites 'for your hardness of heart' – in other words, it was to preserve them from worse excesses. The intention of the Old Testament law is the same as that of Jesus, to uphold the purity of marriage, and to see that it is exercised in faith in God. But purity or chastity is safeguarded amongst those who follow Jesus and share his life.

Being concerned exclusively with the perfect purity, that is to say, the chastity of his disciples, Jesus also approves of absolute celibacy for the sake of the kingdom of heaven. But he lays down no definite programme for his disciples, whether of celibacy or of marriage, only he delivers them from the perils of πορνεία (i.e. any sexual irregularity inside or outside of the married life). Such irregularity is a sin, not only against our own bodies, but against the Body of Christ (I Cor. 6.13-15). Even our bodies belong to Christ and have their part in the life of discipleship, for they are members of his Body. Jesus, the Son of God, bore a human body, and since we enjoy fellowship with that Body, fornication is a sin against Christ's own Body.

The body of Jesus was crucified. St Paul, speaking of those who belong to Christ, says that they have crucified their body with its affections and lusts (Gal. 5.24). Here we have another instance of an Old Testament law finding its truest fulfilment in the crucified body of Jesus Christ. As they contemplate this body which was given for them, and as they share its life, the disciples receive strength for the chastity which Jesus requires.

11 TRUTHFULNESS

> Again, ye have heard that it was said to them of old time, Thou shalt not forswear thyself, but shalt perform unto the Lord thine oaths: but I say unto you, Swear not at all; neither by the heaven, for it is the throne of God; nor by the earth, for it is the footstool of his feet; nor by Jerusalem, for it is the city of the great King. Neither shalt thou swear by thy head, for thou canst not make one hair white or black. But let your speech be, Yea, yea; Nay, nay: and whatsoever is more than these is of the evil one. (Matt. 5.33-37)

THE Christian Church has until now been strangely uncertain about the interpretation of this passage. Since the time of the primitive Church, commentators have oscillated between a rigorism which rejects every oath as a sin, and a more liberal position which rejects only frivolous oaths and downright perjury. In the early Church the commonest interpretation was that 'perfect' Christians were forbidden to swear at all, but the weaker brethren were allowed to swear within certain limits. Augustine represents this latter point of view. He found himself in agreement with the teaching of Plato, the Pythagoreans, Epictetus, Marcus Aurelius, and other pagan philosophers, who maintained that oaths were beneath the dignity of gentlemen. In the Reformation Confessions it is expressly affirmed that there can be no question of Jesus prohibiting oaths exacted by the state in a court of law. Were not such oaths expressly enjoined in the Old Testament? Jesus himself had sworn before a court of law, and St Paul frequently employs expressions of an oath-like character. Next to scriptural proof, the distinction between the spiritual and worldly realms was of decisive importance for the Reformers.

What is an oath? It is an appeal made to God in public, calling upon him to witness a statement made in connection with an event or fact, past, present or future. By means of the oath, men invoke the omniscient deity to avenge the truth. How can Jesus say that such an oath is 'sin', 'from the evil one', ἐκ τοῦ πονηροῦ, 'satanic'? The answer is to be sought in his concern for complete truthfulness.

The very existence of oaths is a proof that there are such things as lies. If lying were unknown, there would be no need for oaths. Oaths are intended as a barrier against untruthfulness. But it goes further than that: for there, where alone the oath claims final truth, is space in life given to the lie, and it is granted a certain right of life. The Old Testament had expressed its condemnation of the lie by the use of the oath. But Jesus destroys the lie by forbidding oaths altogether. Here as there it is the same question, one and undivided, of the destruction of untruth in the life of the believer. The oath which the Old Testament set against the lie is seized by the lie itself and pressed into service. It is thus able through the oath to establish itself and to take the law into its own hands. So the lie must be seized by Jesus in the very place to which it flees, in the oath. Therefore the oath must go, since it is a protection for the lie.

There are two ways in which untruthfulness can undermine the oath: either it may actually insinuate itself into the oath (perjury), or else disguise itself in the form of an oath by invoking some secular or divine power instead of the living God. When once the lie had entrenched itself behind the oath, there was no other way of ensuring complete truthfulness but by abolishing the oath altogether.

'Let your speech be Yea, yea, and Nay, nay.' This is not to say that the disciples are no longer answerable to the omniscient God for every word they utter, it means that *every* word they utter is spoken in his presence, and not only those words which are accompanied by an oath. Hence they are forbidden to swear at all. Since they always speak the whole truth and nothing but the truth, there is no need for an oath, which would only throw doubt on the veracity of all their other statements. That is why the oath is 'of the evil one'. But a disciple must be a light even in his words.

It is clear that the only reason why Jesus prohibits the swearing of oaths lies in this concern for truthfulness. It also goes without laying that he admits no exceptions, however high the court of saw may be. But at the same time it must be admitted that the abolition of oaths is in itself no guarantee that the truth will be told, indeed it may only lead to its concealment. No general rule can be laid down to enable us to decide where this is so, i.e. where an oath is desirable precisely in the interests of the truth; each case must be decided on its own merits. The Churches of the Reformation were convinced that every oath demanded by the state was covered by this exception. But it is questionable whether it is possible to lay down a general rule like that.

There is, however, no question that when such a case appears to arise, an oath can only be sworn where all its implications are first made clear beyond all doubt. Secondly, a distinction must be drawn between oaths which apply to past or present facts, which are known, and oaths which pledge us with reference to the future. Since the profession of Christianity does not confer an infallible knowledge of the past, the invocation of almighty God will serve only to establish the integrity of his mind and conscience but not to confirm a statement which after all may be open to error. Moreover, since he is never lord of his own future, he will always be extremely cautious about giving a pledge (e.g. an oath of allegiance), for he is aware how dangerous it is to do so. And if his own future is outside his own control, how much more is the future of the authority which demands the oath of allegiance! For the sake of the truth, therefore, and for the sake of his following of Christ, he cannot swear such an oath without the proviso, 'God willing'. For the Christian no earthly obligation is absolutely binding, and any oath which makes an unconditional demand on him will for him be a lie which proceeds 'from the evil one'. In such a case the utmost an oath can do is to testify to the fact that the Christian is bound to the will of God alone, and that every other obligation is for the sake of Jesus conditional upon that will. If in a doubtful case this proviso is not explicitly stated or acknowledged, the oath cannot then be sworn, otherwise the Christian would be deceiving the authority. Let your speech, however, be: Yea, yea, Nay, nay.

The commandment of complete truthfulness is really only another name for the totality of discipleship. Only those who follow Jesus and cleave to him are living in complete truthfulness. Such men have nothing to hide from their Lord. Their life is revealed before him, Jesus has recognized them and led them into the way of truth. They cannot hide their sinfulness from Jesus, for they have not revealed themselves to Jesus, but he has revealed himself to them by calling them to follow him. At the moment of their call Jesus showed up their sin and made them aware of it. Complete truthfulness is only possible where sin has been uncovered, and forgiven by Jesus. Only those who are in a state of truthfulness through the confession of their sin to Jesus are not ashamed to tell the truth wherever it must be told. The truthfulness which Jesus demands from his followers is the self-abnegation which does not hide sin. Nothing is then hidden, everything is brought forth to the light of day.

In this question of truthfulness, what matters first and last is that a man's whole being should be exposed, his whole evil laid bare in the sight of God. But sinful men do not like this sort of truthfulness, and they resist it with all their might. That is why they persecute it and crucify it. It is only because we follow Jesus that we can be genuinely truthful, for then he reveals to us our sin upon the cross. The cross is God's truth about us, and therefore it is the only power which can make us truthful. When we know the cross we are no longer afraid of the truth. We need no more oaths to confirm the truth of our utterances, for we live in the perfect truth of God.

There is no truth towards Jesus without truth towards man. Untruthfulness destroys fellowship, but truth cuts false fellowship to pieces and establishes genuine brotherhood. We cannot follow Christ unless we live in revealed truth before God and man.

12 REVENGE

> Ye hath heard that it was said, An eye for an eye, and a tooth for a tooth: but I say unto you, Resist not him that is evil: but whosoever smiteth thee on thy right cheek, turn to him the other also. And if any man would go to law with thee, and take away thy coat, let him have thy cloke also. And whosoever shall compel thee to go one mile, go with him twain. Give to him that asketh thee, and from him that would borrow of thee turn not thou away. (Matt. 5.38-42)

JESUS classes this saying about an eye for an eye and a tooth for a tooth with the commandments which he has already quoted from the Old Testament, for instance, the sixth commandment against murder. He recognizes this saying, like the sixth commandment, as the veritable law of God. This law, like all the others, is not to be abrogated, but fulfilled to the last iota. Jesus will not countenance the modern practice of putting the decalogue on a higher level than the rest of the Old Testament law. For him the law of the Old Testament is a unity, and he insists to his disciples that it must be fulfilled.

The followers of Jesus for his sake renounce every personal right. He calls them blessed because they are meek. If after giving up everything else for his sake they still wanted to cling to their own rights, they would then have ceased to follow him. This passage therefore is simply an elaboration of the beatitudes.

In the Old Testament personal rights are protected by a divinely established system of retribution. Every evil must be requited. The aim of retribution is to establish a proper community, to convict and overcome evil and eradicate it from the body politic of the people of God. That is the purpose of the law which is maintained by retribution.

Jesus takes up this declaration of the divine will and affirms the power of retribution to convict and overcome evil and to ensure the fellowship of the disciples as the true Israel. By exercising the right kind of retribution evil is to be overcome and thus the true disciple will prove himself.

The right way to requite evil, according to Jesus, is not to resist it.

This saying of Christ removes the Church from the sphere of politics and law. The Church is not to be a national community like the old Israel, but a community of believers without political or national ties. The old Israel had been both – the chosen people of God *and* a national community, and it was therefore his will that they should meet force with force. But with the Church it is different: it has abandoned political and national status, and therefore it must patiently endure aggression. Otherwise evil will be heaped upon evil. Only thus can fellowship be established and maintained.

At this point it becomes evident that when a Christian meets with injustice, he no longer clings to his rights and defends them at all costs. He is absolutely free from possessions and bound to Christ alone. Again, his witness to this exclusive adherence to Jesus creates the only workable basis for fellowship, and leaves the aggressor for him to deal with.

The only way to overcome evil is to let it run itself to a standstill because it does not find the resistance it is looking for. Resistance merely creates further evil and adds fuel to the flames. But when evil meets no opposition and encounters no obstacle but only patient endurance, its sting is drawn, and at last it meets an opponent which is more than its match. Of course this can only happen when the last ounce of resistance is abandoned, and the renunciation of revenge is complete. Then evil cannot find its mark, it can breed no further evil, and is left barren.

By willing endurance we cause suffering to pass. Evil becomes a spent force when we put up no resistance. By refusing to pay back the enemy in his own coin, and by preferring to suffer without resistance, the Christian exhibits the sinfulness of contumely and insult. Violence stands condemned by its failure to evoke counter-violence. When a man unjustly demands that I should give him my coat, I offer him my cloak also, and so counter his demand; when he requires me to go the other mile, I go willingly, and show up his exploitation of my service for what it is. To leave everything behind at the call of Christ is to be content with him alone, and to follow only him. By his willingly renouncing self-defence, the Christian affirms his absolute adherence to Jesus, and his freedom from the tyranny of his own ego. The exclusiveness of this adherence is the only power which can overcome evil.

We are concerned not with evil in the abstract, but with the evil *person*. Jesus bluntly calls the evil person evil. If I am assailed, I am not to condone or justify aggression. Patient endurance of evil does not mean a recognition of its rights. That is sheer sentimentality, and Jesus will have nothing to do with it. The shameful assault, the deed of violence and the act of exploitation are still evil. The disciple must realize this, and bear witness to it as Jesus did, just because this is the only way evil can be met and overcome. The very fact that the evil which assaults him is unjustifiable makes it imperative that he should not resist it, but play it out and overcome it by patiently enduring the evil person. Suffering willingly endured is stronger than evil, it spells death to evil.

There is no deed on earth so outrageous as to justify a different attitude. The worse the evil, the readier must the Christian be to suffer; he must let the evil person fall into Jesus' hands.

The Reformers offered a decisively new interpretation of this passage, and contributed a new idea of paramount importance. They distinguished between personal sufferings and those incurred by Christians in the performance of duty as bearers of an office ordained by God, maintaining that the precept of non-violence applies to the first but not to the second. In the second case we are not only freed from obligation to eschew violence, but if we want to act in a genuine spirit of love we must do the very opposite, and meet force with force in order to check the assault of evil. It was along these lines that the Reformers justified war and other legal sanctions against evil. But this distinction between person and office is wholly alien to the teaching of Jesus. He says nothing about that. He addresses his disciples as men who have left all to follow him, and the precept of non-violence applies equally to private life and official duty. He is the Lord of all life, and demands undivided allegiance. Furthermore, when it comes to practice, this distinction raises insoluble difficulties. Am I ever acting only as a private person or only in an official capacity? If I am attacked am I not at once the father of my children, the pastor of my flock, and e.g. a government official? Am I not bound for that very reason to defend myself against every attack, for reason of responsibility to my office? And am I not also always an individual, face to face with Jesus, even in the performance of my official duties? Am I not therefore obliged to resist every attack just because of my responsibility for my office? Is it right to forget that the follower of Jesus is always utterly alone, always the individual, who in the last resort can only decide and act for himself? Don't we act most responsibly on behalf of those entrusted to our care if we act in this aloneness?

How then can the precept of Jesus be justified in the light of experience? It is obvious that weakness and defencelessness only invite aggression. Is then the demand of Jesus nothing but an impracticable ideal? Does he refuse to face up to realities – or shall we say, to the sin of the world? There may of course be a legitimate place for such an ideal in the inner life of the Christian community, but in the outside world such an ideal appears to wear the blinkers of perfectionism, and to take no account of sin. Living as we do in a world of sin and evil, we can have no truck with anything as impracticable as that.

Jesus, however, tells us that it is just *because* we live in the world, and just *because* the world is evil, that the precept of non-resistance must be put into practice. Surely we do not wish to accuse Jesus of ignoring the reality and power of evil! Why, the whole of his life was one long conflict with the devil. He calls evil evil, and that is the very reason why he speaks to his followers in this way. How is that possible?

If we took the precept of non-resistance as an ethical blueprint for general application, we should indeed be indulging in idealistic dreams: we should be dreaming of a utopia with laws which the world would never obey. To make non-resistance a principle for secular life is to deny God, by undermining his gracious ordinance for the preservation of the world. But Jesus is no draughtsman of political blue-prints, he is the one who vanquished evil through suffering. It looked as though evil had triumphed on the cross, but the real victory belonged to Jesus. And the cross is the only justification for the precept of non-violence, for it alone can kindle a faith in the victory over evil which will enable men to obey that precept. And only such obedience is blessed with the promise that we shall be partakers of Christ's victory as well as of his sufferings.

The passion of Christ is the victory of divine love over the powers of evil, and therefore it is the only supportable basis for Christian obedience. Once again, Jesus calls those who follow him to share his passion. How can we convince the world by our preaching of the passion when we shrink from that passion in our own lives? On the cross Jesus fulfilled the law he himself established and thus graciously keeps his disciples in the fellowship of his suffering. The cross is the only power in the world which proves that suffering love can avenge and vanquish evil. But it was just this participation in the cross which the disciples were granted when Jesus called them to him. They are called blessed because of their visible participation in his cross.

13 THE ENEMY—THE 'EXTRAORDINARY'

> Ye have heard that it was said, Thou shalt love thy neighbour,
> and hate thine enemy: but I say unto you, Love your enemies,
> and pray for them that persecute you; that ye may be sons of
> your Father which is in heaven: for he maketh his sun to rise
> on the evil and the good, and sendeth rain on the just and the
> unjust. For if ye love them that love you, what reward have ye?
> do not even the publicans the same? And if ye salute your
> brethren only, what do ye more than others? do not even the
> Gentiles the same? Ye therefore shall be perfect, as your
> heavenly Father is perfect. (Matt. 5.43-48)

HERE, for the first time in the Sermon on the Mount, we meet
the word which sums up the whole of its message, the word 'love'.
Love is defined in uncompromising terms as the love of our
enemies. Had Jesus only told us to love our brethren, we might
have misunderstood what he meant by love, but now he leaves us
in no doubt whatever as to his meaning.

The enemy was no mere abstraction for the disciples. They
knew him only too well. They came across him every day. There
were those who cursed them for undermining the faith and trans-
gressing the law. There were those who hated them for leaving
all they had for Jesus' sake. There were those who insulted and
derided them for their weakness and humility. There were those
who persecuted them as prospective dangerous revolutionaries
and sought to destroy them. Some of their enemies were numbered among the champions of the popular religion, who resented
the exclusive claim of Jesus. These last enjoyed considerable power
and reputation. And then there was the enemy which would
immediately occur to every Jew, the political enemy in Rome.
Over and above all these, the disciples also had to contend with
the hostility which invariably falls to the lot of those who refuse
to follow the crowd, and which brought them daily mockery,
derision and threats.

It is true that the Old Testament never explicitly bids us hate our enemies. On the contrary, it tells us more than once that we must love them (Ex. 23.4 f; Prov. 25.21 f; Gen. 45.1 ff; I Sam. 24.7; II Kings 6.22, etc.). But Jesus is not talking of ordinary enmity, but of that which exists between the People of God and the world. The wars of Israel were the only 'holy wars' in history, for they were the wars of God against the world of idols. It is not this enmity which Jesus condemns, for then he would have condemned the whole history of God's dealings with his people. On the contrary, he affirms the old covenant. He is as concerned as the Old Testament with the defeat of the enemy and the victory of the People of God. No, the real meaning of this saying is that Jesus is again releasing his disciples from the political associations of the old Israel. From now on there can be no more wars of faith. The only way to overcome our enemy is by loving him.

To the natural man, the very notion of loving his enemies is an intolerable offence, and quite beyond his capacity: it cuts right across his ideas of good and evil. More important still, to man under the law, the idea of loving his enemies is clean contrary to the law of God, which requires men to sever all connection with their enemies and to pass judgement on them. Jesus however takes the law of God in his own hands and expounds its true meaning. The will of God, to which the law gives expression, is that men should defeat their enemies by loving them.

In the New Testament our enemies are those who harbour hostility against us, not those against whom we cherish hostility, for Jesus refuses to reckon with such a possibility. The Christian must treat his enemy as a brother, and requite his hostility with love. His behaviour must be determined not by the way others treat him, but by the treatment he himself receives from Jesus; it has only one source, and that is the will of Jesus.

By our enemies Jesus means those who are quite intractable and utterly unresponsive to our love, who forgive us nothing when we forgive them all, who requite our love with hatred and our service with derision, 'For the love that I had unto them, lo, they now take my contrary part: but I give myself unto prayer' (Ps.

109.4). Love asks nothing in return, but seeks those who need it. And who needs our love more than those who are consumed with hatred and are utterly devoid of love? Who in other words deserves our love more than our enemy? Where is love more glorified than where she dwells in the midst of her enemies?

Christian love draws no distinction between one enemy and another, except that the more bitter our enemy's hatred, the greater his need of love. Be his enmity political or religious, he has nothing to expect from a follower of Jesus but unqualified love. In such love there is no inner discord between private person and official capacity. In both we are disciples of Christ, or we are not Christians at all. Am I asked how this love is to behave? Jesus gives the answer: bless, do good, and pray for your enemies without reserve and without respect of persons.

'Love your enemies.' The preceding commandment had spoken only of the passive endurance of evil; here Jesus goes further and bids us not only to bear with evil and the evil person patiently, not only to refrain from treating him as he treats us, but actively to engage in heart-felt love towards him. We are to serve our enemy in all things without hypocrisy and with utter sincerity. No sacrifice which a lover would make for his beloved is too great for us to make for our enemy. If out of love for our brother we are willing to sacrifice goods, honour and life, we must be prepared to do the same for our enemy. We are not to imagine that this is to condone his evil; such a love proceeds from strength rather than weakness, from truth rather than fear, and therefore it cannot be guilty of the hatred of another. And who is to be the object of such a love, if not those whose hearts are stifled with hatred?

'Bless them that persecute you.' If our enemy cannot put up with us any longer and takes to cursing us, our immediate reaction must be to lift up our hands and bless him. Our enemies are the blessed of the Lord. Their curse can do us no harm. May their poverty be enriched with all the riches of God, with the blessing of him whom they seek to oppose in vain. We are ready to endure their curses so long as they redound to their blessing.

'*Do good to them that hate you.*' We must love not only in thought and word, but in deed, and there are opportunities of service in every circumstance of daily life. 'If thine enemy hunger, feed him; if he thirst, give him to drink' (Rom. 12.20). As brother stands by brother in distress, binding up his wounds and soothing his pain, so let us show our love towards our enemy. There is no deeper distress to be found in the world, no pain more bitter than our enemy's. Nowhere is service more necessary or more blessed than when we serve our enemies. 'It is more blessed to give than to receive.'

'*Pray for them which despitefully use you and persecute you.*' This is the supreme demand. Through the medium of prayer we go to our enemy, stand by his side, and plead for him to God. Jesus does not promise that when we bless our enemies and do good to them they will not despitefully use and persecute us. They certainly will. But not even that can hurt or overcome us, so long as we pray for them. For if we pray for them, we are taking their distress and poverty, their guilt and perdition upon ourselves, and pleading to God for them. We are doing vicariously for them what they cannot do for themselves. Every insult they utter only serves to bind us more closely to God and them. Their persecution of us only serves to bring them nearer to reconciliation with God and to further the triumphs of love.

How then does love conquer? By asking not how the enemy treats her but only how Jesus treated her. The love for our enemies takes us along the way of the cross and into fellowship with the Crucified. The more we are driven along this road, the more certain is the victory of love over the enemy's hatred. For then it is not the disciple's own love, but the love of Jesus Christ alone, who for the sake of his enemies went to the cross and prayed for them as he hung there. In the face of the cross the disciples realized that they too were his enemies, and that he had overcome them by his love. It is this that opens the disciple's eyes, and enables him to see his enemy as a brother. He knows that he owes his very life to One, who though he was his enemy, treated him as a brother and accepted him, who made him his neighbour, and drew him into fellowship with himself. The disciple can now perceive that even his enemy is the object of God's love, and that he stands like himself beneath the cross of Christ. God asked us nothing about our virtues or our vices, for in his sight even our virtue was ungodliness. God's love sought out his enemies who needed it, and whom he deemed worthy of it. God loves his enemies – that is the glory of his love, as every follower of Jesus knows; through Jesus he has become a partaker in this love. For God allows his sun to shine upon the just and the unjust. But it is not only the earthly sun and the earthly rain: the 'Sun of righteousness' and the rain of God's Word which are on the sinner, and reveal the grace of the Heavenly Father. Perfect, all inclusive love is the act of the Father, it is also the act of the sons of God as it was the act of the only-begotten Son.

'This commandment, that we should love our enemies and forgo revenge will grow even more urgent in the holy struggle which lies before us and in which we partly have already been engaged for years. In it love and hate engage in mortal combat. It is the urgent duty of every Christian soul to prepare itself for it. The time is coming when the confession of the living God will incur not only the hatred and the fury of the world, for on the whole it has come to that already, but complete ostracism from "human society", as they call it. The Christians will be hounded from place to place, subjected to physical assault, maltreatment and death of every kind. We are approaching an age of widespread persecution. Therein lies the true significance of all the movements and conflicts of our age. Our adversaries seek to root out the Christian Church and the Christian faith because they cannot live side by side with us, because they see in every word we utter and every deed we do, even when they are not specifically directed against them, a condemnation of their own words and deeds. They are not far wrong. They suspect too that we are indifferent to their condemnation. Indeed they must admit that it is utterly futile to condemn us. We do not reciprocate their hatred and contention, although they would like it better if we did, and so sink to their own level. And how is the battle to be fought? Soon the time will come when we shall pray, not as isolated individuals, but as a corporate body, a congregation, a Church: we shall pray in multitudes (albeit in relatively small multitudes) and among the thousands and thousands of apostates we shall loudly praise and confess the Lord who was crucified and is risen and shall come again. And what prayer, what confession, what hymn of praise will it be? It will be the prayer of earnest love for these very sons of perdition who stand around and gaze at us with eyes aflame with hatred, and who have perhaps already raised their hands to kill us. It will be a prayer for the peace of these erring, devastated and bewildered souls, a prayer for the same love and peace which we ourselves enjoy, a prayer which will penetrate to the depths of their souls and rend their hearts more grievously than anything they can do to us. Yes, the Church which is really waiting for its Lord, and which discerns the signs of the times of decision, must fling itself with its utmost power and with the panoply of its holy life into this prayer of love.'[1]

What is undivided love? Love which shows no special favour to those who love us in return. When we love those who love us, our brethren, our nation, our friends, yes, and even our own congregation, we are no better than the heathen and the publicans. Such love is ordinary and natural, and not distinctively Christian. We can love our kith and kin, our fellow-countrymen and our friends, whether we are Christians or not, and there is no need for Jesus to teach us that. But he takes that kind of love for granted, and in contrast asserts that we must love our enemies. Thus he shows us what *he* means by love, and the attitude we must display towards it.

How then do the disciples differ from the heathen? What does it really mean to be a Christian? Here we meet the word which controls the whole chapter, and sums up all we have heard so far. What makes the Christian different from other men is the '*peculiar*' the περισσόν, the 'extraordinary', the 'unusual', that which is not 'a matter of course'. This is the quality whereby the better righteousness exceeds the righteousness of the scribes and Pharisees.

[1] A. F. C. Vilmar, 1880.

It is 'the more', the 'beyond-all-that'. The natural is τὸ αὐτὸ (one and the same) for heathen and Christian, the distinctive quality of the Christian life begins with the περισσόν. It is this quality which first enables us to see the natural in its true light. Where it is lacking, the peculiar graces of Christianity are absent. It cannot occur within the sphere of natural possibilities, but only when they are transcended. The περισσόν never merges into the τὸ αὐτὸ. That was the fatal mistake of the false Protestant ethic which diluted Christian love into patriotism, loyalty to friends and industriousness, which in short, perverted the better righteousness into *justitia civilis*. Not in such terms as these does Jesus speak. For him the hall-mark of the Christian is the 'extraordinary'. The Christian cannot live at the world's level, because he must always remember the περισσόν.

What is the precise nature of the περισσόν? It is the life described in the beatitudes, the life of the followers of Jesus, the light which lights the world, the city set on the hill, the way of self-renunciation, of utter love, of absolute purity, truthfulness and meekness. It is unreserved love for our enemies, for the unloving and the unloved, love for our religious, political and personal adversaries. In every case it is the love which was fulfilled in the cross of Christ. What is the περισσόν? It is the love of Jesus Christ himself, who went patiently and obediently to the cross – it is in fact the cross itself. The cross is the differential of the Christian religion, the power which enables the Christian to transcend the world and to win the victory. The *passio* in the love of the Crucified is the supreme expression of the 'extraordinary' quality of the Christian life.

The 'extraordinary' quality is undoubtedly identical with the light which shines before men and for which they glorify the Father which is in heaven. It cannot be hidden under a bushel, it must be seen of men. The community of the followers of Jesus, the community of the better righteousness, is the visible community: it has left the world and society, and counted everything but loss for the cross of Christ.

And how does this quality work out in practice? The 'extraordinary' – and this is the supreme scandal – is something which the followers of Jesus *do*. It must be *done* like the better righteousness, and done so that all men can see it. It is not strict Puritanism, not some eccentric pattern of Christian living, but simple, unreflecting obedience to the will of Christ. If we make the 'extraordinary' our standard, we shall be led into the *passio* of Christ, and in that its peculiar quality will be displayed. This activity itself is ceaseless suffering. In it the disciple endures the suffering of Christ. If this is not so, then *this* is not the activity of which Jesus speaks.

Hence the περισσόν is the fulfilment of the law, the keeping of the commandments. In Christ crucified and in his people the 'extraordinary' becomes reality.

These men are the perfect, the men in whom the undivided love of the Heavenly Father is perfected. It was that love which gave the Son to die for us upon the cross, and it is by suffering in the fellowship of this cross that the followers of Jesus are perfected. The perfect are none other than the blessed of the beatitudes.

14 THE HIDDEN RIGHTEOUSNESS

Take heed that ye do not your righteousness before men, to be seen of them: else ye have no reward with your Father which is in heaven. When therefore thou doest alms sound not a trumpet before thee, as the hypocrites do in the synagogues and in the streets, that they may have glory of men. Verily I say unto you, They have received their reward. But when thou doest alms, let not thy left hand know what thy right hand doeth: that thine alms may be in secret: and thy Father which seeth in secret shall recompense thee. (Matt. 6.1-4)

In chapter 5 we were told how the disciple community is essentially visible in character, and how its visibility culminates in the περισσόν. We saw that the hall-mark of Christianity is our separation from the world, our transcendence of its standards, and our extraordinariness. The next chapter takes up the theme of the περισσόν, and lays bare its ambiguity. How easy it would be for the disciples to misinterpret it! We can well imagine them saying: 'Now we must set to work and build the Kingdom of Heaven on earth' – and in so doing they would ignore and perhaps even overthrow the established order of things. They might adopt an attitude of indifference to this present age, like the enthusiasts, and try to realize the extraordinary quality of the age to come in a visible institution. Their ideal would then be to withdraw radically and uncompromisingly from the world and by means of force to set up a Christian order more compatible with their following of Christ and more in accordance with his extraordinary demand. There was an obvious temptation to mistake Christ's work for a commendation of a new, however novel, free and inspiring, pattern for pious living. How eagerly would the religious embrace a life of poverty, truthfulness and suffering, if only they might thereby satisfy their yearning not only to believe, but to see with their own eyes! One might have been prepared to move the distinctions between the two a little, so that a pious pattern of life and obedience towards God's word might come a little closer together, so that in the end you could really not tell one from the other. After all, they could argue, they were doing it all for the supreme cause, the realization of the 'extraordinary'.

Others on the other hand would be waiting to hear what Jesus had to say about the 'extraordinary', only to pounce upon him with all their fury. Here at last, they would say, the fanatic, the enthusiastic revolutionary has come out in his true colours. Now we know he wants to turn the whole world upside down and bids his disciples leave the world and build a new one. Is *this* obedience to the word of the Old Testament? Is it not rather the most glaring example of self-righteousness? Does not Jesus know that all he demands is bound to come to grief because of the world's sin? Does he not know the manifest laws of God given so that sin might be banished? Does it not prove him a victim of spiritual pride, always the first sign of fanaticism? No, they would say, genuine obedience and humility are only to be found in the ordinary, the commonplace, and the hidden. Had Jesus urged his disciples to return to their own kith and kin, back to duty and calling, back to the obedience of the law as the scribes expounded it, they would then have known that he was devout, humble and obedient. He would then have given his disciples an inspiring incentive to deeper devotion and stricter obedience. He would have taught what the scribes knew already, what they would gladly have heard him emphasize in his preaching, namely that true devotion and righteousness consist not merely in outward behaviour, but in the disposition of the heart, and conversely not only in the disposition of the heart, but also in concrete action. That would have been just the kind of 'better righteousness' the people needed, and one which nobody could have gainsaid. But now Jesus had lost his chance. He had stepped forth not as a humble teacher, but as an arrogant fanatic. Fanatics of course have always known the secret of kindling the enthusiasm of men, especially the noblest and best of them. Did not the doctors of the law know that for all its nobility the heart of man still spoke with the voice of the flesh? Did they now know themselves what power even pious flesh could have over a man? The 'extraordinary' was simply the spontaneous work of devotion and piety. It was the assertion of human freedom against unreflecting obedience to the command of God, the illegitimate self-justification of man, which the law does not permit; the lawless self-sanctification which the law was bound to condemn; free service to God as opposed to bounden duty, the destruction of the Church of God, the denial of faith, blasphemy against the law and against God himself. . . . If the law had its way Jesus would be put to death for teaching the 'extraordinary'.

And how does Jesus answer these objections? He says: 'Take heed that ye do not your righteousness before men, to be seen of them.' The call to the 'extraordinary' is the inevitable risk men must take when they follow Christ. And therefore Jesus warns us to take heed. He calls a halt to the innocent spontaneous joy we get from making our Christianity visible. He calls us to reflect on what we are doing.

The disciples are told that they can possess the 'extraordinary' only so long as they are reflective: they must beware how they use it, and never fulfil it simply for its own sake, or for the sake of ostentation. The better righteousness of the disciples must have a motive which lies beyond itself. Of course it has to be visible, but they must take care that it does not become visible simply for the sake of becoming visible. There are of course proper grounds for insisting on the visible nature of Christian discipleship, but the visibility is never an end in itself; and if it becomes so we have lost sight of our primary aim, which is to follow Jesus. And, having once done that, we should never be able to carry on again where we had left off; we should have to begin all over again at the beginning. And that would bring it home to us that we were no true disciples. We are therefore confronted with a paradox. Our activity must be visible, but never be done for the sake of making it visible. 'Let your light so shine before men' (5.16) and yet: Take care that you hide it! There is a pointed contrast between chapters 5 and 6. That which is visible must also be hidden. The awareness on which Jesus insists is intended to prevent us from reflecting on our extraordinary position. We have to take heed that we do not take heed of our own righteousness. Otherwise the 'extraordinary' which we achieve will not be that which comes from following Christ, but that which springs from our own will and desire.

How is this paradox to be resolved? The first question to ask is: From whom are we to hide the visibility of our discipleship? Certainly not from other men, for we are told to let them see our light. No. We are to hide it from *ourselves*. Our task is simply to keep on following, looking only to our Leader who goes on before, taking no notice of ourselves or of what we are doing. We must be unaware of our own righteousness, and see it only in so far as we look unto Jesus; then it will seem not extraordinary, but quite ordinary and natural. Thus we hide the visible from ourselves in obedience to the word of Jesus. If the 'extraordinary' were important for its own sake, we should, like fanatics, be relying on our own fleshly strength and power, whereas the disciple of Jesus acts simply in obedience to his Lord. That is, he regards the 'extraordinary' as the natural fruit of obedience. According to the word of Jesus it cannot be otherwise: the Christian is a light unto the world, not because of any quality of his own, but only because he follows Christ and looks solely to him. But precisely because the Christian life is of its very nature extraordinary, it is at the same time ordinary, natural, and *hidden*. If not, it is not the Christian life at all, it is not obedience to the will of Jesus Christ.

Secondly, we have to ask how the visible and the invisible aspects of discipleship can be combined, and how the same life can be both visible and hidden. To answer this question, all we need to do is to go back to chapter 5, where the extraordinary and the visible are defined as the cross of Christ beneath which the disciples stand. The cross is at once the necessary, the hidden and the visible – it is the 'extraordinary'.

Thirdly, we have to ask how the contradiction between the fifth and the sixth chapters is to be resolved. The answer lies in the meaning of discipleship. It means an exclusive adherence to him, and that implies first, that the disciple looks only to his Lord and follows him. If he looked only at the extraordinary quality of the Christian life, he would no longer be following Christ. For the disciple this extraordinary quality consists solely in the will of the Lord, and when he seeks to do that will he knows that there is no other alternative, and that what he does is the only natural thing to do.

All that the follower of Jesus has to do is to make sure that his obedience, following and love are entirely spontaneous and un-premeditated. If you do good, you must not let your left hand know what your right hand is doing, you must be quite uncon-scious of it. Otherwise you are simply displaying your own virtue, and not that which has its source in Jesus Christ. Christ's virtue, the virtue of discipleship, can only be accomplished so long as you are entirely unconscious of what you are doing. The genuine work of love is always a hidden work. Take heed therefore that you know it not, for only so is it the goodness of God. If we want to know our own goodness or love, it has already ceased to be love. We must be unaware even of our love for our enemies. After all, when we love them they are no longer our enemies. This voluntary blindness in the Christian (which is really sight illuminated by Christ) is his certainty, and the fact that his life is hidden from his sight is the ground of his assurance.

Thus hiddenness has its counterpart in manifestation. For there is nothing hidden that shall not be revealed. For our God is a God unto whom all hearts are open, and from whom no secrets are hid. God will show us the hidden and make it visible. Manifesta-tion is the appointed reward for hiddenness, and the only question is where we shall receive it and who will give it us. If we want publicity in the eyes of men we have our reward. In other words, it is immaterial whether the publicity we want is the grosser kind, which all can see, or the more subtle variety which we can only see ourselves. If the left hand knows what the right hand is doing, if we become conscious of our hidden virtue, we are forging our own reward, instead of that which God had intended to give us in his own good time. But if we are content to carry on with our life hidden from our eyes, we shall receive our reward openly from God. But what kind of love is this that is so unaware of itself that it can be hidden until the day of judgement? The answer is obvious. Because love is hidden it cannot be avisible virtue or a habit which can be acquired. Take heed, it says, that you do not exchange true love for an amiable virtuousness, a human 'quality'. Genuine love is always self-forgetful in the true sense of the word. But if we are to have it, our old man must die with all his virtues and qualities, and this can only be done where the disciple forgets self and clings solely to Christ. When Jesus said: 'Let not thy left hand know what thy right hand doeth', he was sounding the death-knell of the old man. Once again, who can live a life which combines chapters 5 and 6? Only those who have died after the old man through Christ, and are given a new life by following him and having fellowship with him. Love, in the sense of spontaneous, unreflective action, spells the death of the old man. For man recovers his true nature in the righteousness of Christ and in his fellow-man. The love of Christ crucified, who delivers our old man to death, is the love which lives in those who follow him. 'I live; yet no longer I, but Christ liveth in me' (Gal. 2.20). Henceforth the Christian finds himself only in Christ and in his brethren.

15 THE HIDDENNESS OF PRAYER

And when ye pray, ye shall not be as the hypocrites: for they love to stand and pray in the synagogues and in the corners of the streets, that they may be seen of men. Verily I say unto you, They have received their reward. But thou, when thou prayest, enter into thine inner chamber, and having shut thy door, pray to thy Father which is in secret, and thy Father which seeth in secret shall recompense thee. And in praying use not vain repetitions, as the Gentiles do: for they think that they shall be heard for their much speaking. Be not therefore like unto them: for your Father knoweth what things ye hath need of, before ye ask him. (Matt. 6.5-8)

JESUS teaches his disciples to pray. What does this mean? It means that prayer is by no means an obvious or natural activity. It is the expression of a universal human instinct, but that does not justify it in the sight of God. Even where prayer is cultivated with discipline and perseverance it can still be profitless and void of God's blessing. The disciples are permitted to pray because Jesus tells them they may – and he knows the Father. He promises that God will hear them. That is to say, the disciples pray only because they are followers of Christ and have fellowship with him. Only those who, like them, adhere to Jesus have access to the Father through him. All Christian prayer is directed to God through a Mediator, and not even prayer affords direct access to the Father. Only through Jesus Christ can we find the Father in prayer. Christian prayer presupposes faith, that is, adherence to Christ. He is the one and only Mediator of our prayers. We pray at his command, and to that word Christian prayer is always bound.

We pray to God because we believe in him through Jesus Christ; that is to say, our prayer can never be an entreaty to God, for we have no need to come before him in that way. We are privileged to know that he knows our needs before we ask him. This is what gives Christian prayer its boundless confidence and its joyous certainty. It matters little what form of prayer we adopt or how

145

many words we use, what matters is the faith which lays hold on God and touches the heart of the Father who knew us long before we came to him.

Genuine prayer is never 'good works', an exercise or a pious attitude, but it is always the prayer of a child to a Father. Hence it is never given to self-display, whether before God, ourselves, or other people. If God were ignorant of our needs, we should have to think out beforehand *how* we should tell him about them, *what* we should tell him, and whether we should tell him or not. Thus faith, which is the mainspring of Christian prayer, excludes all reflection and premeditation.

Prayer is the supreme instance of the hidden character of the Christian life. It is the antithesis of self-display. When men pray, they have ceased to know themselves, and know only God whom they call upon. Prayer does not aim at any direct effect on the world; it is addressed to God alone, and is therefore the perfect example of undemonstrative action.

Of course there is a danger even here. Prayer of this kind can seek self-display, it can seek to bring to light that which is hidden. This may happen in public prayer, which sometimes (though not often nowadays) degenerates into an empty noise. But there is no difference; it is even more pernicious if I turn myself into a spectator of my own prayer performance, if I am giving a show for my own benefit. I may enjoy myself just like a pleased spectator or I may catch myself praying and feel strange and ashamed. The publicity of the market place affords only a more naïve form than the publicity which I am providing for myself. I can lay on a very nice show for myself even in the privacy of my own room. That is the extent to which we can distort the word of Jesus. The publicity which I am looking for is then provided by the fact that I am the one who at the same time prays and looks on. I am listening to my own prayer and thus I am answering my own prayer. Not being content to wait for God to answer our prayer and show us in his own time that he has heard us, we provide our own answer. We take note that we have prayed suitably well, and this substitutes the satisfaction of answered prayer. We have our reward. Since we have heard ourselves, God will not hear us. Having contrived our own reward of publicity, we cannot expect God to reward us any further.

Where is the innermost chamber Jesus is thinking of where I can hide, if I cannot be sure of myself? How can I lock it so well that no audience spoils the anonymity of prayer and thus robs me of the reward of hidden prayer? How are we to be protected from ourselves, and our own premeditations? How are we to drive out reflection by reflecting? The only way is by mortifying our own wills which are always obtruding themselves. And the only way to do this is by letting Christ alone reign in our hearts, by surrendering our wills completely to him, by living in fellowship with Jesus and by following him. Then we can pray that his will may be done, the will of him who knows our needs before we ask. Only then is our prayer certain, strong and pure. And then prayer is really and truly *petition*. The child asks of the Father whom he knows. Thus the essence of Christian prayer is not general adoration, but definite, concrete petition. The right way to approach God is to stretch out our hands and ask of One who we know has the heart of a Father.

True prayer is done in secret, but this does not rule out the fellowship of prayer altogether, however clearly we may be aware of its dangers. In the last resort it is immaterial whether we pray in the open street or in the secrecy of our chambers, whether briefly or lengthily, in the Litany of the Church, or with the sigh of one who knows not what he should pray for. True prayer does not depend either on the individual or the whole body of the faithful, but solely upon the knowledge that our heavenly Father knows our needs. That makes God the sole object of our prayers, and frees us from a false confidence in our own prayerful efforts.

After this manner therefore pray ye: Our Father which art in heaven, Hallowed be thy name. Thy kingdom come. Thy will be done, as in heaven, so on earth. Give us this day our daily bread. And forgive us our debts, as we also have forgiven our debtors. And bring us not into temptation, but deliver us from the evil one. For if ye forgive not men their trespasses, neither will your Father forgive your trespasses. (Matt. 6.9-15)

Jesus told his disciples not only *how* to pray, but also *what* to pray. The Lord's Prayer is not merely the pattern prayer, it is the way Christians *must* pray. If they pray this prayer, God will certainly hear them. The Lord's Prayer is the quintessence of prayer. A disciple's prayer is founded on and circumscribed by it. Once again Jesus does not leave his disciples in ignorance; he teaches them the Lord's Prayer and so leads them to a clear understanding of prayer.

'Our Father which art in heaven.' The disciples call upon the heavenly Father as a corporate body, they call upon a Father who already knows his children's needs. The call of Jesus binds them into a brotherhood. In Jesus they have apprehended the loving-kindness of the Father. In the name of the Son of God they are privileged to call God Father. They are on earth, and their Father is in heaven, He looks down on them from above, and they lift up their eyes to him.

'Hallowed be thy name.' God's name of Father, as it has been revealed to the disciples in Jesus Christ, shall be kept holy among them. In this name the whole content of the gospel is embraced. May God protect his holy gospel from being obscured and profaned by false doctrine and unholiness of living, and may he ever make known his holy name to the disciples in Jesus Christ. May he enable all preachers to proclaim the pure gospel of saving grace, defend us against the tempters, and convert the enemies of his name!

'Thy kingdom come.' In Jesus Christ his followers have witnessed the kingdom of God breaking in on earth. They have seen Satan crushed and the powers of the world, sin and death broken. The kingdom of God is still exposed to suffering and strife. The little flock has a share in that tribulation. They stand under the sovereignty of God in the new righteousness, but in the midst of persecution. God grant that the kingdom of Jesus Christ may grow in his Church on earth, God hasten the end of the kingdoms of this world, and establish his own kingdom in power and glory!

'Thy will be done, as in heaven so on earth.' In fellowship with Jesus his followers have surrendered their own wills completely to God's, and so they pray that God's will may be done throughout the world. No creature on earth shall defy him. But the evil will is still alive even in the followers of Christ, it still seeks to cut them off from fellowship with him; and that is why they must also pray that the will of God may prevail more and more in their hearts every day and break down all defiance. In the end the whole world must bow before that will, worshipping and giving thanks in joy and tribulation. Heaven and earth shall be subject to God.

God's name, God's kingdom, God's will must be the primary object of Christian prayer. Of course it is not as if God needed our prayers, but they are the means by which the disciples become partakers in the heavenly treasure for which they pray. Furthermore, God uses their prayers to hasten the coming of the End.

'Give us this day our daily bread.' As long as the disciples are on earth, they should not be ashamed to pray for their bodily needs. He who created men on earth will keep and preserve their bodies. It is not God's will that his creation should be despised. The disciples are told to ask for bread not only for themselves but for all men on the earth, for all men are their brethren. The disciples realize that while it is a fruit of the earth, bread really comes down from above as the gift of God alone. That is why they have to ask for it before they take it. And since it is the bread of God, it is new every day. They do not ask to lay up a store for the future, but are satisfied with what God gives them day by day. Through that bread their lives are spared a little longer, that they may enjoy life in fellowship with Jesus, praising and thanking him for his loving-kindness. This petition is a test of their faith, for it shows whether they believe that all things work together for good to them that love God.

'Forgive us our debts, as we also forgive our debtors.' Every day Christ's followers must acknowledge and bewail their guilt. Living as they do in fellowship with him, they ought to be sinless, but in practice their life is marred daily with all manner of unbelief, sloth in prayer, lack of bodily discipline, self-indulgence of every kind, envy, hatred and ambition. No wonder that they must pray daily for God's forgiveness. But God will only forgive them if they forgive one another with readiness and brotherly affection. Thus they bring all their guilt before God and pray as a body for forgiveness. God forgive not merely *me my* debts, but *us ours*.

'Lead us not into temptation.' Many and diverse are the temptations which beset the Christian. Satan attacks him on every side, if haply he might cause him to fall. Sometimes the attack takes the form of a false sense of security, and sometimes of ungodly doubt. But the disciple is conscious of his weakness, and does not expose himself unnecessarily to temptation in order to test the strength of his faith. Christians ask God not to put their puny faith to the test, but to preserve them in the hour of temptation.

'But deliver us from evil.' The last petition is for deliverance from evil and for the inheritance of the kingdom of heaven. It is a prayer for a holy death and for the deliverance of the Church in the day of judgement.

'For thine is the kingdom. . . .' The disciples are renewed in their assurance that the Kingdom is God's by their fellowship in *Jesus Christ, on whom depends the fulfilment of all their prayers*. In him God's name is hallowed, his kingdom comes and his will is done. For his sake the disciples are preserved in body and receive forgiveness of sin, in his strength they are preserved in all times of temptation, in his power they are delivered and brought to eternal life. His is the kingdom and the power and the glory for ever and ever in the unity of the Father. That is the assurance the disciples have.

As a summing up Jesus emphasizes once more that everything depends on forgiveness of sin of which the disciples may only partake within the fellowship of sinners.

16 THE HIDDENNESS OF THE DEVOUT LIFE

> Moreover when ye fast, be not, as the hypocrites, of a sad countenance: for they disfigure their faces, that they may be seen of men to fast. Verily I say unto you, They have received their reward. But thou, when thou fastest, anoint thy head, and wash thy face; that thou be not seen of men to fast, but of thy Father which is in secret: and thy Father, which seeth in secret, shall recompense thee. (Matt. 6.16-18)

JESUS takes it for granted that his disciples will observe the pious custom of fasting. Strict exercise of self-control is an essential feature of the Christian's life. Such customs have only one purpose – to make the disciples more ready and cheerful to accomplish those things which God would have done. Fasting helps to discipline the self-indulgent and slothful will which is so reluctant to serve the Lord, and it helps to humiliate and chasten the flesh. By practising abstemiousness we show the world how different the Christian life is from its own. If there is no element of asceticism in our lives, if we give free rein to the desires of the flesh (taking care of course to keep within the limits of what seems permissible to the world), we shall find it hard to train for the service of Christ. When the flesh is satisfied it is hard to pray with cheerfulness or to devote oneself to a life of service which calls for much self-renunciation.

So the Christian needs to observe a strict exterior discipline. But we are not to imagine that that alone will crush the will of the flesh, or that there is any way of mortifying our old man other than by faith in Jesus. The real difference in the believer who follows Christ and has mortified his will and died after the old man in Christ, is that he is more clearly aware than other men of the rebelliousness and perennial pride of the flesh, he is conscious of his sloth and self-indulgence and knows that his arrogance must be eradicated. Hence there is a need for daily self-discipline. It is always true of the disciple that the spirit is willing but the flesh is weak, and he must therefore 'watch and pray'. The spirit knows the right way, and desires to follow it, but the flesh lacks courage and finds it too hard, too hazardous and wearisome, and so it stifles the voice of the spirit. The spirit assents when Jesus bids us love our enemies, but flesh and blood are too strong and prevent our carrying it out. Therefore we have to practise strictest daily discipline; only so can the flesh learn the painful lesson that it has no rights of its own. Regular daily prayer is a great help here, and so is daily meditation on the Word of God, and every kind of bodily discipline and asceticism.

The flesh resists this daily humiliation, first by a frontal attack, and later by hiding itself under the words of the spirit (i.e. in the name of 'evangelical liberty'). We claim liberty from all legal compulsion, from self-martyrdom and mortification, and play this off against the proper evangelical use of discipline and asceticism; we thus excuse our self-indulgence and irregularity in prayer, in meditation and in our bodily life. But the contrast between our behaviour and the word of Jesus is all too painfully evident. We forget that discipleship means estrangement from the world, and we forget the real joy and freedom which are the outcome of a devout rule of life. As soon as a Christian recognizes that he has failed in his service, that his readiness has become feeble, and that he has sinned against another's life and become guilty of another's guilt, that all his joy in God has vanished and that his capacity for prayer has quite gone, it is high time for him to launch an assault upon the flesh, and prepare for better service by fasting and prayer (Luke 2.37; 4.2; Mark 9.29; I Cor. 7.5). Any objection that asceticism is wrong, and that all we need is faith, is quite beside the point; it is cruel to suggest such a thing, and it is no help to us at all. When all is said and done, the life of faith is nothing if not an unending struggle of the spirit with every available weapon against the flesh. How is it possible to live the life of faith when we grow weary of prayer, when we lose our taste for reading the Bible, and when sleep, food and sensuality deprive us of the joy of communion with God?

Asceticism means voluntary suffering: it is *passio activa* rather than *passiva*, and it is just there that the danger lies. There is always a danger that in our asceticism we shall be tempted to imitate the sufferings of Christ. This is a pious but godless ambition, for beneath it there always lurks the notion that it is possible for us to step into Christ's shoes and suffer as he did and kill the old Adam. We are then presuming to undertake that bitter work of eternal redemption which Christ himself wrought for us. The motive of asceticism was more limited – to equip us for better service and deeper humiliation. But it can only do that so long as it takes the suffering of Christ as its basis; if not, it degenerates into a dreadful parody of the Lord's own passion. Our whole motive now becomes a desire for ostentation. We want other people to see our achievements and to be put to shame. Our asceticism has now become the way to salvation. Such publicity gives it the reward it seeks.

'Anoint thine head and wash thy face.' Even this might become an occasion for a still subtler form of self-glorification or enjoyment. But that would be to miss the point and make of it a mere pretence. Jesus, however, bids his disciples to persevere in the practices of humiliation, but not to force them on other people as a rule or regulation. They must rejoice and give thanks for the privilege of remaining in the service of their Lord. Jesus does not mean that a smile on the face is to be a sort of stereotyped expression of Christianity; he is referring rather to the proper hiddenness of Christian behaviour, to that humility which is wholly unselfconscious, even as the eye can see other people but can never see itself. Such hiddenness will one day be made manifest, but that will be God's doing, not ours.

17 THE SIMPLICITY OF THE CAREFREE LIFE

Lay not up for yourselves treasures upon the earth, where moth and rust doth consume, and where thieves break through and steal: but lay up for yourselves treasures in heaven, where neither moth nor rust doth consume, and where thieves do not break through nor steal: for where thy treasure is, there will thy heart be also. The lamp of the body is the eye: if therefore thine eye be single, thy whole body shall be full of light. But if thine eye be evil, thy whole body shall be full of darkness. If therefore the light that is in thee be darkness, how great is the darkness! No man can serve two masters: for either he will hate the one and love the other; or else he will hold to one, and despise the other. Ye cannot serve God and mammon. (Matt. 6.19-24)

THE life of discipleship can only be maintained so long as nothing is allowed to come between Christ and ourselves – neither the law, nor personal piety, nor even the world. The disciple always looks only to his master, never to Christ *and* the law, Christ *and* religion, Christ *and* the world. He avoids all such notions like the plague. Only by following Christ alone can he preserve a single eye. His eye rests wholly on the light that comes from Christ, and has no darkness or ambiguity in it. As the eye must be single, clear and pure in order to keep light in the body, as hand and foot can receive light from no other source save the eye, as the foot stumbles and the hand misses its mark when the eye is dim, as the whole body is in darkness when the eye is blind; so the follower of Christ is in the light only so long as he looks simply to Christ and at nothing else in the world. Thus the heart of the disciple must be set upon Christ alone. If the eye sees an object which is not there, the whole body is deceived. If the heart is devoted to the mirage of the world, to the creature instead of the Creator, the disciple is lost.

Worldly possessions tend to turn the hearts of the disciples away from Jesus. What are we really devoted to? That is the question. Are our hearts set on earthly goods? Do we try to combine devotion to them with loyalty to Christ? Or are we devoted exclusively to him? The light of the body is the eye, and the light of the Christian is his heart. If the eye be dark, how great is the darkness of the body! But the heart is dark when it clings to earthly goods, for then, however urgently Jesus may call us, his call fails to find access to our hearts. Our hearts are closed, for they have already been given to another. As the light cannot penetrate the body when the eye is evil, so the word of Jesus cannot penetrate the disciple's heart so long as it is closed against it. The word is choked like the seed which was sown among thorns, choked 'with cares and riches and pleasures of this life' (Luke 8.14).

The singleness of eye and heart corresponds to that 'hiddenness' which knows nothing but the call and word of Christ, and which consists in perfect fellowship with him. How can the disciple have dealings with earthly goods and yet preserve this singleness of heart? Jesus does not forbid the possession of property in itself. He was man, he ate and drank like his disciples, and thereby sanctified the good things of life. These necessities, which are consumed in use and which meet the legitimate requirements of the body, are to be used by the disciple with thankfulness.

> We walk as pilgrims through the earth,
>   With empty hands, bereft and bare;
> To gather wealth were little worth –
>   'Twould only burden life the more.
>
> If men will go the way to death,
>   With them we will part company;
> For God will give us all we need
>   To cover our necessity.
>
> (TERSTEEGEN)

Earthly goods are given to be used, not to be collected. In the wilderness God gave Israel the manna every day, and they had no need to worry about food and drink. Indeed, if they kept any of the manna over until the next day, it went bad. In the same way, the disciple must receive his portion from God every day. If he stores it up as a permanent possession, he spoils not only the gift, but himself as well, for he sets his heart on his accumulated wealth, and makes it a barrier between himself and God. Where our treasure is, there is our trust, our security, our consolation and our God.[1] Hoarding is idolatry.

But where are we to draw the line between legitimate use and unlawful accumulation? Let us reverse the word of Jesus and our question is answered: 'Where thy heart is, there shall thy treasure be also.' Our treasure may of course be small and inconspicuous, but its size is immaterial; it all depends on the heart, on ourselves. And if we ask how we are to know where our hearts are, the answer is just as simple – everything which hinders us from loving God above all things and acts as a barrier between ourselves and our obedience to Jesus is our treasure, and the place where our heart is.

But Jesus knows that the heart of man hankers after a treasure, and so it is his will that he should have one.[2] But this treasure is to be sought in heaven, not on earth. Earthly treasures soon fade, but a treasure in heaven lasts for ever. By this treasure Jesus does not mean the one great treasure of himself, but treasures in the literal sense of the word, treasures accumulated by the disciples for themselves. What a wonderful promise we have here: as we follow Jesus, we win heavenly treasures which are incorruptible; they are waiting for us, and one day we shall enjoy them as our own. Surely these treasures can be none other than the 'extraordinary', the hidden character of the Christian life, none other than the fruits of the passion of Jesus Christ which sustains the lives of his followers.

If our hearts are entirely given to God, it is clear that we *cannot*

[1] It is no accident that the catalogues of vices in the Pauline Epistles associate fornication with covetousness, and designate both as idolatry.

[2] It is to be observed that Jesus does not deprive the human heart of its instinctive needs – treasure, glory and praise. But he gives it higher objects – the glory of God (John 5.44), the glorying in the cross (Gal. 6.14), and the treasure in heaven.

serve two masters; it is simply impossible – at any rate all the time we are following Christ. It would of course be tempting to show how far we had advanced in the Christian life by endeavouring to serve two masters and giving each his due, both God and Mammon. Why should we not be happy children of the world just because we are the children of God? After all, do we not rejoice in his good gifts, and do we not receive our treasures as a blessing from him? No, God and the world, God and its goods are incompatible, because the world and its goods make a bid for our hearts, and only when they have won them do they become what they really are. That is how they thrive, and that is why they are incompatible with allegiance to God. Our hearts have room only for one all-embracing devotion, and we can only cleave to one Lord. Every competitor to that devotion must be hated. As Jesus says, there is no alternative – either we love God or we hate him. We are confronted by an 'either – or': either we love God, or we love earthly goods. If we love God, we hate the world; and if we love the world, we hate God. It makes no difference whether that love be conscious and deliberate or not; in fact it is morally certain that it will be neither, and that our conscious and deliberate desire will be to serve two masters, to love God *and* the good things of life. We shall indignantly repudiate the suggestion that we hate God, and will be firmly convinced that we love him, whereas by trying to combine love for him with love for the world, we are turning our love for him into hatred. And then we have lost the single eye, and our heart is no longer in fellowship with Jesus. Our deliberate intentions make no difference to the inevitable result: Ye cannot serve two masters, if ye be followers of Jesus Christ.

> Therefore I say unto you, Be not anxious for your life, what ye shall eat, or what ye shall drink; nor yet for your body, what ye shall put on. Is not the life more than the food, and the body than the raiment? Behold the birds of the heaven, that they sow not, neither do they reap, nor gather into barns; and your heavenly Father feedeth them. Are not ye of much more value than they? And which of you by being anxious can add one cubit unto his stature? And why are ye anxious concerning

raiment? Consider the lilies of the field, how they grow; they toil not, neither do they spin: yet I say unto you, that even Solomon in all his glory was not arrayed like one of these. But if God doth so clothe the grass of the field, which to-day is, and to-morrow is cast into the oven, shall he not much more clothe you, O ye of little faith? Be not therefore anxious, saying, What shall we eat? or, What shall we drink? or Wherewithal shall we be clothed? For after all these things do the Gentiles seek; for your heavenly Father knoweth that ye have need of all these things. But seek ye first his kingdom, and his righteousness; and all these things shall be added unto you. Be not therefore anxious for the morrow: for the morrow will be anxious for itself. Sufficient unto the day is the evil thereof. (Matt. 6.25-34)

Be not anxious! Earthly possessions dazzle our eyes and delude us into thinking that they can provide security and freedom from anxiety. Yet all the time they are the very source of all anxiety. If our hearts are set on them, our reward is an anxiety whose burden is intolerable. Anxiety creates its own treasures and they in turn beget further care. When we seek for security in possessions we are trying to drive out care with care, and the net result is the precise opposite of our anticipations. The fetters which bind us to our possessions prove to be cares themselves.

The way to misuse our possessions is to use them as an insurance against the morrow. Anxiety is always directed to the morrow, whereas goods are in the strictest sense meant to be used only for to-day. By trying to insure for the next day we are only creating uncertainty to-day. Sufficient unto the day is the evil thereof. The only way to win assurance is by leaving to-morrow entirely in the hands of God and by receiving from him all we need for to-day. If instead of receiving God's gifts for to-day we worry about to-morrow, we find ourselves helpless victims of infinite anxiety. 'Be not anxious for the morrow': either that is cruel mockery for the poor and wretched, the very people Jesus is talking to who, humanly speaking, really will starve if they do not mak provision to-day. Either it is an intolerable law, which men will reject with indignation; or it is the unique proclamation of the gospel of the glorious liberty of the children of God, who have a Father in heaven, a Father who has given his beloved Son. How shall not God with him also freely give us all things?

'Be not anxious for the morrow.' This is not to be taken as a philosophy of life or a moral law: it is the gospel of Jesus Christ, and only so can it be understood. Only those who follow him and know him can receive this word as a promise of the love of his Father and as a deliverance from the thraldom of material things. It is not care that frees the disciples from care, but their faith in Jesus Christ. Only they know that we *cannot* be anxious (verse 27). The coming day, even the coming hour, are placed beyond our control. It is senseless to pretend that we can make provision because we cannot alter the circumstances of this world. Only God can take care, for it is he who rules the world. Since we *cannot* take care, since we are so completely powerless, we *ought* not to do it either. If we do, we are dethroning God and presuming to rule the world ourselves.

But the Christian also knows that he not only cannot and dare not be anxious, but that there is also no need for him to be so. Neither anxiety nor work can secure his daily bread, for bread is the gift of the Father. The birds and lilies neither toil nor spin, yet both are fed and clothed and receive their daily portion without being anxious for them. They need earthly goods only for their daily sustenance, and they do not lay up a store for the future. This is the way they glorify their Creator, not by their industry, toil or care, but by a daily unquestioning acceptance of his gifts. Birds and lilies then are an example for the followers of Christ. 'Man-in-revolt' imagines that there is a relation of cause and effect between work and sustenance, but Jesus explodes that illusion. According to him, bread is not to be valued as the reward for work; he speaks instead of the carefree simplicity of the man who walks with him and accepts everything as it comes from God.

'Now mark ye, no beast worketh for his sustenance, but each hath his proper function, according to which he seeketh and findeth his own food. The bird doth fly and sing, she maketh nests and beareth young. That is her work, but yet she doth not nourish herself thereby. Oxen plough, horses draw carts and fight, sheep give wool, milk, and cheese, for it is their function so to do. But they do not nurture themselves thereby. Nay, the earth bringeth forth grass, and nurtureth them through God's blessing. Likewise it is man's bounden duty to work and do things, and yet withal to know that it is Another who nurtureth him: it is not his own work, but the bounteous blessing of God. It is true that the bird doth neither sow nor reap, yet would she die of hunger if she flew not in search of food. But that she findeth the same is not her work, but the goodness of God. For who put the food there, that she might find it? For where God hath put nought, none findeth, even though the whole world were to work itself to death in search thereof' (Luther). But if the Creator thus sustains the birds and lilies, should he not much more as a Father nourish his own children, who daily pray to him? Should he not be able to grant them the necessities of life, when all earthly goods belong to him, and when he can distribute them according to his pleasure?

> God the Father grant to me
> All my daily needs.
> Why should I not unto him flee,
> When all the birds he feeds?
>
> (CLAUDIUS)

Anxiety is characteristic of the Gentiles, for they rely on their own strength and work instead of relying on God. They do not know that the Father knows that we have need of all these things, and so they try to do for themselves what they do not expect from God. But the disciples know that the rule is 'Seek ye first the kingdom of God and his righteousness, and all these things shall be added unto you.' Anxiety for food and clothing is clearly not the same thing as anxiety for the kingdom of God, however much we should like to persuade ourselves that when we are working for our families and concerning ourselves with bread and houses we are thereby building the kingdom, as though the kingdom could be realized only through our worldly cares. The kingdom of God and his righteousness are sharply distinguished from the gifts of the world which come our way. That kingdom is none other than the righteousness of Matt. 5 and 6, the righteousness of the cross and of following Christ beneath that cross. Fellowship with Jesus and obedience to his commandment come first, and all else follows. Worldly cares are not a part of our discipleship, but distinct and subordinate concerns. Before we start taking thought for our life, our food and clothing, our work and families, we must seek the righteousness of Christ. This is no more than an ultimate summing up of all that has been said before. Again we have here either a crushing burden, which holds out no hope for the poor and wretched, or else it is the quintessence of the gospel, which brings the promise of freedom and perfect joy. Jesus does not tell us what we ought to do but cannot; he tells us what God has given us and promises still to give. If Christ has been given us, if we are called to his discipleship we are given all things, literally *all* things. He will see to it that they are added unto us. If we follow Jesus and look only to his righteousness, we are in his hands and under the protection of him and his Father. And if we are in communion with the Father, nought can harm us. We shall always be assured that he can feed his children and will not suffer them to hunger. God will help us in the hour of need, and he knows our needs.

After he has been following Christ for a long time, the disciple of Jesus will be asked 'Lacked ye anything?' and he will answer 'Nothing, Lord'. How could he when he knows that despite hunger and nakedness, persecution and danger, the Lord is always at his side?

Judge not, that ye be not judged. For with what judgement ye judge, ye shall be judged: and with what measure ye mete, it shall be measured unto you. And why beholdest thou the mote that is in thy brother's eye, but considerest not the beam that is in thine own eye? Or how wilt thou say to thy brother, Let me cast out the mote out of thine eye; and lo, the beam is in thine own eye? Thou hypocrite, cast out first the beam out of thine own eye; and then shalt thou see clearly to cast out the mote out of thy brother's eye.

Give not that which is holy unto the dogs, neither cast your pearls before the swine, lest haply they trample them under their feet, and turn and rend you.

Ask, and it shall be given you; seek, and ye shall find; knock, and it shall be opened unto you: for every one that asketh receiveth; and he that seeketh findeth; and to him that knocketh it shall be opened. Or what man is there of you, who, if his son shall ask him for a loaf, will give him a stone; or if he shall ask for a fish, will give him a serpent? If ye then, being evil, know how to give good gifts unto your children, how much more shall your Father which is in heaven give good things to them that ask him? All things therefore whatsoever ye would that men should do unto you, even so do ye also unto them: for this is the law and the prophets. (Matt. 7.1-12)

THERE is a continuous thread running through chapters 5 and 6; it passes through these verses, and on to the grand finale of the Sermon on the Mount. Chapter 5 dealt with the extraordinary quality of the Christian life, περισσόν, and chapter 6 with the hidden single-hearted righteousness of the disciples (ἁπλοῦς). In both its aspects, discipleship betokened the separation of the disciples from all their old ties, and an exclusive adherence to Jesus Christ. The frontier between the old life and the new was clearly drawn. But this raises the question of the relation between the Christians and their non-Christian neighbours. Does their separation from the rest of society confer on them special rights and privileges? Do Christians enjoy power, gifts and standards of judgement which qualify them to exert a peculiar authority over others? How easy it would have been for the disciples to adopt a superior attitude, to pass unqualified condemnation on the rest of the world, and to persuade themselves that this was the will of God! That is why Jesus has to make it clear beyond all doubt that such misunderstandings would seriously imperil their discipleship. The disciples are not to judge. If they do so, they will themselves be judged by God. The sword wherewith they judge their brethren will fall upon their own heads. Instead of cutting themselves off from their brother as the just from the unjust, they find themselves cut off from Jesus.

Why should this be so? The source of the disciple's life lies exclusively in his fellowship with Jesus Christ. He possesses his righteousness only within that association, never outside it. That is why his righteousness can never become an objective criterion to be applied at will. He is a disciple not because he possesses such a new standard, but only because of Jesus Christ, the Mediator and very Son of God. That is to say, his righteousness is hidden from himself in fellowship with Jesus. He cannot, as he could once, be a detached observer of himself and judge himself, for he can only see Jesus, and be seen by him, judged by him, and reprieved by him. It is not an approved standard of righteous living that separates a follower of Christ from the unbeliever, but it is Christ who stands between them. Christians always see other men as brethren to whom Christ comes; they meet them only by going to them with Jesus. Disciple and non-disciple can never encounter each other as free men, directly exchanging their views and judging one another by objective criteria. No, the disciple can meet the non-disciple only as a man to whom Jesus comes. Here alone Christ's fight for the soul of the unbeliever, his call, his love, his grace and his judgement comes into its own. Discipleship does not afford us a point of vantage from which to attack others; we come to them with an unconditional offer of fellowship, with the single-mindedness of the love of Jesus.

When we judge other people we confront them in a spirit of detachment, observing and reflecting as it were from the outside. But love has neither time nor opportunity for this. If we love, we can never observe the other person with detachment, for he is always and at every moment a living claim to our love and service. But does not the evil in the other person make me condemn him just for his own good, for the sake of love? Here we see the depth of the dividing line. Any misguided love for the sinner is ominously close to the love of sin. But the love of Christ for the sinner in itself is the condemnation of sin, is his expression of extreme hatred of sin. The disciples of Christ are to love unconditionally. Thus they may effect what their own divided and judiciously and conditionally offered love never could achieve, namely the radical condemnation of sin.

If the disciples make judgements of their own, they set up standards of good and evil. But Jesus Christ is not a standard which I can apply to others. He is judge of myself, revealing my own virtues to me as something altogether evil. Thus I am not permitted to apply to the other person what does not apply to me. For, with my judgement according to good and evil, I only affirm the other person's evil, for he does exactly the same. But he does not know of the hidden iniquity of the good but seeks his justification in it. If I condemn his evil actions I thereby confirm him in his apparently good actions which are yet never the good commended by Christ. Thus we remove him from the judgement of Christ and subject him to human judgement. But I bring God's judgement upon my head, for I then do not live any more on and out of the grace of Jesus Christ, but out of my knowledge of good and evil which I hold on to. To everyone God is the kind of God he believes in.

Judgement is the forbidden objectivization of the other person which destroys single-minded love. I am not forbidden to have my own thoughts about the other person, to realize his shortcomings, but only to the extent that it offers to me an occasion for forgiveness and unconditional love, as Jesus proves to me. If I withhold my judgement I am not indulging in *tout comprendre c'est tout pardonner* and confirm the other person in his bad ways. Neither I am right nor the other person, but God is always right and shall proclaim both his grace and his judgement.

Judging others makes us blind, whereas love is illuminating. By judging others we blind ourselves to our own evil and to the grace which others are just as entitled to as we are. But in the love of Christ we know all about every conceivable sin and guilt; for we know how Jesus suffered, and how all men have been forgiven at the foot of the cross. Christian love sees the fellow-man under the cross and therefore sees with clarity. If when we judged others, our real motive was to destroy evil, we should look for evil where it is certain to be found, and that is in our own hearts. But if we are on the look-out for evil in others, our real motive is obviously to justify ourselves, for we are seeking to escape punishment for our own sins by passing judgement on others, and are assuming by implication that the Word of God applies to ourselves in one way, and to others in another. All this is highly dangerous and misleading. We are trying to claim for ourselves a special privilege which we deny to others. But Christ's disciples have no rights of their own or standards of right and wrong which they could enforce with other people; they have received nothing but Christ's fellowship. Therefore the disciple is not to sit in judgement over his fellow-man because he would wrongly usurp the jurisdiction.

But the Christian is not only forbidden to *judge* other men: even the word of salvation has its limits. He has neither power nor right to force it on other men in season and out of season. Every attempt to impose the gospel by force, to run after people and proselytize them, to use our own resources to arrange the salvation of other people, is both futile and dangerous. It is futile, because the swine do not recognize the pearls that are cast before them, and dangerous, because it profanes the word of forgiveness, by causing those we fain would serve to sin against that which is holy. Worse still, we shall only meet with the blind rage of hardened and darkened hearts, and that will be useless and harmful. Our easy trafficking with the word of cheap grace simply bores the world to disgust, so that in the end it turns against those who try to force on it what it does not want. Thus a strict limit is placed upon the activities of the disciples, just as in Matt. 10 they are told to shake the dust off their feet where the word of peace is refused a hearing. Their restless energy which refuses to recognize any limit to their activity, the zeal which refuses to take note of resistance, springs from a confusion of the gospel with a victorious ideology. An ideology requires fanatics, who neither know nor notice opposition, and it is certainly a potent force. But the Word of God in its weakness takes the risk of meeting the scorn of men and being rejected. There are hearts which are hardened and doors which are closed to the Word. The Word recognizes opposition when it meets it, and is prepared to suffer it. It is a hard lesson, but a true one, that the gospel, unlike an ideology, reckons with impossibilities. The Word is weaker than any ideology, and this means that with only the gospel at their command the witnesses are weaker than the propagandists of an opinion. But although they are weak, they are ready to suffer with the Word and so are free from that morbid restlessness which is so characteristic of fanaticism.

The disciples can even yield their ground and run away, provided they do so with the Word, provided their weakness is the weakness of the Word, and provided they do not leave the Word in the lurch in their flight. They are simply the servants and instruments of the Word; they have no wish to be strong where the Word chooses to be weak. To try and force the Word on the world by hook or by crook is to make the living Word of God into a mere idea, and the world would be perfectly justified in refusing to listen to an idea for which it had no use. But at other times, the disciples must stick to their guns and refuse to run away, though of course only when the Word so wills. If they do not realize this weakness of the Word, they have failed to perceive the mystery of the divine humility. The same weak Word which is content to endure the gainsaying of sinners is also the mighty Word of mercy which can convert the hearts of sinners. Its strength is veiled in weakness; if it came in power that would mean that the day of judgement had arrived. The great task of the disciples is to recognize the limits of their commission. But if they use the Word amiss it will certainly turn against them.

What are the disciples to do when they encounter opposition

and cannot penetrate the hearts of men? They must admit that in no circumstances do they possess any rights or powers over others, and that they have no direct access to them. The only way to reach others is through him in whose hands they are themselves like all other men. We shall hear more about this as we proceed. The disciples are taught to pray, and so they learn that the only way to reach others is by praying to God. Judgement and forgiveness are always in the hands of God. He closes and he opens. But the disciples must ask, they must seek and knock, and then God will hear them. They have to learn that their anxiety and concern for others must drive them to intercession. The promise Christ gives to their prayer is the doughtiest weapon in their armoury.

The difference between the disciples' seeking and the Gentiles' quest for God is that the disciples know what they are looking for. We can only seek God when we know him already. How can you look for something or find it if you do not know what you are looking for? The disciples seek a God whom they have found in the promise they have received from Jesus.

To sum up: it is clear from the foregoing that the disciple has no special privilege or power of his own in all his intercourse with others. The mainspring of his life and work is the strength which comes from fellowship with Jesus Christ. Jesus offers his disciples a simple rule of thumb which will enable even the least sophisticated of them to tell whether his intercourse with others is on the right lines or not. All he need do is to say 'I' instead of 'Thou', and put himself in the other man's place. 'All things whatsoever ye would that men should do unto you, even so do ye also unto them: for this is the law and the prophets.' The moment he does that, the disciple forfeits all advantage over other men, and can no longer excuse in himself what he condemns in others. He is as strict in condemning evil in himself as he was before with others, and as lenient with the evil in others as he was before to himself. The evil in the other person is exactly the same evil as in ourselves. There is only *one* judgement, *one* law, and *one* grace. Henceforth the disciple will look upon other men as forgiven sinners who owe their lives to the love of God. 'This is the law and the prophets' – for this is none other than the supreme commandment: to love God above all things and our neighbours as ourselves.

19 THE GREAT DIVIDE

Enter ye in by the narrow gate: for wide is the gate, and broad is the way, that leadeth to destruction, and many be they that enter in thereby. For narrow is the gate, and straitened the way, that leadeth unto life, and few be they that find it.

Beware of false prophets, which come to you in sheep's clothing, but inwardly are ravening wolves. By their fruits ye shall know them. Do men gather grapes of thorns, or figs of thistles? Even so every good tree bringeth forth good fruit; but the corrupt tree bringeth forth evil fruit. A good tree cannot bring forth evil fruit, neither can a corrupt tree bring forth good fruit. Every tree that bringeth not forth good fruit is hewn down, and cast into the fire. Therefore by their fruits ye shall know them. Not everyone that saith unto me, Lord, Lord, shall enter into the kingdom of heaven; but he that doeth the will of my Father which is in heaven. Many will say to me in that day, Lord, Lord, did we not prophesy by thy name, and by thy name cast out devils, and by thy name do many mighty works? And then will I profess unto them, I never knew you: depart from me, ye that work iniquity. (Matt. 7.13-23)

THE Church of Jesus cannot arbitrarily break off all contact with those who refuse his call. It is called to follow the Lord by promise and commandment. That must suffice. All judgement of others and separation from them must be left to him who chose the Church according to his good purpose, and not for any merit or achievement of its own. The separation of Church and world is not effected by the Church itself, but by the word of its calling.

A little band of men, the followers of Christ, are separated from the rest of the world. The disciples are few in number, and will always be few. This saying of Jesus forestalls all exaggerated hopes of success. Never let a disciple of Jesus pin his hopes on large numbers. 'Few there be. . . .' The rest of the world are many, and will always be many. But they are on the road to perdition. The only comfort the disciples have in face of this prospect is the promise of life and eternal fellowship with Jesus.

The path of discipleship is narrow, and it is fatally easy to miss one's way and stray from the path, even after years of discipleship. And it is hard to find. On either side of the narrow path deep chasms yawn. To be called to a life of extraordinary quality, to live up to it, and yet to be unconscious of it is indeed a narrow way. To confess and testify to the truth as it is in Jesus, and at the same time to love the enemies of that truth, his enemies and ours, and to love them with the infinite love of Jesus Christ, is indeed a narrow way. To believe the promise of Jesus that his followers shall possess the earth, and at the same time to face our enemies unarmed and defenceless, preferring to incur injustice rather than to do wrong ourselves, is indeed a narrow way. To see the weakness and wrong in others, and at the same time refrain from judging them; to deliver the gospel message without casting pearls before swine, is indeed a narrow way. The way is unutterably hard, and at every moment we are in danger of straying from it. If we regard this way as one we follow in obedience to an external command, if we are afraid of ourselves all the time, it is indeed an impossible way. But if we behold Jesus Christ going on before step by step, we shall not go astray. But if we worry about the dangers that beset us, if we gaze at the road instead of at him who goes before, we are already straying from the path. For he is himself the way, the narrow way and the strait gate. He, and he alone, is our journey's end. When we know that, we are able to proceed along the narrow way through the strait gate of the cross, and on to eternal life, and the very narrowness of the road will increase our certainty. The way which the Son of God trod on earth, and the way which we too must tread as citizens of tow worlds on the razor edge between this world and the kingdom of heaven, could hardly be a broad way. The narrow way is bound to be right.

Verses 15-20. The separation of Church and world is now complete. But the word of Jesus forces its way into the Church herself, bringing judgement and decision. The separation is never permanently assured: it must constantly be renewed. The disciples of Jesus must not fondly imagine that they can simply run away from the world and huddle together in a little band. False prophets will rise up among them, and amid the ensuing confusion they will feel more isolated than ever. There is someone standing by my side, who looks just like a member of the Church. He is a prophet and a preacher. He looks like a Christian, he talks and acts like one. But dark powers are mysteriously at work; it was these who sent him into our midst. Inwardly he is a ravening wolf: his words are lies and his works are full of deceit. He knows only too well how to keep his secret dark, and go ahead with his work. It is not faith in Jesus Christ which made him one of us, but the devil. Maybe he hopes his intellectual ability or his success as a prophet will bring him power and influence, money and fame. His ambitions are set on the world, not on Jesus Christ. Knowing that Christians are credulous people, he conceals his dark purpose beneath the cloak of Christian piety, hoping that his innocuous disguise will avert detection. He knows that Christians are forbidden to judge, and he will remind them of it at the appropriate time. After all, other men's hearts are always a closed book. Thus he succeeds in seducing many from the right way. He may even be unconscious himself of what he is doing. The devil can give him every encouragement and at the same time keep him in the dark about his own motives.

Such a pronouncement of Christ's could cause his disciples great anxiety. Who knows his neighbour? Who knows whether the outward appearance of a Christian conceals falsehood and deception underneath? No wonder if mistrust, suspicion and censoriousness crept into the Church. And no wonder if every brother who falls into sin incurred the uncharitable criticism of his brethren, now that Jesus has said this. All this distrust would ruin the Church but for the word of Jesus which assures us that the bad tree will bring forth bad fruit. It is bound to give itself away sooner or later. There is no need to go about prying into the hearts of others. All we need do is to wait until the tree bears fruit, and we shall not have to wait long. This is not to say that we must draw a distinction between the words of the prophet and his deeds: the real distinction is that between appearance and reality. Jesus tells us that men cannot keep up appearances for long. The time of vintage is sure to come, and then we shall be able to sift the good from the bad. Sooner or later we shall find out where a man stands. It is no use the tree refusing to bear any fruit, for the fruit comes of its own accord. Any day the time may come to decide for the world or for the Church. We may have to decide, not in some spectacular matter, but in quite trivial, everyday affairs. And then we shall see and discern the good from the bad. In that day the reality will stand the test, not appearances.

In such times as these, Jesus requires his disciples to distinguish between appearance and reality, between themselves and pseudo-Christians. They will then rise above all inquisitive examination of others, but they will need a sincere determination to recognize the verdict of God when it comes. At any moment the nominal Christians may be separated from the real ones. We may even find that we are nominal Christians ourselves. Here is a challenge to closer fellowship with Jesus and to a more loyal discipleship. The bad tree is cut down and cast into the fire. All its display of finery proves ultimately to be of no avail.

Verse 21. The separation which the call of Jesus creates goes deeper still. After the division between Church and world, between nominal Christians and real ones, the division now enters into the very heart of the confessional body. St Paul says: 'No man can say, Jesus is Lord, but in the Holy Spirit' (I Cor. 12.3). It is impossible to surrender our lives to Jesus or call him Lord of our own free will. St Paul is deliberately reckoning with the possibility that men may call Jesus Lord without the Holy Spirit, that is, without having received the call. It was harder to understand this in days when it brought no earthly gain to be a Christian and when Christianity was a dangerous profession. 'Not every one that saith unto me, Lord, Lord, shall enter the kingdom of heaven. . . .' 'Lord, Lord' is the Church's confession of faith. But not everyone who makes this confession will enter the kingdom of heaven. The dividing line will run right through the confessing Church. Even if we make the confession of faith, it gives us no title to any special claim upon Jesus. We can never appeal to our confession or be saved simply on the ground that we have made it. Neither is the fact that we are members of a Church which has a right confession a claim to God's favour. To think thus is to fall into the sin of Israel, which thought the grace of God's call gave it a special privilege in his sight. That would be a sin against God's gracious call. God will not ask us in that day whether we were good Protestants, but whether we have done his will. We shall be asked the same question as everybody else. The Church is marked off from the world not by a special privilege, but by the gracious election and calling of God. $Π\hatα\varsigma$ $ό$ $λέγων$ and $άλλ'$ $ό$ $ποιῶν$, 'say' and 'do' – this does not mean the ordinary contrast between word and deed, but two different relations between man and God. $Ὁ$ $λέγων$ $κύριε$ – the man who says 'Lord, Lord' – means the man who puts forward a claim on the ground that he has said 'it', $ό$ $ποιῶν$ – the doer – is the man of humble obedience. The first is the one who justifies himself through his confession, and the second, the doer, the obedient man who builds his life on the grace of God. Here a man's speaking denotes self-righteousness, his doing is a token of grace, to which there can be no other response save that of humble and obedient service. The man who says 'Lord, Lord' has either called himself to Jesus without the Holy Spirit, or else he has made out of the call of Jesus a personal privilege. But our doer of the will of God is called and endued with grace, he obeys and follows. He understands his call not as his right, but as an act of God's judgement and grace, as the will of God, which alone he must obey. The grace of Jesus is a demand upon the doer, and so his doing becomes the true humility, the right faith, and the right confession of the grace of the God who calls.

Verse 22. Confessor and doer are separated from one another. And now the division is carried to its furthest extent. Only those are now speaking who have survived the test so far. They are numbered among the doers, but they appeal not to their confession, but to the deeds they have done. They have performed deeds in the name of Jesus. They know that confession does not justify, and so they have gone and made the name of Jesus great among the people by their deeds. Now they appear before Jesus and tell him what they have done.

At this point Jesus reveals to his disciples the possibility of a demonic faith which produces wonderful works quite indistinguishable from the works of the true disciples, works of charity, miracles, perhaps even of personal sanctification, but which is nevertheless a denial of Jesus and of the life of discipleship. This is just what St Paul means in I Cor. 13, when he says that it is possible to preach, to prophesy, to have all knowledge, and even faith so as to remove mountains, and all this without love, that is to say, without Christ, without the Holy Spirit. More than this, St Paul must even reckon with the possibility that the very works of Christian charity, giving away one's goods, and even martyrdom, may be done without love, without Christ, without the Holy Spirit. Without love: that is to say, in all this activity the activity of discipleship is absent, namely that activity the doer of which is in the last resort none other than Jesus Christ himself. Here is the most serious, most incredible satanic possibility in the Church, the final division, which only occurs at the last day. But Christ's followers must ask by what ultimate criterion Jesus will accept or reject them. Who will pass the test, and who will not? The answer lies in the words of Jesus to the last of the rejected: 'I have never known you.' Here we are at last, here is the secret we have been waiting for since the Sermon on the Mount began. Here is the crucial question – has Jesus known us or not? First came the division between Church and world, then the division within the Church, and then the final division on the last day. There is nothing left for us to cling to, not even our confession or our obedience. There is only his word: 'I have known thee', which is his eternal word and call. The end of the Sermon on the Mount echoes the beginning. The word of the last judgement is foreshadowed in the call to discipleship. But from beginning to end it is always *his* word and *his* call, his alone. If we follow Christ, cling to his word, and let everything else go, it will see us through the day of judgement. His word is his grace.

20 THE CONCLUSION

Every one therefore which heareth these words of mine, and doeth them, shall be likened unto a wise man, which built his house upon the rock: and the rain descended, and the floods came, and the winds blew, and beat upon that house; and it fell not: for it was founded upon the rock. And every one that heareth these words of mine, and doeth them not, shall be likened unto a foolish man, which built his house upon the sand: and the rain descended, and the floods came, and the winds blew, and smote upon that house; and it fell: and great was the fall thereof.

And it came to pass, when Jesus ended these words, the multitudes were astonished at his teaching: for he taught them as one having authority, and not as their scribes. (Matt. 7.24-29)

WE have listened to the Sermon on the Mount and perhaps have understood it. But who has heard it aright? Jesus gives the answer at the end. He does not allow his hearers to go away and make of his sayings what they will, picking and choosing from them whatever they find helpful, and testing them to see if they work. He does not give them free rein to misuse his word with their mercenary hands, but gives it to them on condition that it retains exclusive power over them. Humanly speaking, we could understand and interpret the Sermon on the Mount in a thousand different ways. Jesus knows only one possibility: simple surrender and obedience, not interpreting it or applying it, but doing and obeying it. That is the only way to hear his word. But again he does not mean that it is to be discussed as an ideal, he really means us to get on with it.

This word, whose claim we recognize, this word which issues from his saying 'I have known thee', this word which sets us at once to work and obedience, is the rock on which to build our house. The only proper response to this word which Jesus brings with him from eternity is simply to do it. Jesus has spoken: his is the word, ours the obedience. Only in the doing of it does the word of Jesus retain its honour, might and power among us. Now the storm can rage over the house, but it cannot shatter that union with him, which his word has created.

There is only one other possibility, that of failing to do it. It is impossible to want to do it and yet not do it. To deal with the word of Jesus otherwise than by doing it is to give him the lie. It is to deny the Sermon on the Mount and to say No to his word. If we start asking questions, posing problems, and offering interpretations, we are not doing his word. Once again the shades of the rich young man and the lawyer of Luke 10 are raising their heads. However vehemently we assert our faith, and our fundamental recognition of his word, Jesus still calls it 'not-doing'. But the word which we fail to do is no rock to build a house on. There can then be no union with Jesus. He has never known us. That is why as soon as the hurricane begins we lose the word, and find that we have never really believed it. The word we had was not Christ's, but a word we had wrested from him and made our own by reflecting on it instead of doing it. So our house crashes in ruins, because it is not founded on the word of Jesus Christ.

'The multitudes were astonished. . . .' What had happened? The Son of God had spoken. He had taken the judgement of the world into his own hands. And his disciples were standing at his side.

Part Three

THE MESSENGERS

Matthew 9.35-10.42

21 THE HARVEST

And Jesus went about all the cities and villages, teaching in their synagogues and preaching the gospel of the kingdom, and healing all manner of sickness. But when he saw the multitudes, he was moved with compassion for them, because they were distressed and scattered, as sheep not having a shepherd. Then saith he unto his disciples, the harvest truly is plenteous but the labourers are few. Pray ye therefore the Lord of the harvest, that he send forth labourers into his harvest. (Matt. 9.35-38)

THE saviour looks with compassion on his people, the people of God. He could not rest satisfied with the few who had heard his call and followed. He shrank from the idea of forming an exclusive little coterie with his disciples. Unlike the founders of the great religions, he had no desire to withdraw them from the vulgar crowd and initiate them into an esoteric system of religion and ethics. He had come, he had worked and suffered for the sake of all his people. But the disciples wanted to keep him to themselves, as they showed when the young children were brought to him, and on several occasions when he was accosted by beggars on the road-side (Mark 10.48). The disciples had to learn that Jesus would not be hemmed in by them in his service. His gospel of the kingdom of God and his power of healing belonged to the sick and poor, wherever they were to be found among the people. God's beloved people had been ill-treated and laid low and the guilt belonged to those who had failed to minister to them in the service of God. The Romans had not done this, but the chosen ministers of the Word, and their misuse of that Word. There were no longer any shepherds in Israel. No one led the flock to fresh waters to quench their thirst, no one protected them from the wolf. They were harassed, wounded and distraught under the dire rod of their shepherds, and lay prostrate upon the ground. Such was the condition of the people when Jesus came. There were questions but no answers, distress but no relief, anguish of conscience but no deliverance, tears but no consolation, sin but no forgiveness. Where was the good shepherd they needed so badly? What good was it when the scribes herded the people into the schools, when the devotees of the law sternly condemned sinners without lifting a finger to help them? What use were all these orthodox preachers and expounders of the Word, when they were not filled by boundless pity and compassion for God's maltreated and injured people? What is the use of scribes, devotees of the law, preachers and the rest, when there are no shepherds for the flock? What they need is good shepherds, good 'pastors'. 'Feed my lambs' was the last charge Jesus gave to Peter. The Good Shepherd protects his sheep against the wolf, and instead of fleeing he gives his life for the sheep. He knows them all by name and loves them. He knows their distress and their weakness. He heals the wounded, gives drink to the thirsty, sets upright the falling, and leads them gently, not sternly, to pasture. He leads them on the right way. He seeks the one lost sheep, and brings it back to the fold. But the bad shepherds lord it over the flock by force, forgetting their charges and pursuing their own interests. Jesus is looking for good shepherds, and there are none to be found.

The prospect grips his heart, and his divine pity goes out to this erring flock, these multitudes who surge around him. From the human point of view everything looks hopeless, but Jesus sees things with different eyes. Instead of the people maltreated, wretched and poor, he sees the ripe harvest field of God. 'The harvest is great.' It is ripe enough to be gathered into the barns. The hour has come for these poor and wretched folk to be fetched home to the kingdom of God. Jesus beholds the promise of God descending on the multitudes where the scribes and zealots saw only a field trampled down, burnt and ravaged. Jesus sees the fields waving with corn and ripe for the kingdom of God. The harvest is great, but only Jesus in his mercy can see it.

There is now no time to lose: the work of harvest brooks no delay. 'But the labourers are few.' It is hardly surprising that so few are granted to see things with the pitying eyes of Jesus, for only those who share the love of his heart have been given eyes to see. And only they can enter the harvest field.

Jesus is looking for help, for he cannot do the work alone. Who will come forward to help him and work with him? Only God knows, and he must give them to his Son. No man dare presume to come forward and offer himself on his own initiative, not even the disciples themselves. Their duty is to pray the Lord of the harvest to send forth labourers at the right moment, for the time is ripe.

22 THE APOSTLES

And he called unto him his twelve disciples, and gave them power over unclean spirits, to cast them out, and to heal all manner of disease and all manner of sickness. Now the names of the twelve apostles are these: The first, Simon, who is called Peter, and Andrew his brother; James the son of Zebedee, and John his brother; Philip, and Bartholomew; Thomas, and Matthew the publican; James the son of Alphæus, and Thaddeus; Simon the Cananaean, and Judas Iscariot, who also betrayed him. (Matt. 10.1-4)

THE prayer has been heard. The Father has revealed his will to the Son. Jesus calls his twelve disciples and sends them into the harvest. He makes them his 'apostles', his messengers and fellow-workers. 'And gave them power', for the power is all-important. It is not a word or a doctrine they receive, but effective power, without which the work could not be done. They need a power stronger than that of the Prince of this world, the devil. The disciples know the devil's power well enough, although it is his cleverest trick to deny his power and to pretend that he does not exist. It is just this supreme cunning of his that must be countered: he must be brought to light, and overcome through the power of the Christ. In this work the apostles stand by the side of Christ himself, and help him to do his work. So Jesus imparts to them a share in the highest gift he possesses, his power over unclean spirits, and over the devil who has taken possession of the human race. In virtue of this commission the disciples have become like Christ. They do the works of Christ.

The names of the first messengers are preserved for all time. Just as the people of God had consisted of twelve tribes, so it is twelve messengers who are to complete the work of Christ towards that people. Twelve thrones will be prepared for them in the kingdom of God, and they will sit on them judging the twelve tribes of Israel (Matt. 19.28). The heavenly Jerusalem will have twelve gates through which the holy nation will enter in, with the names of the twelve tribes inscribed on them, and the walls of the city have twelve foundations bearing the names of the twelve apostles (Rev. 21.12, 14).

The only bond of unity between the twelve is their choice and call. Simon the Rock-man, Matthew the publican, Simon the Zealot, the champion of law and justice against the oppression of the Gentiles, John the beloved disciple, who lay on Jesus' breast, and the others, of whom we know nothing except their names, then lastly Judas Iscariot, who betrayed him. No power in the world could have united these men for a common task, save the call of Jesus. But that call transcended all their previous divisions, and established a new and steadfast fellowship in Jesus. Even Judas went forth to the Christ-work, and the fact that he did so will always be a dark riddle and an awful warning.

> These twelve Jesus sent forth, and charged them, saying, Go not
> into any way of the Gentiles, and enter not into any city of the
> Samaritans; but go rather to the lost sheep of the house of Israel.
> (Matt. 10.5, 6)

ALL the activity of the disciples is subject to the clear precept of
their Lord. They are not left free to choose their own methods or
adopt their own conception of their task. Their work is to be
Christ-work, and therefore they are absolutely dependent on the
will of Jesus. Happy are they whose duty is fixed by such a precept,
and who are therefore free from the tyranny of their own ideas
and calculations.

In his very first word Jesus lays down a limitation of their work,
a circumstance which they must inevitably have found strange and
difficult. The choice of field for their labours does not depend on
their own impulses or inclinations, but on where they are sent.
This makes it quite clear that it is not their own work they are
doing, but God's. How much they would have liked to go to the
heathen and the Samaritans, who needed the glad tidings far more
than anyone else. That may be quite true, but they receive no
injunctions to go to them. The work of God cannot be done
without due authorization, otherwise it is devoid of promise. Does
it therefore follow that the promise and commission are not uni-
versally valid? Both are valid only where God authorizes them.
But does not the very love of Christ constrain us to set no limit
to its proclamation? The love of Jesus is something very different
from our own zeal and enthusiasms because it adheres to its
mission. What is the urge which drives us to proclaim the saving
truths of the gospel? It is not just love for our fellow-countrymen
or for the heathen in foreign lands: it is the Lord's commission as
he delivered it in his missionary charge. It is only that commission
which can show us the place where the promise lies. If Christ will

not let us preach the gospel in any particular place, we must give up the attempt and abide by his will and word. Thus the disciples are bound to the word and to the terms of their commission. They can only go where the word of Christ and his commission direct them, 'Go not into any way of the Gentiles, and enter not into any city of the Samaritans: but go rather to the lost sheep of the house of Israel.'

We, who are of the Gentiles, were once shut out from the message of the gospel. It was first necessary for Israel to hear and reject it before it could come to the Gentiles, and a Church of Gentile Christians be established according to the commission of Jesus. Not until after his resurrection does Jesus charge his apostles to go out into all the world. The disciples found it hard to understand this limitation of their commission, but in the end it turned out to be a means of grace for the Gentiles. When they received the good news, it was the good news of a crucified and risen Lord. Such was the way of God's wisdom. All that is left to us is the commission.

And as ye go, preach, saying, The kingdom of heaven is at hand. Heal the sick, raise the dead, cast out devils; freely ye have received, freely give. (Matt. 10.7, 8)

The proclamation and activity of the messengers are identical with that of Christ himself. To them has been granted a portion of his power. They are charged to proclaim the advent of the kingdom of heaven, and to confirm their message by performing signs. They must heal the sick, cleanse the lepers, raise the dead and drive out devils. The message becomes an event, and the event confirms the message. The kingdom of God, Jesus Christ, the forgiveness of sins, the justification of the sinner through faith, all this is identical with the destruction of the devil's power, the healing of the sick and raising of the dead. The proclamation of the apostles is the Word of the Almighty God, and therefore it is an act, an event, a miracle. It is the *one* Christ who passes through the land in the person of his twelve messengers and performs his work. The sovereign grace with which they are equipped is the creative and redemptive Word of God.

Get you no gold, nor silver, nor brass in your purses; no wallet for your journey, neither two coats, nor shoes, nor staff: for the labourer is worthy of his food. (Matt. 10.9-10)

Since the authorization and equipment of the messengers is absolutely dependent on the word of Jesus, it is essential that nothing should obscure their royal mission or make it incredible. The messengers are to deliver their testimony to the riches of their Lord in royal poverty. The gifts they have received are no personal possessions which they could trade for other goods. 'Freely ye have received.' To be a messenger of Jesus Christ confers no personal privileges, no title to power or renown. This is true, even where the free messengers of Jesus have turned into a regular ministry in the Church. The rights of a university education and social standing mean nothing to those who have become messengers of Jesus. 'Freely ye have received.' Or was there something else in addition to the call of Jesus which drew us into his service without any merit of our own? 'Freely give,' he says, moreover: 'Show men that you have plenty of riches to give away, but desire nothing for yourselves, neither possessions, nor admiration nor regard, and least of all their gratitude.' Whence could you have any claim on it? Any honours that come our way are only stolen from him to whom alone they really belong, the Lord who sent us. The poverty of Christ's messengers is the proof of their freedom. There is a slight difference between the Matthean and Lukan accounts of what the disciples were allowed or forbidden to take with them, but we are not to draw any conclusion from this discrepancy. The point is that as they go forth to be the plenipotentiaries of his word, Jesus enjoins strict poverty upon them. Note that this is an explicit command, and that the possessions the disciples are allowed to take with them are specified down to the last detail. They are not to go about like beggars and call attention to themselves, nor are they to burden other people like parasites. They are to go forth in the battle-dress of poverty, taking as little with them as a traveller who knows he will get board and lodging with friends at the end of the day. This shall be an expression of their faith, not in men, but in their heavenly father who sent them and will care for them. It is this that will make their gospel credible, for they proclaim the coming Kingdom of God. The same freedom which informs their service allows them to accept board and lodging, not as charity, but as a due reward for their labours. Jesus calls his messengers 'workmen'. If they are idle, they certainly deserve no food. And if this battle with the powers of Satan for the souls of men, this renunciation of all personal dignity, and of the goods and joy of the world for the sake of the poor and miserable and ill-used, is not work, what is? God had himself endured toil and labour for man's sake (Isa. 43.24), and the soul of Jesus laboured on the cross for our salvation even unto death (Isa. 53.11). The disciples are given a share in this work, in the proclamation, in the defeat of Satan, and in intercessory prayer. If men cannot see this, they have as yet failed to discern the true nature of the service of the messengers of Jesus. These messengers are not ashamed to receive the daily reward for their labour, and to remain as poor as ever for the sake of their ministry.

> And into whatsoever city or village ye shall enter, search out in it who is worthy; and there abide until ye go forth. And as ye enter into the house, salute it. And if the house be worthy, let your peace come upon it: but if it be not worthy, let your peace return to you. And whosoever shall not receive you, nor hear your words, as ye go forth out of that house or city, shake off the dust of your feet. Verily I say unto you, it shall be more tolerable for the land of Sodom and Gomorrah in the day of judgement than for that city. (Matt. 10.11-15)

Their work among the people is to begin with those houses which are worthy to give them lodging. There are still people praying and waiting for God in every place, and those people will give the disciples humble and cheerful welcome in the name of their Lord. They will support their work with their prayers, and indeed they are a little flock already in being, the advance guard of the whole Church of Christ. To forestall jealousy among the brethren, and covetousness on the part of the disciples, Jesus bids them stay in the same house throughout their sojourn in that place. As soon as they set foot in the house or city, they must come straight to the point. Time is precious, and multitudes are still waiting for the message of the gospel. As they enter the house they are to use the same word of greeting as their Master: 'Peace be to this house' (Luke 10.5). This is no empty formula, for it immediately brings the power of the peace of God on those who 'are worthy of it'. Their proclamation is clear and concise. They simply announce that the kingdom of God has drawn nigh, and summon men to repentance and faith. They come with the full authority of Jesus of Nazareth, they deliver a command and make an offer with the support of the highest credentials. And that is all. The whole message is staggering in its simplicity and clarity, and since the cause brooks no delay, there is no need for them to enter into any further discussion to clear the ground or to persuade their hearers. The King stands at the door, and he may come in at any moment. Will you bow down and humbly receive him, or do you want him to destroy you in his wrath? Those who have ears to hear have heard all there is to hear. They cannot detain the messengers any longer, for they must be off to the next city. If however men refuse to hear, they have lost their chance, the time of grace is passed, and they have pronounced their own doom. 'To-day if ye shall hear his voice, harden not your hearts' (Heb. 4.7). That is evangelical preaching. Is this ruthless speed? Nothing could be more ruthless than to make men think there is still plenty of time to mend their ways. To tell men that the cause is urgent, and that the kingdom of God is at hand is the most charitable and merciful act we can perform, the most joyous news we can bring. The messenger cannot wait and repeat it to every man in his own language. God's language is clear enough. It is not for the messenger to decide who will hear and who will not, for only God knows who is 'worthy'; and those who are worthy will hear the Word when the disciple proclaims it. But woe to the city and woe to the house which rejects the messenger of Christ. They will incur a dreadful judgement; Sodom and Gomorrah, the cities of inchastity and perversion, will be judged more graciously than those cities of Israel who reject the word of Jesus. Vice and sin may be forgiven, according to the word of Jesus, but the man who rejects the word of salvation has thrown away his last chance. To refuse to believe in the gospel is the worst sin imaginable, and if that happens the messengers can do nothing but leave the place. They go because the Word cannot remain there. They must recognize in fear and amazement both the power and the weakness of the Word of God. But the disciples must not force any issue contrary to or beyond the word of Christ. Their commission is not a heroic struggle, a fanatical pursuit of a grand idea or a good cause. That is why they stay only where the Word stays, and if it is rejected they will be rejected with it, and shake off the dust from their feet as a sign of the curse which awaits that place. This curse will not harm the disciples, but the peace they brought returns to them. 'This is a great consolation for ministers of the Church when they are troubled because their work seems void of success. You must not be depressed, for what others refuse will prove an even greater blessing for yourselves. To such the Lord says: "They have scorned it, so keep it for yourselves" ' (Bengel).

Behold, I send you forth as sheep in the midst of wolves: be ye therefore wise as serpents, and harmless as doves. But beware of men: for they will deliver you up to councils, and in their synagogues they will scourge you, yea, and before governors and kings shall ye be brought for my sake, for a testimony to them and to the Gentiles. But when they deliver you up, be not anxious how or what ye shall speak: for it shall be given you in that hour what ye shall speak. For it is not ye that speak, but the Spirit of your Father that speaketh in you. And brother shall deliver up brother to death, and the father his child: and children shall rise up against parents, and cause them to be put to death. And ye shall be hated of all men for my name's sake: but he that endureth to the end, the same shall be saved. But when they persecute you in this city, flee into the next: for verily I say unto you, Ye shall not have gone through the cities of Israel, till the Son of man be come. A disciple is not above his master, nor a servant above his lord. It is enough for the disciple that he be as his master, and the servant as his lord. If they have called the master of the house Beelzebub, how much more shall they call them of his household! (Matt. 10.16-25)

NEITHER failure nor hostility can weaken the messenger's conviction that he has been sent by Jesus. That his word may be their strength, their stay and their comfort, Jesus repeats it. 'Behold, I send you.' For this is no way they have chosen themselves, no undertaking of their own. It is, in the strict sense of the word, a *mission*. With this the Lord promises them his abiding presence, even when they find themselves as sheep among wolves, defenceless, powerless, sore pressed and beset with great danger. Nothing can happen to them without Jesus knowing of it. 'Be ye therefore wise as serpents, and harmless as doves.' How often have the ministers of Jesus made wrong use of this saying! However willing they may be, it is indeed difficult for them to preserve a true understanding of this word, and to adhere to the path of obedience. How difficult it is to draw the line with certainty between spiritual wisdom and worldly astuteness! Are we not all prepared at heart to do without 'worldly wisdom' and much prefer the harmlessness of the doves and thus again fall into disobedience? Who is there to let us know when we are running away from suffering through cowardice, or running after it through temerity? Who shows us the hidden frontier? It is just as bad to appeal to the commandment of simplicity against that of wisdom, as to appeal to the commandment of wisdom against that of simplicity. There is no one in the world who has a perfect knowledge of his own heart. But Jesus never called his disciples into a state of uncertainty, but to one of supreme certainty. That is why his warning can only summon them to abide by the word. Where the word is, there shall the disciple be. Therein lies his true wisdom and his true simplicity. If it is obvious that the word is being rejected, if it is forced to yield its ground, the disciple must yield with it. But if the word carries on the battle, the disciple must also stand his ground. In each case he will be combining wisdom with simplicity. But wisdom, however spiritual it may be, must never lead the disciple along a path which cannot stand the test of the word of Jesus. Only the truth of that word will enable him to discern what is wise. But to deviate from the truth for the sake of some prospect or hope of our own can never be wise, however slight that deviation may be. It is not our judgement of the situation which can show us what is wise, but only the truth of the Word of God. Here alone lies the promise of God's faithfulness and help. It will always be true that the wisest course for the disciple is always to abide solely by the Word of God in all simplicity.

The Word of God will also give the messengers an unerring insight into human nature. 'Beware of men.' The disciples are not expected to show fear of men, nor malice, nor mistrust, still less a sour misanthropy, nor that gullible credulity which believes that there is good in every man: they are expected rather to display an unerring insight into the mutual relation of the Word and man. If they are content not to pitch their hopes too high, they will not be perturbed when Jesus warns them that their way among men will be one of suffering. But there is a miraculous power

latent in this suffering. Whereas the criminal has to suffer his
punishment in secret, the disciples will have to stand before
governors and kings 'for my sake, for a testimony to them and
to the Gentiles'. This suffering will help forward their testimony.
It is all part of God's plan and the will of Jesus, and that is why
they will be given power to make a good confession and deliver
a fearless testimony even in the hour when they make answer
before thrones and judgement seats. The Holy Ghost himself will
stand by their side, and make them invincible. He will give them
'a mouth and a wisdom which all your adversaries will not be
able to withstand or to gainsay' (Luke 21.15). Because the disciples
remain true to the Word in their sufferings, the Word will remain
true to them. To self-sought martyrdom this promise would not
apply, but there is no doubt whatever that it does apply to
suffering with the Word.

The messengers of Jesus will be hated to the end of time. They
will be blamed for all the divisions which rend cities and homes.
Jesus and his disciples will be condemned on all sides for undermining family life, and for leading the nation astray; they will be
called crazy fanatics and disturbers of the peace. The disciples will
be sorely tempted to desert their Lord. But the end is also near,
and they must hold on and persevere until it comes. Only he will
be blessed who remains loyal to Jesus and his word until the end.
But when the end comes, the hostility towards Jesus and his
disciples will be made manifest the whole world over, and only
then must the messengers flee from city to city, in order that they
may proclaim the Word where it can still find a hearing. If they
run away then, they will not be running away from the Word,
but holding fast to it.

The Church has never forgotten Christ's promise of his immi-
nent return, and she has always believed that this promise is true.
The exact manner of its fulfilment remains obscure, but that is
not a problem for us to solve. This much is clear and all-important
for us to-day that the return of Jesus will take place suddenly.
That fact is more certain than that we shall be able to finish our
work in his service, more certain than our own death. This

assurance that in their suffering they will be as their master is the greatest consolation the messengers of Jesus have. As is the master, so shall the disciple be, and as the Lord, so the servant. If they called Jesus a devil, how much more shall they call the servants of his household devils. Thus Jesus will be with them, and they will be in all things like unto him.

25 THE DECISION

Fear them not therefore: for there is nothing covered, that shall not be revealed; and hid, that shall not be known. What I tell you in the darkness, speak ye in the light: and what ye hear in the ear, proclaim upon the housetops. And be not afraid of them which kill the body, but are not able to kill the soul: but rather fear him which is able to destroy both soul and body in hell. Are not two sparrows sold for a farthing? and not one of them shall fall on the ground without your Father: but the very hairs of your head are all numbered. Fear not therefore; ye are of more value than many sparrows. Every one therefore who shall confess me before men, him will I also confess before my Father which is in heaven. But whosoever shall deny me before men, him will I also deny before my Father which is in heaven.

Think not that I came to send peace on the earth: I came not to send peace, but a sword. For I came to set a man at variance against his father, and the daughter against her mother, and the daughter-in-law against her mother-in-law: and a man's foes shall be they of his own household. He that loveth father or mother more than me is not worthy of me; and he that loveth son or daughter more than me is not worthy of me. And he that doth not take up his cross and follow after me, is not worthy of me. He that findeth his life shall lose it; and he that loseth his life for my sake shall find it. (Matt. 10.26–39)

THE messengers abide by the Word, and the Word abides by the messengers, now and in all eternity. Three times Jesus encourages his disciples by saying, 'Fear not.' Although their sufferings are now secret, they will not always be so: some day they will be made manifest before God and man. However secret these sufferings are at present, they have their Lord's promise that they will be eventually brought to the light of day. And that will mean glory for the messengers and judgement for their persecutors. Nor is the testimony of the messengers intended always to remain in obscurity. The gospel is not to take the form of hole-in-the-corner sectarianism, it must be set forth by public preaching. For the time being it may have to be delivered secretly, but in the last

194

day this preaching will fill the whole world spelling salvation and rejection. The Revelation of St John contains this prediction: 'And I saw another angel flying in mid heaven, having an eternal gospel to proclaim unto them that dwell on the earth, and unto every nation and tribe and tongue and people' (14.6). Therefore 'Fear not.'

They must not fear men. Men can do them no harm, for the power of men ceases with the death of the body. But they must overcome the fear of death with the fear of God. The danger lies not in the judgement of men, but in the judgement of God, not in the death of the body, but in the eternal destruction of body and soul. Those who are still afraid of men have no fear of God, and those who have fear of God have ceased to be afraid of men. All preachers of the gospel will do well to recollect this saying daily.

The power which men enjoy for a brief space on earth is not without the cognizance and the will of God. If we fall into the hands of men, and meet suffering and death from their violence, we are none the less certain that everything comes from God. The same God who sees no sparrow fall to the ground without his knowledge and will, allows nothing to happen, except it be good and profitable for his children and the cause for which they stand. We are in God's hands. Therefore, 'Fear not.'

The time is short. Eternity is long. It is the time of decision. Those who are true to the word and confession on earth will find Jesus Christ standing by their side in the hour of judgement. He will acknowledge them and come to their aid when the accuser demands his rights. All the world will be called to witness as Jesus pronounces our name before his heavenly Father. If we have been true to Jesus in this life, he will be true to us in eternity. But if we have been ashamed of our Lord and of his name, he will likewise be ashamed of us and deny us.

The final decision must be made while we are still on earth. The peace of Jesus is the cross. But the cross is the sword God wields on earth. It creates division. The son against the father, the daughter against her mother, the member of the house against the head – all this will happen in the name of God's kingdom and his peace. That is the work which Christ performs on earth. It is hardly surprising that the harbinger of God's love has been accused of hatred of the human race. Who has a right to speak thus of love for father and mother, for son and daughter, but the destroyer of all human life on the one hand, or the Creator of a new life on the other? Who dare lay such an exclusive claim to man's love and devotion, but the enemy of mankind on the one hand, and the Saviour of mankind on the other? Who but the devil, or Christ, the Prince of Peace, will carry the sword into men's houses? God's love for man is altogether different from the love of men for their own flesh and blood. God's love for man means the cross and the way of discipleship. But that cross and that way are both life and resurrection. 'He that loseth his life for my sake shall find it.' In this promise we hear the voice of him who holds the keys of death, the Son of God, who goes to the cross and the resurrection, and with him takes his own.

26 THE FRUIT

He that receiveth you receiveth me, and he that receiveth me
receiveth him that sent me. He that receiveth a prophet in the
name of a prophet shall receive a prophet's reward; and he that
receiveth a righteous man in the name of a righteous man shall
receive a righteous man's reward. And whosoever shall give to
drink unto one of these little ones a cup of cold water only, in
the name of a disciple, verily I say unto you, he shall in no wise
lose his reward. (Matt. 10.40-42)

THE bearers of Jesus' word receive a final word of promise for
their work. They are now Christ's fellow-workers, and will be
like him in all things. Thus they are to meet those to whom they
are sent as if they were Christ himself. When they are welcomed
into a house, Christ enters with them. They are bearers of his
presence. They bring with them the most precious gift in the
world, the gift of Jesus Christ. And with him they bring God the
Father, and that means indeed forgiveness and salvation, life and
bliss. That is the reward and fruit of their toil and suffering. Every
service men render them is service rendered to Christ himself.
This means grace for the Church and grace for the disciple in
equal measure. The Church will be readier to give them its service
and honour, for with them the Lord himself has entered into their
midst. But the disciples are given to understand that when they
enter into a house they do not enter in vain. They bring with
them an incomparable gift. It is a law of the kingdom of God that
every man shall participate in the gift which he willingly receives
as a gift from God. The man who receives a prophet and knows
what he is doing will participate in the prophet's cause, his gift
and his reward. He who receives a righteous man will receive the
reward of a righteous man, for he has become a partner in his
righteousness. He who offers a cup of cold water to the weakest
and poorest who bears no honourable name has ministered to
Christ himself, and Jesus Christ will be his reward.

Thus the disciples are bidden lastly to think, not about their own way, their own sufferings and their own reward, but of the goal of their labours, which is the salvation of the Church.

Part Four

THE CHURCH OF JESUS CHRIST &
THE LIFE OF DISCIPLESHIP

27 PRELIMINARY QUESTIONS

W HEN Jesus came to his first disciples, he came to them with his word, and was present with them in bodily form. But this same Jesus died and rose again. How is his call handed on to us to-day? To call us: 'Follow me,' Jesus no longer passes us in bodily form as he passed by Levi the publican. What right have we then to leave all and follow him, however earnestly we desire to hear his call? For the men of the New Testament the call was unmistakable but for us it is a highly problematical, and uncontrollable decision. How could we apply Levi's call directly to our own lives? Did not Jesus adapt his words to suit different men and different occasions? What about the paralytic? He received forgiveness and healing. What about Lazarus? *He* was raised from the dead. He did not call *them* to leave their work and follow him, but instead he left them at home with their families and their jobs. Does it follow that he loved these less than his disciples? Who are we to come forward and volunteer for such an extraordinary and unusual life? Who is there to tell me and others, for that matter, that we are not acting on our own initiative and following our own wild fancies? But that would not be discipleship. There is something wrong about all these questions. Every time we ask them we are retreating from the presence of the living Christ and forgetting that Jesus Christ is not dead, but alive and speaking to us to-day through the testimony of the Scriptures. He comes to us to-day, and is present with us in bodily form and in his word. If we would hear his call to follow, we must listen where he is to be found, that is, in the Church through the ministry of Word and Sacrament. The preaching of the Church and the administration of the sacraments is the place where Jesus Christ is present. If you would hear the call of Jesus you need no personal revelation: all you have to do is to hear the sermon and receive the sacrament, that is, to hear the gospel of Christ crucified and risen. Here he is, the same Christ whom the disciples encountered, the same Christ whole and entire. Yes, here he is already, the glorified, victorious and living Lord. Only Christ himself can call us to follow him. But discipleship never consists in this or that specific action: it is always a decision, either for or against Jesus Christ. Hence our situation is not a whit less clear than that of the disciple or the publican in the gospel. When Jesus called his first disciples, they obeyed and followed him because they recognized him as the Christ. But his Messiahship was as hidden to them as it is to us. By itself the call of Jesus could be taken in many different ways. How we take it depends on what we think of him, and he can be recognized only by faith. That was as true for the first disciples as it is for us. *They* saw the rabbi and the wonderworker, and believed on Christ. *We* hear the Word and believe on Christ.

But surely there is another way in which the disciples really had the advantage over us. When they had recognized the Christ, they were immediately given a simple and direct command from his very lips, telling them exactly what to do. But just at this crucial point of Christian obedience we are given no help whatever. Does not Christ speak to us differently now? If that were true, we should certainly be in a hopeless predicament. But it is far from true. Christ speaks to us exactly as he spoke to them. It was not as though they first recognized him as the Christ and then received his command. They believed his word and command and recognized him as the Christ – in that order. There was no other way for them to know Christ, but by his plain word. And therefore the converse is also true – we cannot know Jesus without at the same time knowing his will. So far from obscuring the disciple's realization of his action, his knowledge of the person of Jesus Christ made it all the more certain. If Christ is the living Lord of my life, my encounter with him discloses his word for me, and indeed I have no other means of knowing him, but through his plain word and command. You may of course object that our trouble is that we should like to know Christ and believe on him, but have no means of knowing his will. But such an objection only shows that our knowledge of him is neither genuine nor clear. To know Christ means to know him by his word as the Lord and Saviour of my life. But that knowledge includes a recognition of his plain word directed to me.

Suppose then we say finally that whereas the commandment the disciples received was plain and clear enough, *we* have to decide for ourselves which of his words applies to our particular case. That again is a complete misunderstanding of the situation of the disciples, and of our own situation too. The object of Jesus' command is always the same – to evoke whole-hearted faith, to make us love God and our neighbour with all our heart and soul. This is the only unequivocal feature in his command. Every time we try to perform the commandment of Jesus in some other sense, it is another sign that we have misunderstood his word and are disobeying it. But this does not mean that we have no means whatever of ascertaining what he would have us do in any concrete situation. On the contrary, we are told quite clearly what we have to do every time we hear the word of Christ proclaimed; yet in such a way that we understand that there is no other way of fulfilling it, but by faith in Jesus Christ alone. Thus the gift Jesus gave to his disciples is just as available for us as it was for them. In fact it is even more readily available for us now that he has left the world, because we know that he is glorified, and because the Holy Spirit is with us.

It is therefore abundantly clear that we cannot play off the various accounts of the calling of the disciples against other parts of the gospel narrative. It is not a question of stepping into the shoes of the disciples, or of any other of the New Testament characters. The only constant factor throughout is the sameness of Christ and of his call then and now. His word is one and the same, whether it was addressed during his earthly life to the paralysed or the disciples, or whether it is speaking to us to-day. Here, as there, we receive the gracious summons to enter his kingdom and his glory. It is dangerous to ask whether we are to draw a parallel between ourselves and the disciples or ourselves and the paralytic. We may not compare ourselves to either. All we have to do is to hear the word and obey the will of Christ, in whatever part of the scripture testimony it is proclaimed. The Scriptures do not present us with a series of Christian types to be imitated according to choice: they preach to us in every situation the one Jesus Christ. To him alone must I listen. He is everywhere one and the same.

To the question – where to-day do we hear the call of Jesus to discipleship, there is no other answer than this: Hear the Word, receive the Sacrament; in it hear him himself, and you will hear his call.

28 BAPTISM

In the Synoptic Gospels the relationship between the disciples and their Lord is expressed almost entirely in terms of following him. In the Pauline Epistles this conception recedes into the background. In the first place St Paul has far less to say about the earthly life of our Lord, and far more about the presence of the risen and glorified Christ and his work in us. He therefore needs a new set of terms peculiar to himself. It is born out of his particular subject and aims to stress the unity of the gospel of one Lord who lived, died and rose again. The terms St Paul uses confirm those of the Synoptists, and vice versa. Neither set of terms is intrinsically preferable to the other. After all, we are not 'of Paul, or of Apollos, or of Cephas, or of Christ'. Our faith rests upon the unity of the scriptural testimony. It is destructive of the unity of the Scriptures to say that the Pauline Christ is more alive for us than the Christ of the Synoptists. Of course such language is commonly regarded as genuine Reformation and historico-critical doctrine, but it is in fact the precise opposite of that, and indeed it is the most perilous kind of enthusiasm. Who tells us that the Pauline Christ is as alive for us to-day as he was for St Paul? We get this assurance only from the Scriptures. Or are we talking about a presence of Christ which is free and unbound by the Word? No, the Scriptures are the only witness we have of Christ's presence, and that witness is a unity, which also means that the presence they speak of includes the presence of Jesus Christ as he is presented in the Synoptic Gospels. The Jesus of the Synoptists is neither nearer nor further from us than the Christ of St Paul. The Christ who is present is the Christ of the whole Scripture. He is the incarnate, crucified, risen and glorified Christ, and he meets us in his word. The difference between the terminology of the Synoptists and the witness of St Paul does not involve any break in the unity of the scriptural testimony.[1] (*footnote overleaf*)

Where the synoptic Gospels speak of Christ calling men and their following him, St Paul speaks of *Baptism*.

Baptism is not an offer made by man to God, but an offer made by Christ to man. It is grounded solely on the will of Jesus Christ, as expressed in his gracious call. Baptism is essentially passive – *being baptized, suffering* the call of Christ. In baptism man becomes Christ's own possession. When the name of Christ is spoken over the candidate, he becomes a partaker in this Name, and is baptized '*into* Jesus Christ' (εἰς, Rom. 6.3; Gal. 3.27; Matt. 28.19). From that moment he belongs to Jesus Christ. He is wrested from the dominion of the world, and passes into the ownership of Christ.

Baptism therefore betokens a *breach*. Christ invades the realm of Satan, lays hands on his own, and creates for himself his Church. By this act past and present are rent asunder. The old order is passed away, and all things have become new. This breach is not effected by man's tearing off his own chains through some un-

---

[1] The direct testimony of the Scriptures is frequently confounded with ontological propositions. This error is the essence of fanaticism in all its forms. For example, if we take the statement that Christ is risen and present as an ontological proposition, it inevitably dissolves the unity of the Scriptures, for it leads us to speak of a mode of Christ's presence which is different e.g. from that of the synoptic Jesus. The truth that Jesus Christ is risen and present to us is then taken as an independent statement with an ontological significance which can be applied critically to other ontological statements, and it is thus exalted into a theological principle. This procedure is analogous to the fanatical doctrine of perfectionism, which arises from a similar ontological misunderstanding of the scriptural utterances on the subject of sanctification. In this instance the assertion that he who is in God does not sin is made a starting-point for further speculation. But this is to tear it from its scriptural context and raise it to the status of an independent truth which can be experienced. The proclamation of the scriptural testimony is of quite a different character. The assertion that Christ is risen and present, is, when taken strictly as a testimony given in the Scriptures, true only as a word of the Scriptures. This word is the object of our faith. There is no other conceivable way of approach to this truth except through this word. But this word testifies to the presence of both the Synoptic and the Pauline Christ. Our nearness to the one or to the other is defined solely by the Word, i.e. by the scriptural testimony. Of course this is not to deny the obvious fact that the Pauline testimony and that of the Synoptists differ in respect both of their object and their terminology, but both have to be interpreted in the light of the Scriptures as a whole.

This conclusion is not merely a piece of *a priori* knowledge based on a rigid doctrine of the canon of Scripture. The legitimacy of our view must be put to the test in every instance. Thus in the ensuing argument, our purpose is to show how St Paul takes up the Synoptic notion of following Christ and subjects it to further development.

quenchable longing for a new life of freedom. The breach has been effected by Christ long since, and in baptism it is effected in our own lives. We are now deprived of our direct relationship with all God-given realities of life. Christ the Mediator has stepped in between us and them. The baptized Christian has ceased to belong to the world and is no longer its slave. He belongs to Christ alone, and his relationship with the world is mediated through him.

The breach with the world is complete. It demands and produces the death of the old man.[1] In baptism a man dies together with his old world. This death, no less than baptism itself, is a passive event. It is not as though a man must achieve his own death through various kinds of renunciation and mortification. That would never be the death of the old man which Christ demands. The old man cannot will his own death or kill himself. He can only die in, through and with Christ. Christ is his death. For the sake of fellowship with Christ, and in that fellowship alone a man dies. In fellowship with Christ and through the grace of baptism he receives his death as a gift.[2] This death is a gift of grace: a man can never accomplish it by himself. The old man and his sin are judged and condemned, but out of this judgement a new man arises, who has died to the world and to sin. Thus this death is not the act of an angry Creator finally rejecting his creation in his wrath, but the gracious death which has been won for us by the death of Christ; the gracious assumption of the creature by his creator. It is death in the power and fellowship of the cross of Christ. He who becomes Christ's own possession must submit to his cross, and suffer and die with him. He who is granted fellowship with Jesus must die the baptismal death which is the fountain of grace, for the sake of the cross which Christ lays upon his disciples. The cross and death of Christ were cruel and hard but the yoke of our cross is easy and light because of our fellowship with him. The cross of Christ is the death which we undergo

[1] Even Jesus himself referred to his death as a baptism, and promised that his disciples would share this baptism of death (Mark 10.39; Luke 12.50).

[2] Schlatter also takes I Cor. 15.29 as a reference to the baptism of martyrdom.

once and for all in our baptism, and it is a death full of grace. The cross to which we are called is a daily dying in the power of the death which Christ died once and for all. In this way baptism means sharing in the cross of Christ (Rom. 6.3 ff; Col. 2.12). The believer passes under the yoke of the cross.

Baptismal death means *justification from sin*. The sinner must die that he may be delivered from his sin. If a man dies he is justified from sin (Rom. 6.7; Col. 2.20). Sin has no further claim on him, for death's demand has been met, and its account settled. Justification from (ἀπό) sin can only happen through death. Forgiveness of sin does not mean that the sin is overlooked and forgotten, it means a real death on the part of the sinner and his separation from (ἀπό) sin. But the only reason why the sinner's death can bring justification and not condemnation is that this death is a sharing of the death of Christ. It is baptism into the death of Christ which effects the forgiveness of sin and justification, and completes our separation from sin. The fellowship of the cross to which Jesus invited his disciples is the gift of justification through that cross, it is the gift of death and of the forgiveness of sins. The disciple who followed in the fellowship of the cross received exactly the same gift as the believer who was baptized after he had heard the teaching of St Paul.

Although for the candidate baptism is a passive event, it is never a mechanical process. This is made abundantly clear by the connection of baptism with the Spirit (Matt. 3.11; Acts 10.47; John 3.5; I Cor. 12.11-13). The gift of baptism is the Holy Spirit. But the Holy Spirit is Christ himself dwelling in the hearts of the faithful (II Cor. 3.17; Rom. 8.9-11, 14 ff; Eph. 3.16 f). The baptized are the house where the Holy Spirit has made his dwelling (οἰκεῖ). The Spirit is the pledge of the abiding presence of Jesus, and of our fellowship with him. He imparts true knowledge of his being (I Cor. 2.10) and of his will, He teaches us and reminds us of all that Christ said on earth (John 14.26). He guides us into all truth (John 16.13), so that we are not without knowledge of Christ and of the gifts which God has given us in him (I Cor. 2.12; Eph. 1.9). The gift which the Holy Spirit creates in us is not uncertainty, but assurance and discernment. Thus we are enabled to walk in the Spirit (Gal. 5.16, 18, 25; Rom. 8.2, 4), and to walk in assurance. The certainty which the disciples enjoyed in their intercourse with Jesus was not lost after he left them. Through the sending of the Spirit into the hearts of the believers that certainty is not only perpetuated, but strengthened and increased, so intimate is the fellowship of the Spirit (Rom. 8.16; John 16.12 f).

When he called men to follow him, Jesus was summoning them to a *visible act of obedience*. To follow Jesus was a public act. Baptism is similarly a public event, for it is the means whereby a member is grafted on to the visible body of Christ (Gal. 3.27 f; I Cor. 12.13). The breach with the world which has been effected in Christ can no longer remain hidden; it must come out into the open through membership of the Church and participation in its life and worship. When he joins the Church the Christian steps out of the world, his work and family, taking his stand visibly in the fellowship of Jesus Christ. He takes this step alone. But he recovers what he has surrendered – brothers, sisters, houses, and fields. Those who have been baptized live in the visible community of Christ. We shall endeavour to draw out the full import of this statement in the next two chapters, the first of which deals with the 'Body of Christ' and the second with the 'Visible Community'.

Baptism and the gifts it confers are characterized by a certain finality. The baptism of Christ can never be repeated.[1] It is just this finality and uniqueness which the Epistle to the Hebrews is trying to express in that obscure passage about the impossibility of a second repentance after baptism and conversion (Heb. 6.4 ff). By baptism we are made partakers in the death of Christ. Through our baptismal death we have been condemned to death and have died, just as Christ died once and for all. There can be no repetition of his sacrifice, therefore the baptized person dies in Christ once and for all. Now he is dead. The daily dying of the Christian life is merely the consequence of the one baptismal death, just as the tree dies after its roots have been cut away. Henceforth the law

---

[1] Contrast the baptism of John, which must be renewed through baptism into Christ (Acts 19.5).

which governs the life of the baptized is: 'Likewise reckon ye yourselves to be dead indeed unto sin' (Rom. 6.11). From now on the baptized can know themselves only as dead men, in whom everything necessary for salvation has already been accomplished. The baptized live, not by a literal repetition of this death, but by a constant renewal of their faith in the death of Christ as his act of grace in us. The source of their faith lies in the once-and-for-allness of Christ's death, which they have experienced in their baptism.

This element of finality in baptism throws significant light on the question of infant baptism.[1] The problem is not whether infant baptism is baptism at all, but that the final and unrepeatable character of infant baptism necessitates certain restrictions in its use. It was certainly not a sign of a healthy church life in the second and third century when believing Christians deferred their baptism until they reached old age or were on their death beds, but all the same it shows a clear insight into the nature of baptismal grace, an insight which we sadly lack to-day. As far as infant baptism is concerned, it must be insisted that the sacrament should be administered only where there is a firm faith present which remembers Christ's deed of salvation wrought for us once and for all. That can only happen in a living Christian community. To baptize infants without a Church is not only an abuse of the sacrament, it betokens a disgusting frivolity in dealing with the souls of the children themselves. For baptism can never be repeated.

The call of Jesus was no less final and unrepeatable for those who heard it in the days of his earthly life. When men followed him they died to their previous life. That is why he expected them to leave all that they had. The irrevocable nature of the decision was thus put beyond all doubt. But it also showed how complete and entire was the gift they had received from their Lord. 'If the salt have lost its savour, wherewith shall it be salted?' No clearer

---

[1] To the usual passages quoted as evidence for the practice of infant baptism in New Testament times, we may perhaps add I John 2.12 ff. The use of the three forms of address – children, fathers, and young men – would seem to justify our taking τεκνία in verse 12 not as a general term for the Christian community, but as a reference to 'children' in the literal sense of the word.

expression could be given to the finality of the gift of Jesus than this. Having taken their life from them, he sought to confer on them a new life, a life so perfect and complete that he gave them the gift of his cross. That was the gift of baptism to the first disciples.

THE first disciples lived in the bodily presence and communion of Jesus. In what manner is that communion and fellowship still possible for us to-day? St Paul tells us that we are made members of the Body of Christ through baptism. But this is such a difficult statement that it requires further elucidation.

It means that although Jesus has died and risen again, the baptized can still live in his bodily presence and enjoy communion with him. So far from impoverishing them his departure brings a new gift. The disciples enjoyed exactly the same bodily communion as is available for us to-day, nay rather, our communion with him is richer and more assured than it was for them, for the communion and presence which we have is that of the glorified Lord. Our faith must be aware of the greatness of this gift. The Body of Christ is the ground and assurance of that faith. It is the one and perfect gift whereby we become partakers of salvation. It is indeed newness of life. In the Body of Christ we are caught up into eternity by the act of God.

After the fall of Adam, God never ceased to send his Word to sinful men. He sought after them in order to take them to himself. The whole purpose for which the Word came was to restore lost mankind to fellowship with God. The Word of God came both as a promise and as a law. It became weak and of no account for our sake. But men rejected the Word, refusing to be accepted by God. They offered sacrifices and performed works which they fondly imagined God would accept in place of themselves, but with these they wanted to buy themselves out. Then the supreme miracle occurs. The Son of God becomes man. The Word is made flesh. He who had existed from all eternity in the glory of the Father, he who in the beginning was the agent of creation (which means that the created world can be known only through him and in him), he who was very God (I Cor. 8.6; II Cor. 8.9; Phil.

2.6 ff; Eph. 1.4; Col. 1.16; John 1.1 ff; Heb. 1.1 ff) accepts human-ity by taking upon himself our human nature, 'sinful flesh' as the Bible calls it, and human form (Rom. 8.3; Gal. 4.4; Phil. 2.6 ff). God takes humanity to himself, not merely as heretofore through the spoken word, but in the Body of Jesus. Of his mercy God sends his Son in the flesh, that therein he may bear the whole human race and bring it to himself. The Son of God takes to himself the whole human race bodily, that race which in its hatred of God and in the pride of its flesh had rejected the incorporeal, invisible Word of God. Now this humanity, in all its weakness, is, by the mercy of God, taken up in the Body of Jesus in true bodily form.

As they contemplated the miracle of the Incarnation, the early Fathers passionately contended that while it was true to say that God took human nature upon him, it was wrong to say that he chose a perfect individual man and united himself to him. God was made man, and while that means that he took upon him our entire human nature with all its infirmity, sinfulness and corrup-tion, the whole of apostate humanity, it does not mean that he took upon him the man Jesus. Unless we draw this distinction we shall misunderstand the whole message of the gospel. The Body of Jesus Christ, in which we are taken up with the whole human race, has now become the ground of our salvation.

It is *sinful* flesh that he bears, though he was himself without sin (II Cor. 5.21; Heb. 4.15). In his human body he takes all flesh upon himself. 'Surely he hath borne our griefs, and carried our sorrows.' It is solely in virtue of the Incarnation that Jesus was able to heal the diseases and pains of human nature, because he bore upon his own body all these ills (Matt. 8.15-17). 'He was wounded for our transgressions, he was bruised for our iniquities.' He bore our sins, and was able to forgive them because he had 'taken up' our sinful flesh in his Body. Similarly, Jesus received sinners and took them to himself (Luke 15.2) because he bore them in his own body. With the coming of Christ the 'acceptable (δεκτόν) year of the Lord' had dawned (Luke 4.19).

Consequently the incarnate Son of God existed so to speak in

213

two capacities – in his own person, and as the representative of the new humanity. Every act he wrought was performed on behalf of the new humanity which he bore in his body. That is why he is called the Second Adam or the last Adam (I Cor. 15.45). Like Christ himself, the first Adam had been both an individual man and the representative of the whole human race. He too bore the whole race in himself. In him the human race fell, in Adam (which means 'man' in Hebrew) man fell (Rom. 5.19). Christ is the Second Man (I Cor. 15.47) in whom the new humanity is created. He is the 'New Man'.

We must start at this point if we wish to understand the nature of that bodily fellowship and communion which the disciples enjoyed with their Master. It is no accident that to follow him meant cleaving to him bodily. That was the natural consequence of the Incarnation. Had he been merely a prophet or a teacher, he would not have needed followers, but only pupils and hearers. But since he is the incarnate Son of God who came in human flesh, he needs a community of followers, who will participate not merely in his teaching, but also in his Body. The disciples have communion and fellowship in the Body of Christ. They live and suffer in bodily communion with him. That is why they must bear the burden of the cross. In him they are all borne and taken up.

The earthly body of Jesus underwent crucifixion and death. In that death the new humanity undergoes crucifixion and death. Jesus Christ had taken upon him not a man, but the human 'form', sinful flesh, human 'nature', so that all whom he bore suffer and die with him. It is all our infirmities and all our sin that he bears to the cross. It is *we* who are crucified with him, and we who die with him. True, his earthly body undergoes death, but only to rise again as an incorruptible, glorious body. It is the same body – the tomb was empty – and yet it is a new body. And so as he dies, Jesus bears the human race, and carries it onward to resurrection. Thus, too, he bears for ever in his glorified body the humanity which he had taken upon him on earth.

How then do we come to participate in the Body of Christ, who did all this for us? It is certain that there can be no fellowship or communion with him except through his Body. For only through that Body can we find acceptance and salvation. The answer is, through the two sacraments of his Body, baptism and the Lord's Supper. Note how in recording the incident of the water and blood which issued from the side of the crucified body of Christ, St John refers unmistakably to the elements of the two sacraments (John 19.34, 35). St Paul corroborates this when he rivets our membership of the Body of Christ exclusively to the two sacraments.[1] The sacraments begin and end in the Body of Christ, and it is only the presence of that Body which makes them what they are. The word of preaching is insufficient to make us members of Christ's Body; the sacraments also have to be added. Baptism incorporates us into the unity of the Body of Christ, and the Lord's Supper fosters and sustains our fellowship and communion (κοινωνία) in that Body. Baptism makes us members of the Body of Christ. We are 'baptized into' Christ (Gal. 3.27; Rom. 6.3); we are 'baptized into one body' (I Cor. 12.13). Our death in baptism conveys the gift of the Holy Spirit, and gains the redemption which Christ wrought for us in his body. The communion of the Body of Christ, which we receive as the disciples received it in the early days, is the sign and pledge that we are 'with Christ' and 'in Christ', and that he is 'in us'. Rightly understood, the doctrine of the Body is the clue to the meaning of these expressions.

All men are 'with Christ' as a consequence of the Incarnation, for in the Incarnation Jesus bore our whole human nature. That is why his life, death and resurrection are events which involve all men (Rom. 5.18 ff; I Cor. 15.22; II Cor. 5.14). But Christians are 'with Christ' in a special sense. For the rest of mankind to be with Christ means death, but for Christians it is a means of grace. Baptism is their assurance that they are 'dead with Christ' (Rom. 6.8), 'crucified with him' (Rom. 6.6; Col. 2.20), 'buried with him' (Rom. 6.4; Col. 2.12), 'planted together in the likeness of his death' (Rom. 6.5). All this creates in them the assurance that they will also live with him (Rom. 6.8; Eph. 2.5; Col. 2.12;

---

[1] Eph. 3.6 likewise embraces the whole gift of salvation – the Word, Baptism, and the Lord's Supper.

II Tim. 2.11; II Cor. 7.3). 'We with Christ' – for Christ is Emmanuel, 'God with us'. Only when we know Christ in this way is our being with him the source of grace. The Christian who is baptized into (εἰς) Christ is baptized into the fellowship of his sufferings. Thus not only does the individual become a member of the Body of Christ, but the fellowship of the baptized becomes a body which is identical with Christ's own Body. The Christians are 'in Christ' (ἐν) and 'Christ in them'. They are no longer 'under the law' (Rom. 2.12; 3.19), no longer 'in the flesh' (Rom. 7.5; 8.3, 8, 9; II Cor. 10.3), no longer 'in Adam' (I Cor. 15.22), but are henceforth 'in Christ' in the totality of their being and life, whatever form it may take.

It was St Paul's achievement to express the miracle of the Incarnation in an infinite variety of ways. All the foregoing may be summed up in the single phrase – Christ is 'for us', not only in word and in his attitude towards us, but in his bodily life. He occupies in his body the place where we should be before God. He suffers and dies in our stead, and can do so because of the Incarnation (II Cor. 5.21; Gal. 3.13; 1.4; Tit. 2.14; I Thess. 5.10, etc.). The Body of Christ is in the strictest sense of the word 'for us' as it hangs on the cross, and 'for us' as it is given to us in the Word, in baptism and in the Lord's Supper. This is the ground of all bodily fellowship with Jesus Christ.

The Body of Christ is identical with the new humanity which he has taken upon him. It is in fact the Church. Jesus Christ is at once himself and his Church (I Cor. 12.12). Since the first Whit Sunday the Life of Christ has been perpetuated on earth in the form of his Body, the Church. Here is his body, crucified and risen, here is the humanity he took upon him. To be baptized therefore means to become a member of the Church, a member of the Body of Christ (Gal. 3.28; I Cor. 12.13). To be in Christ therefore means to be in the Church. But if we are in the Church we are verily and bodily in Christ. Now we perceive the whole wealth of meaning which lies behind the idea of the Body of Christ.

Since the ascension, Christ's place on earth has been taken by his Body, the Church. The Church is the real presence of Christ.

Once we have realized this truth we are well on the way to recovering an aspect of the Church's being which has been sadly neglected in the past. We should think of the Church not as an institution, but as a *person*, though of course a person in a unique sense.

The Church is One Man. All who are baptized are 'one in Christ' (Gal. 3.28; Rom. 12.5; I Cor. 10.17). The Church is 'Man', the 'New Man' (καινός ἄνθρωπος). The Church is created as the new man through Christ's death on the cross. On the cross the enmity between Jew and Gentile was abolished, that enmity which rent the world in two, 'that he might create in himself of the twain one new man, so making peace' (Eph. 2.15). The 'new man' is one, not many. Beyond the confines of the Church, the new man, there is only the old humanity with all its divisions.

This new man, the Church, is 'after God created in righteousness and true holiness' (Eph. 4.24). It is 'being renewed unto knowledge after the image of him that created him' (Col. 3.10). In this passage Christ alone is identified with the image of God. Adam was the first man to be created after the image of the Creator, but he forfeited that image at the Fall. Now a Second Man, a Last Adam, is created after the divine image – Jesus Christ (I Cor. 15.47). Hence the new man is both Christ and the Church. Christ is the new humanity in the new man. Christ is the Church.

The relation of the individual believer to the new man is expressed in terms of 'putting on' the new man.[1] The new man is like a garment made to cover the individual believer. He must clothe himself with the image of God, that is, with Christ and the Church. In baptism a man puts on Christ, and that means the same as being incorporated into the body, into the one man, in

---

[1] The analogy of ἐνδύσασθαι implies the spatial metaphor of being housed or clothed. Perhaps II Cor. 5.1 ff is also to be interpreted in this light. Here we find ἐνδύσασθαι associated with the heavenly οἰκητήριον, without which man is γυμνός, naked, and naturally ashamed before God. He is not covered, but longs for a covering. That happens when he is clothed with the heavenly οἰκητήριον. Should not the putting on of the οἰκητήριον of the Church in this world find its complement in our being clothed with the heavenly Church for which Paul longs? In both cases it is the one Church we are clothed with, the tabernacle of God, the place occupied by the divine presence. It is the body of Christ which covers us.

whom there is neither Greek nor Jew, neither bond nor free. No one can become a new man except by entering the Church, and becoming a member of the Body of Christ. It is impossible to become a new man as a solitary individual. The new man means more than the individual believer after he has been justified and sanctified. it means the Church, the Body of Christ, in fact it means Christ himself.

Through his Spirit, the crucified and risen Lord exists as the Church, as the new man. It is just as true to say that his Body is the new humanity as to say that he is God incarnate dwelling in eternity. As the fulness of the Godhead dwells in Christ bodily, so the Christian believers are filled with Christ (Col. 2.9; Eph. 3.19). Indeed, they are themselves that fulness in so far as they are in the Body and in so far as it is he alone who filleth all in all.

When we have recognized the unity between Christ and his Body, the Church, we must also hold fast to the complementary truth of Christ's Lordship over the Body. That is why St Paul, as he comes to develop the theme of the Body of Christ, calls him the Head of the Body (Eph. 1.22; Col. 1.18; 2.19). This assertion symbolizes and preserves the truth that Christ stands over against his Church. The historical fact in the story of our redemption which makes this truth essential, and rules out any idea of a mystical fusion between Christ and his Church, is the Ascension of Christ (and his Second Coming). The same Christ who is present in his Church will also come again. It is the same Lord and the same Church in both places, and it is one and the same Body, whether we think of his presence on earth or of his coming again on the clouds of heaven. But it makes a great deal of difference whether we are here or there. So it is necessary to give due weight both to the unity of Christ and his Church and to their distinction.

The Church is one man; it is the Body of Christ. But it is also many, a fellowship of members (Rom. 12.5; I Cor. 12.12 ff). Since the Church is a body made up of many members, no separate member, such as hand or eye or foot, can transcend its own individuality. That is the meaning of St Paul's analogy of the body. The hand can never take the place of the eye, or the eye the place of the ear. Each preserves its separate identity and function. On the other hand, they all preserve that identity and function only as members of the one body, as a fellowship united in service. It is the unity of the whole Church which makes each member what he is and the fellowship what it is, just as it is Christ and his Body which makes the Church what it is. Here we encounter the office and work of the Holy Spirit. It is the Spirit who brings Christ to each several member (Eph. 3.17; I Cor. 12.3), who builds up the Church by gathering the individual members together, although the whole building is already complete in Christ (Eph. 2.22; 4.12; Col. 2.2). He creates the fellowship (II Cor. 13.14) of the members of the Body (Rom. 15.30; 5.5; Col. 1.8; Eph. 4.3). The Lord is the Spirit (II Cor. 3.17). The Church of Christ is the presence of Christ through the Holy Spirit. In this way the life of the Body of Christ becomes our own life. In Christ we no longer live our own lives, but he lives his life in us. The life of the faithful in the Church is indeed the *Life of Christ in them* (Gal. 2.20; Rom. 8.10; II Cor. 13.5; I John 4.15).

In the fellowship of the crucified and glorified body of Christ we participate in his suffering and glory. His cross is the burden which is laid on his Body, the Church. All its sufferings borne beneath this cross are the sufferings of Christ himself. This suffering first takes the form of the baptismal death, and after that the daily dying of the Christians (I Cor. 15.31) in the power of their baptism. But there is a far greater form of suffering than this, one which bears an ineffable promise. For while it is true that only the suffering of Christ himself can atone for sin, and that his suffering and triumph took place 'for us', yet to some, who are not ashamed of their fellowship in his body, he vouchsafes the immeasurable grace and privilege of suffering 'for him', as he did for them. No greater glory could he have granted to his own, no higher privilege can the Christian enjoy, than to suffer 'for Christ'. When that happens, something comes to pass which is inconceivable under the law. For according to the law we can only be punished for our own sins. Under the law there is nothing that a man can suffer for his own *good*, still less for the good of another, and least of all for the good of Christ. The body of Christ, which was given for us, which suffered the punishment of our sins, makes us free to take our share of suffering and death 'for Christ'. Now we may work and suffer for Christ, for the sake of him who did everything possible for us. This is the miracle of grace we enjoy in our fellowship in the Body of Christ (Phil. 1.25; 2.17; Rom. 8.35 ff; I Cor. 4.10; II Cor. 4.10; 5.20; 13.9). Although Christ has fulfilled all the vicarious suffering necessary for our redemption, his suffering on earth is not finished yet. He has, in his grace, left a residue (ὑστερήματα) of suffering for his Church to fulfil in the interval before his Second Coming (Col. 1.24). This suffering is allowed to benefit the Body of Christ, the Church. Whether we have any right to assume that this suffering has power to atone for sin (cf. I Pet. 4.1), we have no means of knowing. But we do at least know that the man who suffers in the power of the body of Christ suffers in a representative capacity 'for' the Church, the Body of Christ, being privileged to endure himself what others are spared. ' . . . Always bearing about in the body the dying of Jesus, that the life also of Jesus may be manifested in our body. For we which live are always delivered unto death for Jesus' sake, that the life also of Jesus may be manifested in our mortal flesh' (II Cor. 4.10-12; cf. 1.5-7; 13.9; Phil. 2.17). The Body of Christ has its own allotted portion of suffering. God grants one man the grace to bear special suffering in place of another, and this suffering must at all costs be endured and overcome. Blessed is he whom God deems worthy to suffer for the Body of Christ. Such suffering is joy indeed (Col. 1.24; Phil. 2.17), enabling the believer to boast that he bears the dying of Jesus Christ and the marks of Christ in his body (II Cor. 4.10; Gal. 6.17). The Christian may now serve so that 'Christ may be magnified in my body, whether by life or by death' (Phil. 1.20). Such vicarious activity and passivity on the part of the members of the Body is the very life of Christ, who wills to be formed in his members (Gal. 4.19).

There is nothing new in all this. We are simply following in the steps of the first disciples of Christ.

It would be appropriate to conclude this chapter by summarizing the witness of the Scriptures as a whole to the doctrine of the Body of Christ. The New Testament doctrine of the Body of Christ is the fulfilment of the Old Testament prophecy concerning the temple of God. We are to understand the temple, not from the Hellenistic usage, but from the teaching of the prophets. First, we find David proposing to build a temple for God. But when he consults the prophet, he is told what God thinks of his design: 'Shalt thou build me an house to dwell in? . . . the Lord telleth thee that the Lord will make thee an house' (II Sam. 7.5, 11). Only God can build a temple for himself. Yet, paradoxically, David receives the promise that one sprung from his seed shall build the house, and that his seed shall endure for ever (verses 12 and 13). 'I will be his father, and he shall be my son' (verse 14). Solomon, the 'son of peace', the peace of God with the house of David, claimed this promise for himself. He built a temple and his action was approved by God. But this temple was not enough to fulfil the promise. It was built by the hands of men, and so was doomed to destruction. The prophecy still awaited fulfilment. Still the People of God look for a temple built by the Son of David whose kingdom shall endure for ever. The temple at Jerusalem was destroyed more than once, a sign that it was not the temple of God's promise. Where then was the true temple? Christ himself answers that question by applying the prophecy to his Body. 'The Jews therefore said, Forty and six years was this temple in building, and wilt thou raise it up in three days? But he spake of the temple of his body. When therefore he was raised from the dead, his disciples remembered that he spake this: and they believed the word which Jesus had said' (John 2.20 ff). The temple which the Jews were looking for was the Body of Christ, of which the temple of the Old Testament was but the shadow (Col. 2.17; Heb. 10.1; 8.5). Jesus was speaking of his human body. He knows that the temple of his earthly body will be destroyed, like the temple of Jerusalem. But he will rise again, and the new temple, the eternal temple, will be his risen and glorified body. This is the house which God builds for his Son; but it is also built by the Son for the Father. In this house God dwells verily and indeed, as does also the new humanity, the Church of Christ. The incarnate Christ is himself the temple of the fulfilment. Similarly Revelation, speaking of the New Jerusalem, says that there is no temple in heaven, 'for the Lord God Almighty, and the lamb are the temple thereof' (21.22).

The temple is the place where the gracious presence of God condescends to dwell among men, and also the place where God receives his people. Both aspects of the temple are fulfilled only in the Incarnation. Here is the real presence of God in bodily form, as well as the new humanity, for Christ has taken that humanity upon himself in his own body. From this it follows that the Body of Christ is the place of acceptance, the place of atonement and peace between God and man. God finds man in the Body of Christ, and man finds himself accepted by God in that same body. The Body of Christ is the spiritual temple (οἶκος πνευματικός) built out of living stones (I Pet. 2.5 ff). Christ is its sole foundation and corner-stone (Eph. 2.20; I Cor. 3.11) but at the same time he is in his Person the temple (οἰκοδομή, Eph. 2.21), in whom the Holy Spirit dwells, replenishing and sanctifying the hearts of the faithful (I Cor. 3.16; 6.19). The temple of God is the holy people in Jesus Christ. The Body of Christ is the living temple of God and of the new humanity.

THE Body of Christ takes up space on earth. That is a consequence of the Incarnation. Christ came into his own. But at his birth they gave him a manger, for 'there was no room in the inn'. At his death they thrust him out, and his Body hung between earth and heaven on the gallows. But despite all this, the Incarnation does involve a claim to a space of its own on earth. Anything which claims space is visible. Hence the Body of Christ can only be a visible Body, or else it is not a Body at all. The physical body of the man Jesus is visible to all, his divine sonship only to the eye of faith, just as that Body as the Body of God incarnate is visible only to faith. That Jesus was in the flesh was visible fact, but that he *bore* our flesh is a matter of faith. 'To this man shalt thou point and say, Here is God' (Luther).

A truth, a doctrine, or a religion need no space for themselves. They are disembodied entities. They are heard, learnt and apprehended, and that is all. But the incarnate Son of God needs not only ears or hearts, but living men who will follow him. That is why he called his disciples into a literal, bodily following, and thus made his fellowship with them a visible reality. That fellowship was founded and sustained by Jesus Christ, the incarnate Lord himself. It was the Word made flesh which had called them and created their bodily fellowship with him. Having been called, they could no longer remain in obscurity, for they were the light that must shine, the city set on the hill which must be seen. Their fellowship with him was visibly overshadowed by the cross and passion of Jesus Christ. In order that they might enjoy that fellowship with him, the disciples must leave everything else behind, and submit to suffering and persecution. Yet even in the midst of their persecutions they receive back all they had lost in visible form – brethren, sisters, fields and houses in his fellowship. The Church consisting of Christ's followers manifest to the whole world as a visible community. Here were bodies which acted, worked and suffered in fellowship with Jesus.

The body of the exalted Lord is also a visible body in the shape of the Church. How is this body made visible? In the first place, through the preaching of the word. 'They continued in the apostles' teaching' (Acts 2.42). Every word in this sentence is significant. Teaching (διδαχή) means preaching, and is contrasted with all kinds of religious addresses. It means the act of reporting certain concrete events. The matter to be conveyed is objective and constant, and all it needs is to be communicated in 'teaching'. By definition the term 'report' is limited to facts which are as yet unknown to the hearers. Once they have been communicated, there is no need to report them again. It is of the essence of teaching that it seeks to render itself superfluous. But in striking contrast we read here that the Church 'continued' in the apostles' teaching – in other words, teaching did not render itself superfluous, and constant repetition was the very thing it required. There must be some inner necessity for this association of 'teaching' with 'continuing'. We must also note that the teaching spoken of is the teaching *of the apostles*. Now the apostles were the men chosen by God to bear witness to the events of his revelation in Jesus Christ. They were men who lived in bodily fellowship with Jesus, men who saw the incarnate, crucified and risen Christ, and who handled his Body with their hands (I John 1.1). They were the witnesses employed by God the Holy Spirit to proclaim the Word. The teaching of the apostles is the witness to the physical event of God revealing himself in Christ. Hence the apostles and prophets are the foundation on which the Church is built, while the corner-stone is Jesus Christ (Eph. 2.20). Since the days of the apostles the preaching of the Church has always had to be 'apostolic', in the sense of being based on the same foundation. Thus the unity between us and the first congregation is established. In what way does apostolic teaching necessitate continuous 'hearing'? The word spoken by the apostles is verily and indeed the Word of God spoken through the word of men (I Thess. 2.13). It is therefore a word which seeks to take man to itself, and has the power to achieve its purpose. The Word of God seeks a *Church* to take unto itself. It has its being *in* the Church. It enters the Church by its own self-initiated movement. It is wrong to suppose that there is so to speak a Word on the one hand and a Church on the other, and that it is the task of the preacher to take that Word into his hands and move it so as to bring it into the Church and apply it to the Church's needs. On the contrary, the Word moves of its own accord, and all the preacher has to do is to assist that movement and try to put no obstacles in its path. The Word comes forth to take men to itself; the apostles knew that and it was the burden of their message. They had seen the Word of God for themselves, they had seen how it came and took flesh, and in this flesh the whole human race. Now the burden of their testimony was simply this – the Word of God had become flesh, it had come to take sinners to itself, to forgive and to sanctify. It is this same Word which now makes its entry into the Church. This Word made flesh, this Word which already bears the whole human race, can no longer exist without the humanity it has assumed. Furthermore, when this Word comes, the Holy Spirit comes, showing to Christians, both individually and corporately, the gifts of the incarnate Christ to man. He produces faith in his hearers, that they may discern in the preaching the entry of Jesus Christ. He opens their eyes to see Christ coming into their midst in the power of his Body to tell us that he has received us and will receive us again to-day.

The word of the apostles' preaching is the same Word which bore the sins of the whole world in his Body. That Word is the presence of Christ through the Holy Spirit. 'Christ in his Church' is the sum of the apostles' teaching, the apostolic preaching. This teaching never renders itself superfluous. It creates for itself a Church which remains steadfast in it, because it has been accepted by the Word, and is daily confirmed in its faith. This teaching creates for itself a visible Church. But preaching is not the only means whereby the Church takes visible form. That is also done by the sacraments of baptism and the Lord's supper, both of which flow from the true humanity of our Lord Jesus Christ. In the two sacraments he encounters us bodily and makes us partakers in the fellowship and communion of his Body, and they are both closely linked to his word. Both proclaim the death of Christ for us (Rom. 6.3 ff; I Cor. 11.26). In both we receive the Body of Christ. Baptism makes us members of the Body, and the Lord's Supper confers bodily fellowship and communion (κοινωνία) with the Body of the Lord whom we receive, and through it the bodily fellowship with the other members of his Body. Thus through the gift of his Body we become one body with him. Both baptism and the Lord's Supper give us far more than the forgiveness of our sins. It would be better to describe the gift of the sacraments as the gift of the very Body of Christ in the Church. But the forgiveness of sins is certainly a *part* of the gift of the Body of Christ considered in its aspect as the Church. Now we can see why, in contrast to our present practice, the administration of the two sacraments was not combined by the apostles with the proclamation of the Word in New Testament times, but was performed by the congregation itself (I Cor. 1.1, 14 ff; 11.17 ff). Baptism and the Lord's Supper belong to the fellowship of the body of Christ alone, whereas the Word is intended not only for believers but also for unbelievers. The sacraments belong exclusively to the Church. Hence the congregation is in a true sense a baptismal and eucharistic congregation, and only secondarily a preaching congregation.

It has been demonstrated that the Church of Jesus Christ claims space in the world for its proclamation. The Body of Christ becomes visible to the world in the congregation gathered round the Word and Sacrament.

The Church or congregation is an articulated organism. When we speak of the Church as the Body of Christ, we include its articulation and order. These are essential to the Body and are of divine appointment. An unarticulated body is doomed to perish. According to St Paul's teaching, the Body of Christ has an articulated form (Rom. 12.5; I Cor. 12.12 ff). In this context all distinctions between form and content, reality and appearance are impossible. To insist on them is to deny the Body of Christ, which is equivalent to denying the incarnate Lord himself (I John 4.3). Thus the Church claims space for its church order as well as for its proclamation.

Church order is divine both in origin and character, though of course it is meant to serve and not to rule. The offices of the Church are 'ministries' (διακονίαι, I Cor. 12.5). They are appointed in the Church of God (I Cor. 12.28), by Christ (Eph. 4.11) and by the Holy Spirit (Acts 20.28). They are not appointed *by* the Church. Even where the Church makes itself responsible for distributing offices, it does so only under the guidance of the Holy Spirit (Acts 13.2 etc.). Both ministry and Church spring from the triune God. The offices exist to serve the Church, and their spiritual rights only originate from this service. That is why the Church has to adapt its offices to the varying needs of time and place. The offices in the Church at Jerusalem had to be different from those in St Paul's missionary Churches. Though the articulation of the Church is of divine appointment, its form is adaptable to varying needs and subject only to the spiritual judgement of the Church itself as it ordains its members for service. In a similar way the 'charismata' which the Holy Spirit confers on individual members of the Church are subject to the strict discipline of the ministry in the Body, for God is not a God of confusion but of peace (I Cor. 14.32 f). By ensuring that everything is done for the well-being of the Church, the Holy Spirit makes himself visible (φανέρωσις, I Cor. 12.7). Apostles, prophets, teachers, overseers (bishops), deacons, elders, presidents and helps (I Cor. 12.28 ff; Eph. 2.20; 4.11) are ministers of the Church, the Body of Christ. They are ordained for service to the Church, and their office is of divine origin and character. Only the Church can release them from their ministry. Thus, although the Church is at liberty to adapt the form of its order according to contemporary needs, any attack on that order from without means an attack on the visible form of the Body of Christ itself.

Of all the offices of the Church, the uncorrupted ministry of the Word and Sacraments is of paramount importance. In this connection we must take note of the following considerations.

227

Proclamation may take different forms according to the commission and gifts of the preacher. But whether it be of Paul, or of Peter, or of the Apostles, or of Christ, the one indivisible Christ must be recognized in them all (I Cor. 1.11 ff). It is essential that they all work hand in hand (I Cor. 3.6). The emergence of partisanship will lead to party strife, and then everyone will pursue his own interests (I Tim. 6.5, 20; II Tim. 2.16; 3.8; Titus 1.10). It is fatally easy to prostitute divine salvation to material gain, in the shape of prestige, power or filthy lucre. Similarly it is all too easy for the natural inclination to pose and discuss problems, which, once they flare up, only distract men's minds from the pure and simple truth of the gospel (II Tim. 3.7). Instead of obeying the commandment of God men try to get their own way. In contrast to this, the aim of proclamation is always the same – namely, healthy and wholesome doctrine (II Tim. 4.3; I Tim. 1.10; 4.16; 6.1; Titus 1.9, 13; 2.1; 3.8), and the guarantee of true order and unity.

It is not always easy to see where a legitimate school of thought ends and heresy begins. That is why a doctrine may be tolerated in one Church and proscribed as heresy in another (Rev. 2.6, 15 ff). But once a heresy has become an open scandal it must of necessity be proscribed. The heretical teacher must be excommunicated, and all personal intercourse with him avoided (Gal. 1.8; I Cor. 16.22; Titus 3.10; II John 10 ff). The word of pure proclamation must visibly bind and loose. The space which the Church claims for its proclamation and order is thus made clear as an ordinance of divine appointment.

We must now ask whether we have adequately described the visible nature of the Church, or whether it claims further space in the world. The New Testament gives a clear and definite answer. The Church needs space not only for her liturgy and order, but also for the daily life of her members in the world. That is why we must now speak of the living-space (*Lebensraum*) of the visible Church.

The fellowship between Jesus and his disciples covered every aspect of their daily life. Within the fellowship of Christ's disciples the life of each individual was part of the life of the brotherhood. This common life bears living testimony to the concrete humanity of the Son of God. The bodily presence of God demands that for him and with him man should stake his own life in his daily existence. With all the concreteness of his bodily existence, man belongs to him who for his sake took upon him the human body. In the Christian life the individual disciple and the body of Jesus belong inseparably together.

All this is confirmed in the earliest record of the life of the Church in the Acts of the Apostles (Acts 2.42 ff; 4.32 ff). 'They continued steadfastly in the apostles' teaching and fellowship, in the breaking of bread and the prayers.' – 'They that believed were of one heart and soul and . . . had all things in common.' It is instructive to note that the fellowship (κοινωνία) is mentioned between Word and Sacrament. This is no accident, for fellowship always springs from the Word and finds its goal and completion in the Lord's Supper. The whole common life of the Christian fellowship oscillates between Word and Sacrament, it begins and ends in worship. It looks forward in expectation to the final banquet in the kingdom of God. When a community has such a source and goal it is a perfect communion of fellowship, in which even material goods fall into their appointed place. In freedom, joy and the power of the Holy Spirit a pattern of common life is produced where 'neither was there among them any that lacked', where 'distribution was made unto each according as anyone had need', where 'not one of them said that aught of the things which he possessed was his own'. In the everyday quality of these events we see a perfect picture of that evangelical liberty where there is no need of compulsion. They were indeed 'of one heart and soul'.

This infant Church was a visible community which all the world could see, and strange to say, 'they had favour with all the people' (Acts 2.47). Was this due to the blindness of Israel, which could not see that the secret of this common life was the cross of Christ? Was it an anticipation of the day in which all the nations of the earth should glorify the People of God? Or was it on account of God's loving-kindness, which he so often displays in the tender years of growth, and in times of bitter strife and conflict between believers and unbelievers, by drawing round the Church a fence of ordinary human good-will, of human sympathy with its fortunes? Or was it simply that the Church found favour with the people who cried 'Hosanna' but not 'crucify'? 'And the Lord added to them day by day those that were being saved.' This visible Church, with its perfect common life, invades the world and robs it of its children. The daily growth of the Church is a proof of the power of the Lord who dwells in it.

The first disciples learnt the truth of the saying that where their Lord is, there they must also be, and where they are, there also will their Lord be until the world comes to an end. Everything the disciple does is part of the common life of the Church of which he is a member. That is why the law, which governs the life of the Body of Christ, is that where one member is, there the whole body is also. There is no department of life in which the member may withdraw from the Body nor should he desire so to withdraw. Wherever we are, whatever we do, everything happens 'in the body', in the Church, 'in Christ'. The Christian is strong or weak 'in Christ' (Phil. 4.13; II Cor. 13.4), he works and rejoices 'in the Lord' (Rom. 16.9, 12; I Cor. 15.58; Phil. 4.4), he speaks and admonishes 'in Christ' (II Cor. 2.17; Phil. 2.1), he shows hospitality 'in Christ' (Rom. 16.2), he marries 'in the Lord' (I Cor. 7.39), he is in prison 'in the Lord' (Phil. 1.13, 23), is a slave 'in the Lord' (I Cor. 7.22). Among Christians the whole range of human relationships is embraced by Christ and the Church.

It is their baptism into the Body of Christ which assures all Christians of their full share in the life of Christ and the Church. It is wrong, and contrary to the New Testament, to limit the gift of baptism to participation in the sermon and the Lord's Supper, i.e. to participation in the means of grace, or to the right to hold office or perform a ministry in the Church. On the contrary, baptism confers the privilege of participation in all the activities of the Body of Christ in every department of life. To allow a baptized brother to take part in the worship of the Church, but to refuse to have anything to do with him in everyday life, is to subject him to abuse and contempt. If we do that, we are guilty of the very Body of Christ. And if we grant the baptized brother the right to the gifts of salvation, but refuse him the gifts necessary to earthly life or knowingly leave him in material need and distress, we are holding up the gifts of salvation to ridicule and behaving as liars. If the Holy Ghost has spoken and we listen instead to the call of blood and nature, or to our personal sympathies or antipathies, we are profaning the sacrament. When a man is baptized into the Body of Christ not only is his personal status as regards salvation changed, but also the relationships of daily life.

The slave Onesimus had run away from his Christian master, Philemon, after grievously wronging him. Now Onesimus has been baptized, and Philemon is asked to receive him back again for ever (Philemon 15), 'no longer as a servant, but more than a servant, a brother beloved . . . both in the flesh and in the Lord' (verse 16). 'In the flesh' a brother, says St Paul with emphasis, thus warning Philemon against those misunderstandings to which all 'privileged' Christians are liable. Such Christians are prepared to tolerate the society of Christians of lower social standing in church, but outside they give them the cold shoulder. Instead, Philemon must welcome Onesimus as a brother, nay, as if he were St Paul himself (verse 17), and since Onesimus is his brother, he must not seek repayment for the damage he suffered at his hands (verse 18). St Paul asks Philemon to do this voluntarily, though if necessary he would not shrink from ordering him to do it outright (verses 8-14). Probably Philemon will exceed in kindness beyond what is asked of him (verse 21). Onesimus is a brother in the flesh because he has been baptized. Whether he stays on as a slave or not, the whole relationship between master and slave has been radically changed. And how had this come to pass? Master and slave are now both members of the Body of Christ. Their common life is now a tiny cell in the Body of Christ, the Church. 'As many of you as were baptized into Christ did put on Christ. There can be neither Jew nor Greek, there can be neither bond nor free, there can be no male nor female: for ye are all one man in Christ Jesus' (Gal. 3.27 f; Col. 3.11). In the Church men look upon one another no longer as free men or slaves, as men or women, but as members of Christ's body. To be sure this does not mean that the slave is no longer a slave nor the man a man. But it does mean that in the Church no one has to be considered in his special capacity, whether he be Jew or Greek, freeman or bondservant. Any such respect of persons must be excluded at all costs. We take account of each other only with regard to our membership in the Body of Christ, that is to say, that we are all one in Christ. Jew and Greek, freedman and bondservant, man and woman now stand within the fellowship as part of the community of the Body of Christ. Wherever Christians live together, conversing and dealing with one another, there is the Church, there they are in Christ. This is what transforms the whole character of their fellowship. The wife obeys her husband 'in the Lord'; by serving his master the slave serves God, and the master knows that he too has a Lord in heaven (Col. 3.18-4.1), but they are all brethren 'in the flesh and in the Lord'.

This is how the Church invades the life of the world and conquers territory for Christ. For whatever is 'in Christ' has ceased to be subject to the world of sin and the law. No law of the world can interfere with this fellowship. The realm of Christian love is subject to Christ, not to the world. The Church can never tolerate any limits set to the love and service of the brethren. For where the brother is, there is the Body of Christ, and there is his Church. And there we must also be.

The member of the Body of Christ has been delivered from the world and called out of it. He must give the world a visible proof of his calling, not only by sharing in the Church's worship and discipline, but also through the new fellowship of brotherly living. If the world despises one of the brethren, the Christian will love and serve him. If the world does him violence, the Christian will succour and comfort him. If the world dishonours and insults him, the Christian will sacrifice his own honour to cover his brother's shame. Where the world seeks gain, the Christian will renounce it. Where the world exploits, he will dispossess himself, and where the world oppresses, he will stoop down and raise up the oppressed.

If the world refuses justice, the Christian will pursue mercy, and if the world takes refuge in lies, he will open his mouth for the dumb, and bear testimony to the truth. For the sake of the brother, be he Jew or Greek, bond or free, strong or weak, noble or base, he will renounce all fellowship with the world. For the Christian serves the fellowship of the Body of Christ, and he cannot hide it from the world. He is called out of the world to follow Christ.

But 'let each man abide in that calling wherein he was called. Wast thou called being a bondservant? care not for it: but if thou canst become free, use it rather' (i.e. remain a slave). 'For he that was called in the Lord, being a bondservant, is the Lord's freedman: likewise he that was called, being free, is Christ's bondservant. Ye were bought at a price; become not the servants of men. Brethren, let each man, wherein he was called, therein abide with God' (I Cor. 7.20-24). How different it all sounds from the calling of the first disciples! *They* had to leave everything and follow Jesus. *Now* we are told: 'Let each man abide in the calling wherein he was called.' How are we to reconcile the contradiction? Only by recognizing the underlying motive both of the call of Jesus and of the exhortation of the apostle. In both cases it is the same – to bring their hearers into the fellowship of the Body of Christ. The only way the first disciples could enter that fellowship was by going with Jesus. But now through Word and Sacrament the Body of Christ is no longer confined to a single place. The risen and exalted Lord had returned to the earth to be nearer than ever before. The Body of Christ has penetrated into the heart of the world in the form of the Church. The baptized Christian is baptized into that Body. Christ has come to him and taken his life into his own, thus robbing the world of its own. If a man is baptized as a slave, he has now as a slave become a partaker in the common life of the Body of Christ. As a slave he is already torn from the world's clutches, and become a freedman of Christ. That is why the slave is told to stay as he is. As a member of the Body of Christ he has acquired a freedom which no rebellion or revolution could have brought him. Of course St Paul does not mean thereby to bind him more closely to the world, or to give him a spiritual anchor so that he can continue his life in the world. When he admonishes the slave to stay as he is, it is not because he wants to make him a better citizen of the world or a more loyal one. It is not as though St Paul were trying to condone or gloss over a black spot in the social order. He does not mean that the class-structure of secular society is so good and godly an institution that it would be wrong to upset it by revolution. The truth of the matter is that the whole world has already been turned upside down by the work of Jesus Christ, which has wrought a liberation for freeman and slave alike. A revolution would only obscure that divine New Order which Jesus Christ has established. It would also hinder and delay the disruption of the existing world order in the coming of the kingdom of God. It would be equally wrong to suppose that St Paul imagines that the fulfilment of our secular calling is itself the living of the Christian life. No, his real meaning is that to renounce rebellion and revolution is the most appropriate way of expressing our conviction that the Christian hope is not set on this world, but on Christ and his kingdom. And so – let the slave remain a slave! It is not reform that the world needs, for it is already ripe for destruction. And so – let the slave remain a slave! He enjoys a better promise. Surely there is enough judgement for the world and comfort for the slave in the fact that God 'took upon himself the form of a slave' (Phil. 2.7), when he came to the earth? If a man was called to be a Christian as a slave, does not the very fact that he is a slave prevent him from loving and desiring and concerning himself too much about the world? Therefore let not the slave suffer in silent rebellion, but as a member of the Church and Body of Christ. He will thereby hasten the end of the world.

'Become not the bondservants of men.' This can happen in two different ways. First, it may happen by a revolution and the over-throw of the established order, and secondly by investing the established order with a halo of spirituality. 'Brethren, let each man, wherein he was called, therein abide with God.' 'With God' – and therefore 'become not bondservants of men', neither by revolution nor by false submission. To stay in the world with

God means simply to live in the rough and tumble of the world and at the same time remain in the Body of Christ, the visible Church, to take part in its worship and to live the life of discipleship. In so doing we bear testimony to the defeat of this world.

'Therefore let every soul be in subjection to the higher powers' (Rom. 13.1 ff). The Christian must not be drawn to the bearers of high office: his calling is to stay below. The higher powers are over ($\dot{v}\pi\dot{\epsilon}\rho$) him, and he must remain under ($\dot{v}\pi\dot{o}$) them. The world exercises dominion, the Christian serves, and thus he shares the earthly lot of his Lord, who became a servant. 'But Jesus called them unto him, and saith unto them, Ye know that they which are accounted to rule over the Gentiles lord it over them; and their great ones exercise authority over them. But it is not so among you: but whosoever would become great among you, shall be your minister: and whosoever would be first among you, shall be servant of all. For verily the Son of man came not to be ministered unto, but to minister, and to give his life a ransom for many' (Mark 10.42-45). 'For there is no power but of God.' These words are addressed to the Christians, not to the powers. The Christians are to know that if they would perceive and do the will of God, they must be content with the subordinate place accorded to them by the powers. They are bidden to be of good cheer: God himself will use the powers to work for their good, and his sovereignty extends even over the powers. This is more than an academic statement about the nature of authority in the abstract ($\dot{\epsilon}\xi ov\sigma\dot{\iota}a$, note the singular): it applies to the position of the Christians under the powers which actually exist ($a\dot{\iota}$ $\delta\dot{\epsilon}$ $ov\sigma a\iota\ldots$). To resist the power is to resist the ordinance of God ($\delta\iota a\tau a\chi\dot{\eta}$ τov $\theta\epsilon ov$), who has so ordered life that the world exercises dominion by force and Christ and Christians conquer by service. Failure to realize this distinction will bring a heavy judgement on the Christian (verse 2): it will mean a lapse into the standards of the world. How then is it so easy for the Christians to find themselves in opposition to the powers? Because they are so easily tempted to resent their blunders and injustices. But if we harbour such resentments we are in mortal danger of neglecting the will of the God we are called to serve. If only Christians will concentrate on perceiving what is good and on doing it as God commands, they can live 'without fear of the authorities'. 'For rulers are not a terror to the good work, but to the evil.' What has the Christian to fear, so long as he remains faithful to his Lord and does that which is good? 'And wouldest thou have no fear of the power? do that which is good.' That is the one thing necessary. It does not matter what others do, but what we do. Do that which is good, without fear, and without limit or reserve. What right have we to blame the government when we do not do that which is good ourselves? How can we pass judgement on others when we invite the same condemnation ourselves? If you want to be fearless, do good. 'And thou shalt receive praise from the same: for he is a minister of God to thee for good.' The point here is not that we should deliberately seek praise: praise is only an afterthought, and will naturally ensue where there is good government. The starting-point of St Paul's thinking is always the Church, and his sole concern is its well-being and manner of life. So much so, he feels obliged to warn the Christians to refrain from any unjust or evil conduct themselves, but does not utter a single word of reproach to the State. 'But if thou do that which is evil, be afraid: for he beareth not the sword in vain: for he is a minister of God, and avenger of wrath to him that doeth evil' (verse 4). On no account must evil occur within the Church. Once again, St Paul is talking to the Christians, not to the State. His concern is that the Christians should persevere in repentance and obedience wherever they may be and whatever conflict should threaten them. He is not concerned to excuse or condemn any secular power. No State is entitled to read into St Paul's words a justification of its own existence. Should any State take to heart these words, they would be just as much a challenge to repentance for that State as they are for the Church. If a ruler ($\check{\alpha}\rho\chi\omega\nu$) were to hear these words, he would not be entitled to take them as a divine authorization of his office, but rather as a commission to be God's minister for the sake of the fellowship of charity. And this would lead him straight to repentance. St Paul certainly does not speak to the Christians in this way because the governments of this world are so good, but because the Church must obey the will of God, whether the State be bad or good. He has no intention to instruct the Christian community about the task and responsibility of government. His entire concern is with the responsibility of the Christian community towards the State.

The Christian should receive praise from authority. If instead of praise he incurs punishment and persecution, what fault is that of his? After all, he was not looking for praise when he did that which brought him punishment, nor did he do good for fear of punishment. If he meets with suffering instead of praise, his conscience is clear in the sight of God and he has nothing to fear. After all, he has not brought shame or discredit on the Church. He obeys the power, not for material profit, but 'for conscience' sake' (verse 5). That is why the government cannot hurt the Christian's conscience even if it makes a mistake. The Christian is still free and has nothing to fear, and he can still pay the State its due by suffering innocently. He knows that when all is said and done, the sovereign power belongs to God and not to the State, which is only his minister. Authority is the minister of God – so says the apostle, who had had frequent occasion to learn what it meant to be imprisoned by that self-same power without having committed any crime. On three separate occasions he had endured the cruel punishment of whipping, and he was well aware how the Jews had been banished from Rome under the Emperor Claudius (Acts 18.1 ff). Authority is the minister of God – so says the man who knew that all power and all authority in the world had long since been stripped of their might, and led in triumph to the cross; so says the man who knew that Christ's victory would soon be made manifest to the whole world.

The whole of Paul's doctrine of the State in Rom. 13 is controlled by the introductory admonition: 'Be not overcome of evil, but overcome evil with good' (Rom. 12.21). It is immaterial whether the power be good or bad, what matters is that the Christian should overcome evil by good. The question of the payment of taxes to the Emperor was a point of temptation with the Jews. They pinned their hopes on the destruction of the Roman Empire, which would enable them to set up an independent dominion of their own. But for Jesus and his followers there was no need to be agitated over this question. 'Render unto Caesar the things that are Caesar's' (Matt. 22.21), says Jesus. 'For this cause pay ye tribute also' (Rom. 13.6), says St Paul at the end of his exposition. So far from contradicting the precept of our Lord, the Pauline charge is identical in meaning – the Christians are to give to Caesar what belongs to him in any case. Yes, they must regard those who insist on the payment of taxes as the 'ministers of God' (λειτουργοί, verse 6). Of course the converse cannot be true. The payment of taxes is not the service of God, but those who impose them render their service to God thereby in their own way, according to St Paul. But not even to this peculiar service of God does St Paul invite the Christians, but to submit themselves to authority and discharge any debts they owe (verses 7 and 8). To oppose or resist at this point would be to show a fatal inability to distinguish between the kingdom of God and the kingdoms of this world.

Let the slave therefore remain a slave. Let the Christian remain in subjection to the powers which exercise dominion over him. Let him not contract out of the world (I Cor. 5.11). But let the slave of course live as a freeman of Jesus Christ. Let him live under authority as a doer of good, let him live in the world as a member of the Body of Christ, the New Humanity. Let him do it without reserve, for his life in the world must be of such a quality as to bear witness to the world's lost condition and to the new creation which has taken place in the Church. Let the Christian suffer only for being a member of the Body of Christ.

Let the Christian remain in the world, not because of the good gifts of creation, nor because of his responsibility for the course of the world, but for the sake of the Body of the incarnate Christ and for the sake of the Church. Let him remain in the world to engage in frontal assault on it, and let him live the life of his secular calling in order to show himself as a stranger in this world all the more. But that is only possible if we are visible members of the Church. The antithesis between the world and the Church must be borne out in the world. That was the purpose of the incarnation. That is why Christ died among his enemies. That is the reason and the only reason why the slave must remain a slave and the Christian remain subject to the powers that be.

This is exactly the conclusion Luther reached with regard to the Christian's secular calling during those critical years when he was turning his back on the cloister. It was not so much the lofty standards of monasticism that he repudiated, as their interpretation in terms of individual achievement. It was not otherworldliness as such that he attacked, but the perversion of otherworldliness into a subtle kind of 'spiritual' worldliness. To Luther's mind that was a most insidious perversion of the gospel. The otherworldliness of the Christian life ought, Luther concluded, to be manifested in the very midst of the world, in the Christian community and in its daily life. Hence the Christian's task is to live out that life in terms of his secular calling. That is the way to die unto the world. The value of the secular calling for the Christian is that it provides an opportunity of living the Christian life with the support of God's grace, and of engaging more vigorously in the assault on the world and everything that it stands for. Luther did not return to the world because he had arrived at a more positive attitude towards it. Nor had he abandoned the eschatological expectation of early Christianity. He intended his action to express a radical criticism and protest against the secularization of Christianity which had taken place within monasticism. By recalling the Christians into the world he called them paradoxically out of it all the more. That was what Luther experienced in his own person. His call to men to return to the world was essentially a call to enter the visible Church of the incarnate Lord. It was no different with St Paul.

We have by now made it clear that for the Christian a life within the terms of a secular calling has a definite limit. It may well happen that after we have been called to a secular profession we shall be called upon to quit it. This of course is to be understood in the way both St Paul and Luther understood it. The limits and claims of the secular calling are fixed by our membership of the visible Church of Christ, and these limits are reached when the space which the Body of Christ claims and occupies in the world for its worship, its offices and the civic life of its members clashes with the world's claim for space for its own activities. We shall at once know when the limit has been reached, for every member of the Church will then be obliged to make a public confession of Christ, and the world will be forced to react, either by calculated restraint or open violence. Now the Christian must suffer openly. Hitherto, since the day he had died with Christ in baptism, his suffering had been in secret. Now he is openly ejected from his secular calling and enters upon a visible participation in the passion of his Lord. Now he needs more than ever all the fellowship and brotherly help the Church can give.

But it is not always the world which ejects the Christian from his secular calling. Even in the first century we find that certain professions were regarded as incompatible with membership of the Christian Church. The actor who had to play the part of pagan gods and heroes, the teacher who was forced to teach pagan mythologies in pagan schools, the gladiator who had to take human life for sport, the soldier who wielded the sword, the policeman and the judge, all had to renounce their heathen professions if they wanted to be baptized. Later the Church – or was it perhaps the world? – found it possible to lift the ban on these professions. More and more the offensive passes from the Church to the world.

The older the world grows, the more heated becomes the conflict between Christ and Antichrist, and the more thorough the efforts of the world to get rid of the Christians. Until now the world had always granted them a lodging-place by allowing them to work for their own food and clothing. But a world that has become one hundred per cent antichristian cannot allow them even this private sphere of work for their daily bread. The Christians are now forced to deny their Lord for every crumb of bread they need. Either they must flee from the world, or go to prison; there is no other alternative. When the Christian community has been deprived of its last inch of space on the earth, the end will be near.

Thus while it is true that the Body of Christ makes a deep invasion into the sphere of secular life, yet at the same time the great gulf between the two is always clear at other points, and must become increasingly so. But whether in the world or out of it, the Christian's choice is determined by obedience to the same word: 'Be not fashioned according to this world: but be ye transformed (μεταμορφοῦσθε) by the renewing of your mind, that ye may prove what is the good and acceptable and perfect will of God' (Rom. 12.2). There is a way of putting oneself on the same level as the world in the world as there is a way of creating one's own spiritual 'world' in a monastery. There is a wrong way of staying in the world and a wrong way of fleeing from it. In both cases we are fashioning ourselves according to the world. But the Church of Christ has a different 'form' from the world. Her task is increasingly to realize this form. It is the form of Christ himself, who came into the world and of his infinite mercy bore mankind and took it to himself, but who notwithstanding did not fashion himself in accordance with it but was rejected and cast out by it. He was not of this world. In the right confrontation with the world, the Church will become ever more like to the form of its suffering Lord.

The brethren must therefore be told that 'the time is short – that those that have wives may be as though they had none; and those that weep, as though they wept not; and those that rejoice, as though they rejoiced not; and those that buy, as though they possessed not; and those that use the world, as not abusing it: for the fashion of this world passeth away. But I would have you to be free from cares' (I Cor. 7.29-32a). Such is the life of the Church in the world. Christians live like other men: they get married, they mourn and rejoice, they buy their requirements and use the world for the purpose of day-to-day existence. But they have everything through Christ alone, in him and for his sake. Thus they are not bound by it. They have everything as though they had it not. They do not set their heart on their possessions, but are inwardly free. That is why they are able to make use of the world without with drawing from it altogether (I Cor. 5.13). And that is also why they can leave the world when it becomes an impediment to discipleship. They get married, though admittedly the apostle would prefer them to remain unmarried so long as they can do so in faith (I Cor. 7.7, 33-40). They sell and engage in commerce, but only to the extent their daily needs require. They do not heap up treasures and set their hearts on them. They work, for they are not allowed to be idle. But their work is certainly no end in itself. Work for work's sake is not a New Testament notion. Everyone must support himself by his own labours, and have something to give away to his brethren (I Thess. 4.11 f; II Thess. 3.11 f; Eph. 4.28). He must be independent of 'them that are without' (I Thess. 4.12), i.e. the heathen, just as St Paul took special pride in working for his bread with his own hands, that he might not be beholden even to his converts (II Thess. 3.8; I Cor. 9.15). This independence gives the preacher an opportunity of showing that he does not preach with a view to personal gain, but solely in the service of the Church. After the commandment to work comes another: 'In nothing be anxious, but in everything by prayer and supplication with thanksgiving let your requests be made known unto God' (Phil. 4.6). The Christians know that 'godliness with contentment is great gain: for we brought nothing into the world, for neither can we carry anything out: but having food and covering we shall be therewith content. But they that desire to be rich fall into temptation and a snare and many foolish and hurtful lusts, such as drown men in destruction and perdition. For the love of money is the root of all kinds of evil: which some reaching after have been led astray from the faith, and have pierced themselves through with many sorrows' (I Tim. 6.6-9). Thus the Christians use worldly goods 'as things which are to perish in the using '(Col. 2.22). They use them with thankfulness and prayer to the Creator of all good things (I Tim. 4.4). But all the while they are free. They may be filled or go hungry, abound or be in want. 'I can do all things through him that strengtheneth me' (Phil. 4.12 f).

The Christians live in the world. They make use of the world, for they are creatures of flesh and blood, and it was for the sake of their flesh that Christ came into the world. They indulge in worldly activities. They get married, but their marriage will look quite different from marriage as the world understands it. Christian marriage will be undertaken 'in the Lord' (I Cor. 7.39). It will be sanctified in the service of the Body of Christ and in the discipline of prayer and self-control (I Cor. 7.5). It will be a parable of the self-sacrificing love of Christ for his Church. It will even be itself a part of the Body of Christ, a Church in miniature (Eph. 5.32). The Christians buy and sell, they engage in trade and commerce, but again in a different spirit from the world. They will not only refrain from driving a hard bargain with one another (I Thess. 4.6), but (what to the world will appear incomprehensible) they will prefer to let others gain unfair advantage over them and do them injustice, rather than take their case to a pagan law-court over 'things that pertain to this life'. Should need arise, they will settle their disputes within the Christian community, and before their own tribunals (I Cor. 6.1-8).

Thus the life of the Christian community in the world bears permanent witness to the truth that 'the fashion of this world passeth away' (I Cor. 7.31), that the time is short (I Cor. 7.29) and the Lord is nigh (Phil. 4.5). This thought fills them with joy unspeakable (Phil. 4.4). The world is growing too small for the Christian community, and all it looks for is the Lord's return. It still walks in the flesh, but with eyes upturned to heaven, whence he for whom they wait will come again. In the world the Christians are a colony of the true home, they are strangers and aliens in a foreign land, enjoying the hospitality of that land, obeying its laws and honouring its government. They receive with gratitude the requirements of their bodily life, and in all things prove themselves honest, just, chaste, gentle, peaceable, and ready to serve. They show the love of God to all men, 'but specially to them that are of the household of faith' (Gal. 6.10; II Pet. 1.7). They are patient and cheerful in suffering, and they glory in tribulation. They live their own life under alien rulers and alien laws. Above all, they pray for all in authority, for that is their greatest service.

But they are only passing through the country. At any moment they may receive the signal to move on. Then they will strike tents, leaving behind them all their worldly friends and connections, and following only the voice of their Lord who calls. They leave the land of their exile, and start their homeward trek to heaven.

Amid poverty and suffering, hunger and thirst, they are meek, merciful, and peacemakers, persecuted and scorned by the world, although it is for their sake alone that the world is allowed to continue, and it is they who protect the world from the wrath and judgement of God. They are strangers and sojourners on earth (Heb. 11.13; 13.14; I Pet. 2.11). They seek those things that are above, not the things that are on the earth (Col. 3.2). For their true life is not yet made manifest, but hidden with Christ in God. Here they see no more than the reflection of what they shall be. Here all that is visible is their dying, their secret daily death unto the old man, and their manifest death before the world. They are still hidden from themselves, and their left hand knows not what their right hand does. Although they are a visible society, they are always unknown even to themselves, looking only to their Lord. He is in heaven, their life is with him, and for him they wait. But when Christ, who is their life shall be manifested, then they too shall be manifested with him in glory (Col. 3.4).

They wander on earth and live in heaven, and although they are weak, they protect the world; they taste of peace in the midst of turmoil; they are poor, and yet they have all they want. They stand in suffering and remain in joy, they appear dead to all outward sense and lead a life of faith within.

'When Christ, their life, shall be manifested, when once he appears in glory, they too will appear in glory with him as princes of the earth. They will reign and triumph with him, and adorn heaven as shining lights. There joy will be shared by all' (C. F. Richter).

That is the Church of the elect, the *Ecclesia*, those who have been *called out*, the Body of Christ on earth, the followers and disciples of Jesus.

31 THE SAINTS

THE *ecclesia Christi*, the disciple community, has been torn from the clutches of the world. Of course it still has to live in the world, but it is made into one body, with its own sphere of sovereignty, and its own claim to living-space. It is the holy Church (Eph. 5.27), the community of the saints (I Cor. 14.33), and its members are called to be saints (Rom. 1.7), sanctified in Jesus Christ (I Cor. 1.2), chosen and set apart before the foundation of the world (Eph. 1.4). The object of their calling in Jesus Christ, and of their election before the foundation of the world, was that they should be holy and without blemish (Eph. 1.4). Christ had surrendered his body to death that he might present his own holy and without blemish and unreproveable before him (Col. 1.22). The fruit of their liberation from sin through the death of Christ is that whereas they once surrendered their members servants to iniquity, they may now use them in the service of righteousness unto sanctification (Rom. 6.19-22).

Only God is holy. He is holy both in his perfect separation from the sinful world and in the establishment of his sanctuary in the midst of that world. This is the burden of the song Moses sang with the children of Israel after the perdition of the Egyptians, as he praised the Lord, who had redeemed his people out of bondage of the world:

'Who is like unto thee, O Lord, among the gods? Who is like thee, glorious in holiness, fearful in praises, doing wonders? Thou stretchest out thy right hand, the earth swallowed them up. Thou in thy mercy hast led the people which thou hast redeemed: thou hast in thy mercy guided them to thy holy habitation. . . . Thou shalt bring them in, and plant them in the mountain of thine inheritance. The place, O Lord, which thou hast made for thee to dwell in, The sanctuary, O Lord, which thy hands have established' (Ex. 15.11 ff). The holiness of God means his coming to dwell in the midst of the world and to establish his sanctuary as the place from which he sends forth his judgement and redemption (Ps. 99 etc.). Moreover, it is in this sanctuary that God enters into a relationship with his people by an act of atonement such as can only be effected in the sanctuary (Lev. 16.16 ff). God makes a covenant with his people and separates them from the world as his own possession, and vouches himself for this covenant. 'Ye shall be holy: for I the Lord your God am holy' (Lev. 19.2), and again, 'I the Lord, which sanctify you, am holy' (Lev. 21.8). This is the foundation on which the covenant is based. All the subsequent legislation presupposes and is intended to maintain the holiness of God and his people.

Like God himself, the Holy One, the people of his sanctuary are also separated from all things profane and from sin. For God has made them the people of his covenant, choosing them for himself, making atonement for them and purifying them in his sanctuary. Now the sanctuary is the temple, and the temple is the Body of Christ. Hence the ultimate purpose of God, which is to establish a holy community, is at last fulfilled in the Body of Christ. For that Body has been separated from the world and from sin, and made the peculiar possession of God and his sanctuary in the world. God dwells in it with the Holy Spirit.

How does all this come to pass? How does God create a community of saints out of sinful men and women? How can he avert the reproach of unrighteousness if he makes a covenant with sinners? How can the sinner become righteous without impairing the righteousness of God? The answer is that God justifies himself by appearing as his own advocate in defence of his own righteousness. And it is in the cross of Christ that this supreme miracle happens (Rom. 3.21 f). It is necessary for the sinner to be parted from his sin and still live before God. But so closely is his life identified with sin that the only way in which that can be achieved is by dying. That is to say, the only way for God to maintain his righteousness is by putting the sinner to death. The problem is, how can the sinner live, and be holy before God?

This problem is solved by God himself becoming man, taking

upon him our flesh in his Son Jesus Christ, and in his body bearing our flesh to the death of the cross. In other words, by putting his own Son, the bearer of our flesh, to death, he puts to death all flesh on earth. Now it is revealed that none is good, save God alone and that none is righteous but he. Thus God has given terrible proof of his own righteousness (ἔνδειξις τῆς δικαιωσύνης αὐτοῦ, Rom. 3.26). In order that he *alone* might be righteous, it was necessary for God to deliver the whole human race to death on the cross in the judgement of his wrath. The death of Jesus is the manifestation of God's righteousness, it is the place where God has given gracious proof of his own righteousness, the place where alone the righteousness of God will dwell. By sharing in this death we too become partakers of that righteousness. For it was *our* flesh Christ took upon him, and our sins which he bore in his body on the tree (I Pet. 2.24). What happened there to him happened to us all. He shared our life and death, that we might partake of his life and death. Since God had to establish his own righteousness in the death of Christ, it follows that we are with him in the place where God's righteousness is to be found, that is, on the cross – for he bore our flesh. Having thus died with him, we become partakers in the righteousness of God through the death of Jesus. This righteousness of God which effects the death of us sinners, is in the death of Jesus his righteousness *for us*. For the death of Jesus establishes not only the righteousness of God, it establishes his righteousness for us who are embodied in the death of Christ: 'that he himself might be just, and the justifier of him that hath faith in Jesus' (Rom. 3.26). The justification of the sinner therefore consists in the sole righteousness of God, wherein the sinner is utterly and completely unrighteous, and has no righteousness whatever of his own, side by side with the righteousness of God. Whenever we desire an independent righteousness of our own we are forfeiting our only chance of justification, which is through God and his righteousness. God alone is righteous. On the cross this truth is apprehended as our condemnation as sinners. But when we are brought to faith in the death of Christ, we receive the righteousness of God triumphant on the cross in the very place where we receive our own condemnation as sinners. We can then receive justification because we willingly renounce every attempt to establish our own righteousness and allow God alone to be righteous. Thus the only way we can be righteous in the sight of God is by recognizing that he only is righteous, and we ourselves sinners in the totality of our being. At bottom, the problem of our righteousness before God, sinners though we be, is the problem of how God alone can be righteous over against us. The only ground for our justification is the justification of God. 'That thou (i.e. God) mightest be justified in thy words, and mightest prevail when thou comest to judgement' (Rom. 3.4).

All that matters is that God's righteousness should prevail over ours, that God's righteousness should be maintained in his own eyes, and that he alone should be righteous. This is the divine victory which is fought and won on the cross, and it is this that makes the cross an act not only of judgement but also of atonement (ἱλαστήριον, verse 25) for all who believe that in the death of Christ God alone is righteous, and who recognize their sins. The righteousness of God itself effects atonement (προέθετο, verse 25). 'God was in Christ reconciling the world unto himself' (II Cor. 5.19). 'Not reckoning unto them their trespasses' – he bore them, and bore the death which they deserved. 'Having committed unto us the word of reconciliation'; this word looks for faith, the faith that God alone is righteous, and in Jesus has become our righteousness. But between the death of Christ and the apostolic gospel of the cross there lay the resurrection, which alone gives the cross its redemptive power. The gospel of Christ crucified is always the gospel of him who was not holden of death. 'We are ambassadors therefore on behalf of God, as though God were entreating you by us: we beseech you on behalf of Christ, be ye reconciled unto God.' The message of the atonement is the word of Christ himself. He is the risen Lord, who bears witness to himself in the word of the apostle as one who was crucified. Discover your true selves, says the apostle, in the death of Jesus, in the righteousness of God which is granted there to us. The man who discovers his true self in the death of Jesus, discovers it in the sole righteousness of God.

'Him who knew no sin he made to be sin on our behalf; that we might be made the righteousness of God in him.' The innocent victim is put to death because he bears our sinful flesh. He is hated by God and men and accursed, made guilty for the sake of our flesh. But *we* find in his death the righteousness of God.

We are in him in virtue of his incarnation. Thus he died for us that we sinners might become in him the righteousness of God, as sinners absolved from sin through the sole righteousness of God. If in the sight of God Christ is our sin (which deserves condemnation) then we are righteousness in him (though of course this righteousness is not our own – ἰδία δικαιοσύνη, Rom. 10.3; Phil. 3.9), but in the strictest sense the righteousness of God and his alone. Hence the righteousness of God means this, that we who are sinners become his righteousness, and our (that is, his) righteousness (Isa. 54.17) means that God alone is righteous, and we are sinners accepted by him. The righteousness of God is Christ himself (I Cor. 1.30). And Christ is 'God with us', 'Immanuel' (Isa. 7.14), The Lord our Righteousness (Jer. 33.16).

The proclamation of the death of Christ for us is the preaching of justification. The means whereby we are incorporated into the Body of Christ, that is, into his death and resurrection, is baptism. Just as Christ died once and for all, so we are baptized and justified once and for all. Both events are in the strictest sense *unrepeatable*. Only repeatable is the recollection of the event that happened for our sake once and for all, and it needs to be repeated daily. But our recollection is always different in kind from the reality itself. If we forfeit reality, we can never recover it. The Epistle to the Hebrews is right in insisting on this (Heb. 6.5 f; 10.26f). 'If the salt have lost its savour, wherewith shall it be salted?' The baptized always stand under the rule 'Know ye not?' (Rom. 6.3; I Cor. 3.16; 6.19), and 'Reckon ye yourselves to be dead unto sin, but alive unto God in Christ Jesus' (Rom. 6.11). All that can happen has happened already, not only on the cross, but also in us. We have been separated from sin, we are dead, we are justified. With that the work of God is complete. He has established his sanctuary on earth in righteousness. This sanctuary is Christ, the Body of

Christ. Our separation from sin has been accomplished through our death as sinners in Jesus Christ. God has prepared himself a people which has been justified from sin. This people is the community of the disciples of Jesus, the community of the saints. They are taken up into his sanctuary, and in fact they are his sanctuary, his temple. They are taken out of the world and live in a new realm of their own in the midst of the world.

Henceforth the New Testament simply calls the Christians 'saints'. It does not, as we might have expected, call them 'the righteous', perhaps because that term hardly does justice to the gift they have received. In any case, its reference is to the unique event of baptism and justification. It is true, of course, that our recollection of that event has daily to be renewed. It is equally true that the saints remain justified sinners. But there is also a further gift than these, the gift of final perseverance, or sanctification. Both gifts have the same source. Jesus Christ and him crucified (I Cor. 1.2; 6.11), and both have the same content, which is fellowship and communion with him. They are inseparably connected, but for that very reason not identical. Justification is the means whereby we appropriate the saving act of God in the past, and sanctification the promise of God's activity in the present and future. Justification secured our entrance into fellowship and communion with Christ through the unique and final event of his death, and sanctification keeps us in that fellowship in Christ. Justification is primarily concerned with the relation between man and the law of God, sanctification with the Christian's separation from the world until the second coming of Christ. Justification makes the individual a member of the Church whereas sanctification preserves the Church with all its members. Justification enables the believer to break away from his sinful past, sanctification enables him to abide in Christ, to persevere in faith and to grow in love. We may perhaps think of justification and sanctification as bearing the same relation to each other as creation and preservation. Justification is the new creation of the new man, and sanctification his preservation until the day of Jesus Christ.

Sanctification is the fulfilment of the divine purpose enunciated in the words, 'Ye shall be holy: for I am holy', and again, 'I the Lord who sanctify you am holy.' The fulfilment is the work of God the Holy Spirit. He is the 'seal' whereby the faithful are sealed as God's possession until the day of redemption. Hitherto they had been kept in ward under the law, enclosed as it were in a prison (Gal. 3.23), but now they are enclosed 'in Christ', sealed with the seal of God, which is the Holy Spirit. This seal may not be broken. God himself has shut the door and holds the key in his hand. In other words, God now has complete possession of those whom he has won in Christ. The circle is closed, and in the Holy Spirit man has become God's own possession. The community of the saints is barred off from the world by an unbreakable seal, awaiting its ultimate deliverance. Like a sealed train travelling through foreign territory, the Church goes on its way through the world. Its journey is like that of the ark, which was 'pitched within and without with pitch' (Gen. 6.14), so that it might come safely through the flood. The saints are sealed that they might have redemption, deliverance and salvation (Eph. 4.30; 1.13 f; I Thess. 5.23; I Pet. 1.5, etc.) at the second coming of Christ. Again, the Spirit is the pledge which gives the sealed assurance of their destiny ' . . . to the end that we should be unto the praise of his glory, we who had hoped in Christ, in whom ye also having heard the word of truth, the gospel of your salvation – in whom having also believed, ye were sealed with the Spirit of promise, which is an earnest of our inheritance, the redemption of God's own possession, unto the praise of his glory' (Eph. 1.12-14).

The sanctification of the Church means its separation from all that is unholy, from sin; and the method by which it is accomplished is by God's sealing the Church and thus making it his own possession, his habitation on earth, the place from which judgement and reconciliation go forth into all the world. Sanctification means that the Christians have been judged already, and that they are being preserved until the coming of Christ and are ever advancing towards it.

All this has a threefold significance for the community of the saints. First, their sanctification will be maintained by their being clearly *separated from the world*. Secondly, it will be maintained through their *walking* in a way which is *worthy* of the holiness of God. Thirdly, their sanctification will be *hidden*, and they must *wait* for the day of Jesus Christ.

Sanctification is therefore possible only within the visible Church. This is the first point, and it is one of the crucial marks of sanctification. The Church's claim to a place of its own in the world, and the consequent line of demarcation between Church and world, prove that the Church is in the state of sanctification. For the Spirit seals off the Church from the world. This seal gives the Church the strength and power to fulfil its duty of vindicating God's claim over the whole of the world. At the same time the Church must claim a definite sphere in the world for itself, and so define clearly the frontier between itself and the world. Now the Church is the city set on the hill and founded on earth by the direct act of God, it is the *'polis'* of Matt. 5.14, and as such it is God's own sealed possession. Hence there is a certain 'political' character involved in the idea of sanctification and it is this character which provides the only basis for the Church's political ethic. The world is the world and the Church the Church, and yet the Word of God must go forth from the Church into all the world, proclaiming that the earth is the Lord's and all that therein is. Herein lies the 'political' character of the Church. If we regard sanctification as a purely personal matter which has nothing whatever to do with public life and the visible line of demarcation between the Church and the world, we shall land ourselves inevitably into a confusion between the pious wishes of the religious flesh and the sanctification of the Church which is accomplished in the death of Christ through the seal of God. This is the deceitful arrogance and the false spirituality of the old man, who seeks sanctification outside the visible community of the brethren. It is contempt of the Body of Christ as a visible fellowship of justified sinners, a contempt which disguises itself as inward humility, whereas it was the good pleasure of Christ to take upon him our flesh visibly and to bear it up to the cross. It is also contempt of the fellowship, for we are then trying to attain sanctification in isolation from our brethren. And it shows contempt for our fellow-sinners, for we are withdrawing from the Church and pursuing a sanctity of our own choosing because we are disgusted by the Church's sinful form. By pursuing sanctification outside the Church we are trying to pronounce ourselves holy.

Because it is sanctified by the seal of the Spirit, the Church is always in the battlefield, waging a war to prevent the breaking of the seal, whether from within or from without, and struggling to prevent the world from becoming the Church and the Church from becoming the world. The sanctification of the Church is really a defensive war, for the place which has been given to the Body of Christ on earth. The separation of the Church and the world from one another is the crusade which the Church fights for the sanctuary of God on earth.

This sanctuary can only exist in the visible Church. But – and here we come to the second point – the very fact that it is separated from the world means that while the Church lives in the sanctuary of God something of the world still lives in the Church. That is why it is the duty of the saints to walk worthily of their calling and of the gospel in every sphere of life (Eph. 4.1; Phil. 1.27; Col. 1.10; I Thess. 2.12). But the only way to do this is by daily re-calling the gospel on which their whole life depends. 'Ye were washed, ye were sanctified, ye were justified' (I Cor. 6.11). It is by living daily on this recollection that the saints are sanctified. And the gospel of which they are to be worthy is that which proclaims the death of the world and the flesh, and their own crucifixion and death with Christ on the cross and through baptism, which pro-claims that sin can no longer have dominion over them because its sovereignty has already been broken, and that it is no longer possible for the Christian to sin. 'Whosoever is begotten of God doeth no sin' (I John 3.9).

Their breach with the past is an accomplished fact. Their 'former' manner of life has come to an end (Eph. 4.22). 'Ye were once darkness, but now are light in the Lord' (Eph. 5.8). Whereas they had once performed the shameful and 'unfruitful works of the flesh', the Spirit now produces in them the fruit of sanctification.

This is why Christians are no longer to be called sinners, in the sense of men who are still living under the dominion of sin (ἁμαρτωλοί – the only apparent exception is in I Tim. 1.15, but that is a personal confession). On the contrary, they were once sinners, ungodly, enemies (Rom. 5.8, 19; Gal. 2.15, 17), but now through Christ they are holy. As saints they are reminded and exhorted to be what they are. But this is not an impossible ideal, it is not sinners who are required to become holy, or that would mean a return to justification by works and would be blasphemy against Christ. No, it is saints who are required to be holy, saints who have been sanctified in Christ Jesus through the Holy Spirit.

The life of the saints emerges from a lurid background. The dark works of the flesh are brought out into the open by the bright light of life in the Spirit: '... fornication, uncleanness, lasciviousness, idolatry, sorcery, enmities, strife, jealousies, wraths, factions, divisions, heresies, envyings, drunkenness, revellings, and such like' (Gal. 5.19). There is no place for such vices in the Church of Christ, for they have been abolished and condemned by the cross, and have ceased to be. As they set out on their new life the Christians are warned that 'they which practise such things shall not inherit the kingdom of God' (Gal. 5.21; Eph. 5.5; I Cor. 6.9; Rom. 1.32). These sins cut men off from eternal salvation. If however one of these vices should rear its ugly head in the Church, there is no alternative but excommunication (I Cor. 5.1 ff).

There is a remarkable agreement in the various catalogues of vices. Almost without exception the lists are headed by the sin of whoredom (πορνεία). Whoredom is incompatible with the new life in Christ. In most instances the sin of covetousness comes second (πλεονεξία, I Cor. 5.10; 6.10; Eph. 4.19; 5.3, 5; Col. 3.5; I Thess. 4.4 ff). Covetousness and whoredom may be summarized as 'uncleanness' or 'idolatry' (I Cor. 5.10; 6.9; Eph. 5.3; Gal. 5.19; Col. 3.5,8). Next come the sins against the brotherhood, and finally revellings.[1] It is certainly no accident that whoredom stands at the head of the lists, not so much on account of the peculiar circum-

---

[1] The dominical word in Mark 7.21 f may well be the source of all these catalogues.

stances of the times but rather because of the peculiar character of the vice. Whoredom is a resurgence of the old Adam, the sin Adam committed when he desired to be as God, to be the creator of life, to rule rather than to serve. It symbolizes the attempt of man to transcend the divinely ordered limits, and to lay aggressive hands on God's creatures. The sin of Israel lay in its constant denial of the faithfulness of its Lord, its fornication with idols (see I Cor. 10.7), and its devotion to them. Whoredom is the first sin against the Creator. For the Christian however, whoredom is in a very special way a sin against the very Body of Christ, for the Christian's body is a member of Christ, and belongs exclusively to him. Bodily union with a harlot dissolves this spiritual unity with Christ, and by robbing Christ of his body and lending it to sin the Christian forfeits his communion and fellowship with him. Whoredom is also sin against our own bodies. The Christian must realize that his body too is a temple of the indwelling Spirit (I Cor. 6.13 ff). So close is the communion between the Christian's body and Christ that his body cannot belong to the world as well as to Christ. Our common life in the Body of Christ forbids us to sin against our own bodies. The whoremonger will assuredly incur the wrath of God (Rom. 1.29; I Cor. 5.1 f; 7.2; 10.7; II Cor. 12.21; Heb. 12.16; 13.4). The Christian is chaste: he devotes his body exclusively to the service of the Body of Christ. He knows that the suffering and death of Christ's Body on the cross is intimately connected with his own body, which, like Christ's, is also given over to death. Our fellowship and communion with the crucified and glorified Body of Christ liberates us from unchastity in our own physical life. In that communion our wild physical passions are daily done to death. The Christian practises chastity and self-control, using his body exclusively in the service of building up the Body of Christ, the Church. He does the same in marriage, and thus makes it also a part of the Body of Christ.

With whoredom covetousness is closely associated. Insatiable desire is a common feature to both, and in both the sinner succumbs to the world. The divine commandment says: 'Thou shalt not covet.' The whoremonger and the covetous person are both perfect embodiments of desire. The whoremonger desires to possess another person, the covetous man material things. The covetous man seeks dominion and power, but only to become a slave of the world on which he has set his heart. Whoredom and covetousness alike bring men into contact with the world in such a way as to defile them and make them unclean. Both vices are idolatry, for their victims have ceased to belong to God and Christ, desiring the goods of their own world instead.

But when we create our own God and our own world, what we are really doing is to deify our own lust. We are then bound to hate our fellow-men, as obstacles standing in the way of our wills. Hatred, jealousy and murder are all of them the fruits of selfish lust. 'Whence come fightings and wars among you? come they not hence, even of the pleasures that war in your members?' (James 4.1 f). The whoremonger and the covetous person cannot know brotherly love. They thrive upon the darkness of their own hearts. In sinning against the Body of Christ, they sin against themselves and their fellow-men. Whoredom and brotherly love are incompatible because of the Body of Christ. By withdrawing our bodies from the Body of Christ, we render them incapable of serving our neighbours. Once again, contempt of our own bodies and those of our fellow-men leads to shameless and ungodly revellings, to rioting and drunkenness. In other words, we fall victims to the flesh, and 'they that are such serve not our Lord Christ, but their own belly' (Rom. 16.18). The ugliness of this sin consists in the attempt of the dead flesh to nurture itself, thereby bringing a shame which shows itself even in a man's outward appearance. The glutton has no part in the Body of Christ.

For the Church, the world and all its vices belong to the past. It has broken off all contact with those that do such things, and it is its duty always to shun them (I Cor. 5.9 ff). For 'what communion hath light with darkness?' (II Cor. 6.14 ff). In the world there are 'the works of the flesh', in the Church 'the fruit of the Spirit' (Gal. 5.19; Eph. 5.9).

What does 'fruit' mean in this context? There are many works of the flesh, but only one fruit of the Spirit. Works are done by human hands, fruit thrusts upward and grows all unbeknown to the tree which bears it. Works are dead, fruit is alive, and bears the seed which will bring forth more fruit. Works can subsist on their own, fruit cannot exist apart from the tree. Fruit is always the miraculous, the created; it is never the result of willing, but always a growth. The fruit of the Spirit is a gift of God, and only he can produce it. They who bear it know as little about it as the tree knows of its fruit. They know only the power of him on whom their life depends. There is no room for boasting here, but only for an ever more intimate union with him. The saints are unconscious of the fruit they bear. The left hand knows not what the right hand does. If the saints desired to know about it, if they wanted to become detached observers of themselves, they would have already severed themselves from the root, and the time of their fruition would be past. 'The fruit of the Spirit is love, joy, peace, longsuffering, kindness, goodness, faithfulness, meekness, temperance' (Gal. 5.22). No clearer expression could be given to the sanctification of the individual, as well as the sanctification of the Church as a whole. But the source of both individual and corporate sanctification is the same, namely, fellowship and communion with Christ in the same body. Just as the separation of Church and world became visible only in their continuous conflict, so also does personal sanctification consist in the conflict of the Spirit against the flesh. The saints are only conscious of the strife and distress, the weakness and sin in their lives; and the further they advance in holiness, the more they feel they are fighting a losing battle and dying in the flesh. 'They that are of Christ Jesus have crucified the flesh with the passions and lusts thereof' (Gal. 5.24). They still live in the flesh, but for that very reason their whole life must be an act of faith in the Son of God, who has begun his life in them (Gal. 2.20). The Christian dies daily (I Cor. 15.31), but although this may mean suffering and decay in the flesh, the inward man is renewed day by day (II Cor. 4.16). The only reason why the saints have to die in the flesh is that Christ through the Holy Spirit has begun to live his life in them. The effect of Christ and his life on the saints is that they die

257

after the flesh. There is no need for them to go out of their way to look for suffering: indeed that would only mean a return to the self-assertion of the flesh. Every day Christ is their death and Christ is their life.

Therefore this triumph song is in full measure applicable to them: he who is born of God has ceased from sin, sin has no more dominion over them, they are dead unto sin and live through the Spirit.[1] 'There is therefore now no condemnation to them that are in Christ Jesus' (Rom. 8.1). God is well pleased in his saints. He is acting in their conflicts and their death, but he uses these to further their sanctification. The saints are meant to be assured that the fruit is there, although it is always hidden from their eyes. Of course this does not mean that so long as the gospel of forgiveness is proclaimed they are free to indulge in whoredom, covetousness, murder and hatred of the brethren, or that it is possible for the fruit of sanctification to remain invisible. But wherever it becomes visible on a large scale, wherever the world looks at the Christians and feels obliged to say, as it said in the earliest days, 'See how these Christians love one another', the saints must then take special care to keep their eyes on him alone,

---

[1] 'I live, says the believer, I live in the sight of God. Through his grace I am acquitted before his judgement seat. I live in his loving kindness, his light and his love. I am wholly delivered from all my sins. There are no further unpaid accounts against my name in his debit book. The law makes no more demands on me, it pursues me no longer, neither does it condemn me. I am righteous before God, even as he is righteous. I am holy and perfect even as my God is holy and as my Father is perfect. The entire goodwill of God embraces me: it is the ground whereon I stand, the roof beneath which I hide. All the blessedness and peace of God raises and bears me aloft. It is the air I breathe, and the nourishment on which I thrive. There is no more sin in me, and I have ceased entirely to commit it. I have a good conscience, and know that I am walking in God's ways and doing his will; I know that my whole life is fashioned in accordance with that will, whether I walk or stand, sit or lie down, am awake or asleep. Every thought I speak and every deed I do I think and do according to his will. Wheresoever I be, at home or abroad, it is according to his gracious will. I am acceptable to him, whether I be at work or at rest. My guilt is forever wiped out, and it is impossible for me to incur fresh guilt which could not be expiated. I am preserved by his grace and can sin no more. Yea, death cannot harm me for I have eternal life like all the angels of God. No longer will my God be wroth with me or rebuke me, for I am eternally redeemed from the wrath to come. The evil one can no longer assail me, neither can the world ensnare me any more. Who can separate us from the love of God? If God be for us, who can be against us?' (Kohlbrugge).

to ignore any good they may have achieved themselves, and to pray fervently for forgiveness. The same Christians who have claimed the privilege of being no longer under the dominion of sin, will confess: 'If we say we have no sin, we deceive ourselves, and the truth is not in us. If we confess our sins, he is faithful and just to forgive us our sins, and to cleanse us from all unrighteousness. If we say that we have not sinned, we make him a liar, and his word is not in us. My little children, these things I write unto you, that ye may not sin. And if any man sin, we have an advocate with the Father, Jesus Christ the righteous' (I John 1.8-2.1). This is exactly how the Lord himself taught us to pray – 'Forgive us our trespasses.' He charged us never to tire of forgiving one another (Eph. 4.32; Matt. 18.21 ff). Brotherly forgiveness makes room for the forgiveness of Jesus to enter into their common life. Instead of seeing their neighbours as men who have injured them, they see them as men for whom Christ has won forgiveness on the cross. They meet on the basis of their common sanctification through the cross of Christ.

The community of the saints is not an 'ideal' community consisting of perfect and sinless men and women, where there is no need of further repentance. No, it is a community which proves that it is worthy of the gospel of forgiveness by constantly and sincerely proclaiming God's forgiveness (which has nothing to do with self-forgiveness). It is a community of men and women who have genuinely encountered the precious grace of God, and who walk worthily of the gospel by not casting that grace recklessly away.

In other words the preaching of forgiveness must always go hand-in-hand with the preaching of repentance, the preaching of the gospel with the preaching of the law. Nor can the forgiveness of sin be unconditional – sometimes sin must be retained. It is the will of the Lord himself that the gospel should not be given to the dogs. He too held that the only way to safeguard the gospel of forgiveness was by preaching repentance. If the Church refuses to face the stern reality of sin, it will gain no credence when it talks of forgiveness. Such a Church sins against its sacred trust and walks unworthily of the gospel. It is an unholy Church, squandering the precious treasure of the Lord's forgiveness. Nor is it enough simply to deplore in general terms that the sinfulness of man infects even his good works. It is necessary to point out concrete sins, and to punish and condemn them. This is the proper use of the *power of the keys* (Matt. 16.19; 18.18; John 20.23), which the Lord bequeathed to his Church. Even the Reformers laid great emphasis on this power. It is essential for the Church to exercise it, for the sake of holiness, for the sake of the sinner and for its own sake. If the Church is to walk worthily of the gospel, part of its duty will be to maintain ecclesiastical discipline. Sanctification means driving out the world from the Church as well as separating the Church from the world.

But the purpose of such discipline is not to establish a community of the perfect, but a community consisting of men who really live under the forgiving mercy of God. Discipline in a congregation is a servant of the precious grace of God. If a member of the Church falls into sin, he must be admonished and punished, lest he forfeit his own salvation and the gospel be discredited. That is why baptism can be administered only on condition that the candidate repents of his sins and confesses his faith in Jesus Christ, and why only those who can 'discern' (I Cor. 11.29) between the true Body and Blood of Christ and any other eating ritual of a symbolic or similar kind can receive the grace of the Holy Communion. That means also that he must be able to give an account of himself regarding his spiritual insights, that he should examine himself or submit to an examination by a brother, to prove that he truly desires the sacrament of Christ's flesh and blood and his forgiveness. In addition to examination of the faith, there is also the sacramental confession, wherein the Christian seeks and finds assurance that his sins are forgiven. Confession is the God-given remedy for self-deception and self-indulgence. When we confess our sins before a brother-Christian, we are mortifying the pride of the flesh and delivering it up to shame and death through Christ. Then through the word of absolution we rise as new men, utterly dependent on the mercy of God. Confession is thus a genuine part of the life of the saints, and one of the gifts of grace. But if it is wrongly used, punishment is bound to ensue. In confession, the Christian is conformed to the death of Christ. 'When I admonish men to come to confession, I am simply urging them to be Christians' (Luther, *Great Catechism*).

The spirit of discipline pervades the whole life of the Church. The various stages in the ministry of grace are carefully arranged, but the basis is throughout the same, namely, the proclamation of the Word under the two keys. The exercise of discipline is not confined to formal assemblies in Church, for the Church's officers are always on duty. 'Preach the word, be instant in season, out of season; reprove, rebuke, exhort, with all long-suffering and teaching' (II Tim. 4.2). Here is the starting-point of church discipline. But it is only sins that have become public which come into consideration. 'Some men's sins are evident, going before unto judgement, and some men also they follow after' (I Tim. 5.24). According to this, the man who is punished under ecclesiastical discipline will be spared the punishment of the day of judgement.

But if already at this stage church discipline breaks down, i.e. at the daily exercise of the pastoral office, everything else is called in question. For the second stage is that of brotherly admonition from the other members of the Church. 'Teach and admonish one another' (Col. 3.16; I Thess. 5.11, 14). Such admonition must also include encouragement of the faint-hearted, support of the weak, and long-suffering toward all men (I Thess. 5.14). This is the only form of protection against our daily trials and temptations, and against apostasy within the congregation.

Where this spirit of brotherhood and service is absent, the third stage will hardly be reached. For if a brother falls into open sin in word or deed, the Church must have sufficient authority to bring formal disciplinary action against him. This also is a lengthy process. The Church must first of all overcome its reluctance to withdraw from communion with the sinner. 'Have no company with him' (II Thess. 3.14). 'Turn away from them' (Rom. 16.17). 'With such an one, no, not to eat' (the Holy Communion? – I Cor. 5.11). 'From these also turn away' (II Tim. 3.5; I Tim. 6.4). 'Now

261

we command you, brethren, in the name of our Lord Jesus Christ, that ye withdraw yourselves from every brother that walketh disorderly, and not after the tradition they received of us' (II Thess. 3.6). The purpose of this is to make the sinner 'ashamed' (II Thess. 3.14), and so win him back again. But although the sinner is temporarily excluded from the activities of the Church, it does not mean the end of all intercourse with him. The Church must go on admonishing him. 'Count him not as an enemy, but admonish him as a brother' (II Thess. 3.15). It is just because he is still a brother that he is punished and admonished by the community. It is brotherly tenderness which impels the Church to discipline him. When punishment is meted out to the stubborn and refractory, it must be administered in a spirit of meekness and patience. 'If peradventure God may give them the spirit of repentance and knowledge of the truth, and they may recover themselves out of the snare of the devil, having been taken captive by the Lord's servant unto the will of God' (II Tim. 2.26). The method of applying this discipline will vary with each individual case, but the aim is constant, namely, to bring the sinner to repentance and reconciliation. If the sin is of such a kind that it can remain a secret between you and the sinner, it is not for you to divulge it, but punish him in private and summon him to repentance, and then 'thou hast gained thy brother'. But if he will not listen to you, and remains obdurate, you must not go and make his sin public, but choose one or two witnesses (Matt. 18.15 f). These witnesses are necessary for two reasons. First they are needed to establish the fact of the sin – that is to say, if the accusation cannot be proved and is denied by the member of the congregation, leave the matter in God's hand; the brethren are meant to be witnesses, not inquisitors! But secondly they are needed to prove the offender's refusal to repent. The secrecy of the disciplinary action is meant to help the sinner towards repentance. But if he still refuses to listen or if his sin is already public property amongst the whole congregation, then the entire congregation must call the sinner to repentance and admonish him (Matt. 18.17; cf. II Thess. 3.14). If the sinner has a special office in the church, he must be charged only on evidence of two or three witnesses. 'Them that sin reprove in the sight of all, that the rest also may be in fear' (I Tim. 5.20). It is now time for the congregation to join its officers in administering the keys. If the verdict is public, both congregation and ministry must be publicly carried out. 'I charge thee in the sight of God and Christ Jesus and the elect angels, that thou observe these things without prejudice' (I Tim. 5.21). Now the judgement of God himself is about to be pronounced upon the sinner. If he shows genuine repentance, and publicly acknowledges his sin, he then receives forgiveness in God's name. But if he is still unrepentant, the Church must retain his sin in that Name. In other words, the sinner must be excommunicated. 'Let him be unto thee as the Gentile and the publican' (Matt. 18.17). 'Verily I say unto you, What things soever ye shall bind on earth shall be bound in heaven: and what things soever ye shall loose on earth shall be loosed in heaven. . . . For where two or three are gathered together in my name, there am I in the midst of them' (Matt. 18.18 ff). But excommunication is really nothing more than the recognition of a state of affairs which already exists, for the unrepentant sinner has condemned himself already (Titus 3.10), and before the community had to exclude him. St Paul calls excommunication 'delivering over to Satan' (I Cor. 5.5; I Tim. 1.20). The sinner is handed back to the world, where Satan rules and deals death. (This sentence is not to be taken as equivalent to capital punishment like that delivered in Acts 5, as may be proved by comparing I Tim. 1.20 and II Tim. 2.17; II Tim. 4.15.) The sinner is ejected from the fellowship of the Body of Christ because he has already separated himself from it. He has no further claim on the community. Yet even this extreme measure has one sole aim, the salvation of the sinner: 'that the spirit may be saved in the day of the Lord Jesus' (I Cor. 5.5), 'that they might be taught not to blaspheme' (I Tim. 1.20). Readmission to the community or salvation is the purpose of church discipline in all its stages: it is throughout a 'pedagogic' procedure. It is absolutely certain that the Church's verdict has an eternal validity where the sinner refuses to repent, and it is equally certain that this verdict (which means the inevitable loss of salvation) is no more than the last offer of restoration to the community and of salvation.[1] Thus the Church maintains its sanctification by

[1] Beyond all exercise of discipline by the congregation, which in itself still is a ministry of charity, even beyond the handing over of the most obdurate sinners to Satan, the New Testament knows as the most fearful punishment of all the curse, the anathema. This penalty is not intended any more to save the sinner but anticipates the divine judgement. The anathema corresponds to the *Cherem* of the Old Testament, which meant final exclusion from the community of Israel, and subsequent execution. This procedure has a double significance. First, any further absolution of the sinner is out of the question, and so he is handed over completely to God. But secondly this means that the sinner is at once accursed and holy. And therefore the community has no longer the power to try and save him. That the anathema means the loss of all hope of salvation is proved by Rom. 9.3, and that it has an eschatological reference is fairly clear from I Cor. 16.22. Gal. 1.8 f shows that the anathema overtakes those who deliberately pervert the gospel. It is no mere accident that the only passage where the anathema is pronounced against specific persons is concerned with heretical teachers. *Doctrina est coelum, vita terra* (Luther).

The difference between doctrinal and ecclesiastical discipline is that the latter is the consequence of right doctrine, that is, the right use of the keys, and the former is directed against the wrong use of doctrine. False doctrine corrupts the life of the Church at its source, and that is why doctrinal sin is more serious than moral. Those who rob the Church of the gospel deserve the ultimate penalty, whereas those who fail in morality have the gospel there to help them. In the first instance doctrinal discipline applies to those who hold a teaching office in the Church. It is always assumed that only those will be admitted to the ministry who are *didactikoi*, able to teach (I Tim. 3.2; II Tim. 2.24; Titus 1.9), 'able to teach others also' (II Tim. 2.2). If hands are laid on any man before he is ready for his office, the responsibility rests with the ordaining minister (I Tim. 5.22). Doctrinal discipline thus starts before the actual ordination. It is a matter of life and death for the Church that the utmost care be exercised with regard to ordinations. But this is only the beginning. When the candidate has been approved and admitted to his office, he must, like Timothy, be admonished unceasingly to maintain the true saving doctrine. In this connection the reading of the Scriptures is especially emphasized. The danger of error is only too strong (II Tim. 3.10, 14; 4.2; 2.15; I Tim. 4.13, 16; Titus 1.9; 3.8). Further the minister must be exhorted to live an exemplary life – 'Give heed to thyself and to the doctrine.' It is certainly no reflection on Timothy's character that he is exhorted to observe chastity, humility, impartiality, and diligence. Thus the discipline of the official ministry comes before ordinary church discipline. It is the responsibility of the minister to disseminate true doctrine in his congregation, and to resist every attempt to pervert it. Should flagrant heresy gain entry, the minister must require those concerned 'not to teach a different doctrine' (I Tim. 1.3) because the office of teaching is his and his is the authority. Again it is his duty to warn his flock to avoid strife of words (II Tim. 2.14). If a teacher of heresy is exposed, he is to 'receive a first and second admonition'. If he will not listen to that, he is to be treated as a heretic and excommunicated (Titus 3.10; I Tim. 6.4 f); for such a man leads the Church astray (II Tim. 3.6 f). 'Whosoever abideth not in the teaching of Christ hath not God.' Even hospitality and the Christian greeting must be refused to him (II John 10).

walking worthily of the gospel. Such a life produces the fruit of
the Spirit, and is ordered by the discipline of the Word. Yet all
the time the Church is still the community of those whose sanctification is Christ alone (I Cor. 1.30), the community which is
advancing towards the day of the Lord's return.

This brings us to our third definition of true sanctification –
that the purpose of it is to make us stand the test in the day of
Jesus Christ. 'Follow after ... the sanctification without which
no man shall see the Lord' (Heb. 12.14). Sanctification is always
related to the End. Its purpose is to enable us to pass not the world's
judgement or our own, but the Lord's. In the world's eyes and in
their own their sanctification may look like sin, their faith like
unbelief, their love like hardness of heart, their discipline like
weakness. Their true sanctification is always hidden. But Christ
himself is preparing his Church so that it may abide before his
judgement. 'Husbands, love your wives, even as Christ also loved
the Church, and gave himself up for it; that he might sanctify it,
having cleansed it by the washing of water with the word, that he
might present the Church to himself a glorious church, not having
spot or wrinkle or any such thing; but that it should be holy, and
without blemish' (Eph. 5.25-27; Col. 1.22; Eph. 1.4). Only the
Church which is sanctified can stand in Christ's sight. Christ
reconciled God's enemies and gave his life for the ungodly, so that
his Church might be holy until his coming again. The Church
becomes holy by being sealed with the Holy Spirit, by which seal
the saints are enclosed in the sanctuary of the Church and preserved there until the day of Jesus Christ. In that day they shall
be found before him without spot or shame, holy and without
blemish in body, soul and spirit (I Thess. 5.23). 'Or know ye not
that the unrighteous shall not inherit the kingdom of God? Be
not deceived: neither fornicators, nor idolaters, nor adulterers, nor

False doctrine is a coming of Antichrist, a term which is not applied to those whose
sins are moral, but which is reserved for teachers of heresy like the anathema of
Gal. 1.9. But both forms of discipline are essential to one another. St Paul therefore rebukes the Corinthians for being so puffed up that they start schisms without
exercising church discipline. It is impossible to separate doctrine and morality in
the Christian Church.

effeminate, nor abusers of themselves with men, nor thieves, nor drunkards, nor revilers, nor extortioners, shall inherit the kingdom of God. And such were some of you: but ye were washed, but ye were sanctified, but ye were justified in the name of the Lord Jesus Christ, and in the Spirit of our God' (I Cor. 6.9-11). If any man therefore chooses to persist in sin, let him not presume upon the grace of God. Only the sanctified community will be delivered from wrath in the day of the Lord Jesus Christ, for 'the Lord will judge every man according to his works, and will have no respect of persons. The works of all will be made manifest and he will render to every man according to what he hath done, whether it be good or bad' (II Cor. 5.10; Rom. 2.6 ff; Matt. 16.26). Nothing which has escaped judgement on earth will be able to elude detection in the day of judgement. Who then will remain? Those who have been found to do the good. Not the hearers, but the doers of the law shall be justified (Rom. 2.13). Christ himself said that only they who do the will of his Heavenly Father will enter into his kingdom.

We shall be judged according to our works – this is why we are exhorted to do good works. The Bible assuredly knows nothing of those qualms about good works, by which we only try to excuse ourselves and justify our evil works. The Bible never draws the antithesis between faith and good works so sharply as to maintain that good works undermine faith. No, it is evil works rather than good works which hinder and destroy faith. Grace and active obedience are complementary. There is no faith without good works, and no good works apart from faith.[1] If the Christian would be saved, he must do good works, for those who are caught doing evil works will not see the kingdom of God. That is why it is a Christian aim to do good. There is only one question of

---

[1] The difference between St Paul and St James is as follows. St James is endeavouring to prevent faith from boasting of its own humility, and St Paul to prevent works from boasting of *their* own humility. St James is not concerned to deny justification by faith alone; rather he is urging the believer not to rest content on the laurels of faith, but to get on with the work of obedience. This is his way of leading him to genuine humility. Both apostles want Christians to have a genuine and complete dependence on grace, rather than on their own achievements.

paramount importance in the Christian life, and that is, how we shall survive the last judgement? And because we shall be judged according to our own works, it is vitally important that we should be trained to do good works. That indeed is the whole purpose of our new creation in Christ 'For by grace ye have been saved through faith, and that not of yourselves: it is the gift of God: not of works, that no man should glory. For we are his workmanship, *created in Christ Jesus for good works*, which God afore prepared that we should walk in them' (Eph. 2.8-10; cf. II Tim. 2.21; 3.17; Titus 1.16; 3.1, 8, 14).

All this is perfectly clear: the aim of the Christian life is to produce those good works which God demands. The law of God is still in force, and still demands fulfilment (Rom. 3.31). And the only way to fulfil the law is by doing good works. But ultimately there is only one good work; the work of God in Christ Jesus. Through God's own action in Christ we have been saved and not through our own works. We can never boast about them, for we are ourselves his workmanship. Yet it remains true that the whole purpose of our new creation in Christ is that in him we might attain unto good works.

But all our good works are the works of God himself, the works for which he has prepared us beforehand. Good works then are ordained for the sake of salvation, but they are in the end those which God himself works within us. They are his gift, but it is *our* task to walk in them at every moment of our lives, knowing all the time that any good works of our own could never help us to abide before the judgement of God. We cling in faith to Christ and his works alone. For we have the promise that those who are in Christ Jesus will be enabled to do good works, which will testify for them in the day of judgement. They will be preserved and sanctified until the last day. All we can do is to believe in God's Word, rely on his promise, and walk in the good works which he has prepared for us.

From this it follows that we can never be conscious of our good works. Our sanctification is veiled from our eyes until the last day, when all secrets will be disclosed. If we want to see some results here and assess our own spiritual state, and have not the patience to wait, we have our reward. The moment we begin to feel satisfied that we are making some progress along the road of sanctification, it is all the more necessary to repent and confess that all our righteousnesses are as filthy rags. Yet the Christian life is not one of gloom, but of ever increasing joy in the Lord. God alone knows our good works, all we know is his good work. We can do no more than hearken to his commandment, carry on and rely on his grace, walk in his commandments, and – sin. All the time our new righteousness, our sanctification, the light which is meant to shine, are veiled from our eyes. The left hand knows not what the right hand does. But we believe, and are well assured, 'that he which began a good work in you will perfect it until the day of Jesus Christ' (Phil. 1.6). In that day Christ will show us the good works of which we were unaware. While we knew it not, we gave him food, drink and clothing and visited him, and while we knew it not we rejected him. Great will be our astonishment in that day, and we shall then realize that it is not our works which remain, but the work which God has wrought through us in his good time without any effort of will and intention on our part (Matt. 25.31 ff). Once again we simply are to look away from ourselves to him who has himself accomplished all things for us and to follow him.

The believer will be justified, the justified will be sanctified and the sanctified will be saved in the day of judgement. But this does not mean that our faith, our righteousness and our sanctification (in so far as they depend on ourselves) could be anything but sin. No, all this is true only because Jesus Christ has become our 'righteousness, and sanctification and redemption, so that he that glorieth let him glory in the Lord' (I Cor. 1.30).

'Whom he foreknew, he also foreordained to be conformed to the image of his Son, that he might be the firstborn among many brethren' (Rom. 8.29). Here is a promise which passes all understanding. Those who follow Christ are destined to bear his image, and to be the brethren of the firstborn Son of God. Their goal is to become 'as Christ'. Christ's followers always have his image before their eyes, and in its light all other images are screened from their sight. It penetrates into the depths of their being, fills them, and makes them more and more like their Master. The image of Jesus Christ impresses itself in daily communion on the image of the disciple. No follower of Jesus can contemplate his image in a spirit of cold detachment. That image has the power to transform our lives, and if we surrender ourselves utterly to him, we cannot help bearing his image ourselves. We become the sons of God, we stand side by side with Christ, our unseen Brother, bearing like him the image of God.

When the world began, God created Adam in his own image, as the climax of his creation. He wanted to have the joy of beholding in Adam the reflection of himself. 'And behold, it was very good.' God saw himself in Adam. Here, right from the beginning, is the mysterious paradox of man. He is a creature, and yet he is destined to be like his Creator. Created man is destined to bear the image of uncreated God. Adam is 'as God'. His destiny is to bear this mystery in gratitude and obedience towards his Maker. But the false serpent persuaded Adam that he must still do something to *become* like God: he must achieve that likeness by deciding and acting for himself. Through this choice Adam rejected the grace of God, choosing his own action. He wanted instead to unravel the mystery of his being for himself, to make himself what God had already made him. That was the Fall of man. Adam became 'as God' – *sicut deus* – in his own way. But now that he had made himself god, he no longer had a God. He ruled in solitude as a creator-god in a God-forsaken subjected world.

But the riddle of human nature was still unsolved. With the loss of the God-like nature God had given him, man had forfeited the destiny of his being, which was to be like God. In short, man had ceased to be man. He must live without the ability to live. Herein lies the paradox of human nature and the source of all our woe. Since that day, the sons of Adam in their pride have striven to recover the divine image by their own efforts. The more serious and devoted their attempt to regain the lost image and the more proud and convincing their apparent success, the greater their contradiction to God. Their misshapen form, modelled after the god they have invented for themselves, grows more and more like the image of Satan, though they are unaware of it. The divine image, which God in his grace had given to man, is lost for ever on this earth.

But God does not neglect his lost creature. He plans to recreate his image in man, to recover his first delight in his handiwork. He is seeking in it his own image so that he may love it. But there is only one way to achieve this purpose and that is for God, out of sheer mercy, to assume the image and form of fallen man. As man can no longer be like the image of God, God must become like the image of man. But this restoration of the divine image concerns not just a part, but the whole of human nature. It is not enough for man simply to recover right ideas about God, or to obey his will in the isolated actions of his life. No, man must be re-fashioned as a living whole in the image of God. His whole form, body, soul and spirit, must once more bear that image on earth. Such is God's purpose and destiny for man. His good pleasure can rest only on his perfected image.

An image needs a living object, and a copy can only be formed from a model. Either man models himself on the god of his own invention, or the true and living God moulds the human form into his image. There must be a complete transformation, a 'metamorphosis' (Rom. 12.2; II Cor. 3.18), if man is to be restored to the image of God. How then is that transformation to be effected?

Since fallen man cannot rediscover and assimilate the form of God, the only way is for God to take the form of man and come to him. The Son of God who dwelt in the form of God the Father, lays aside that form, and comes to man in the form of a slave (Phil. 2.5 ff). The change of form, which could not take place in man, now takes place in God. The divine image which had existed from eternity with God, assumes the image of fallen, sinful man. God sends his Son in the likeness of sinful flesh (Rom. 8.2 f).

God sends his Son – here lies the only remedy. It is not enough to give man a new philosophy or a better religion. A Man comes to men. Every man bears an image. His body and his life become visible. A man is not a bare word, a thought or a will. He is above all and always a *man*, a form, an image, a brother. And thus he does not create around him just a new way of thought, will and action, but he gives us the new image, the new form. Now in Jesus Christ this is just what has happened. The image of God has entered our midst, in the form of our fallen life, in the likeness of sinful flesh. In the teaching and acts of Christ, in his life and death, the image of God is revealed. In him the divine image has been re-created on earth. The Incarnation, the words and acts of Jesus, his death on the cross, are all indispensable parts of that image. But it is not the same image as Adam bore in the primal glory of paradise. Rather, it is the image of one who enters a world of sin and death, who takes upon himself all the sorrows of humanity, who meekly bears God's wrath and judgement against sinners, and obeys his will with unswerving devotion in suffering and death, the Man born to poverty, the friend of publicans and sinners, the Man of sorrows, rejected of man and forsaken of God. Here is God made man, here is man in the new image of God.

We know full well that the marks of the passion, the wounds of the cross, are now become the marks of grace in the Body of the risen and glorified Christ. We know that the image of the Crucified lives henceforth in the glory of the eternal High Priest, who ever maketh intercession for us in Heaven. That Body, in which Christ had lived in the form of a servant, rose on Easter

Day as a new Body, with heavenly form and radiance. But if we would have a share in that glory and radiance, we must first be conformed to the image of the Suffering Servant who was obedient to the death of the cross. If we would bear the image of his glory, we must first bear the image of his shame. There is no other way to recover the image we lost through the Fall.

To be conformed to the image of Christ is not an ideal to be striven after. It is not as though we had to imitate him as well as we could. We cannot transform ourselves into his image; it is rather the form of Christ which seeks to be formed in us (Gal. 4.19), and to be manifested in us. Christ's work in us is not finished until he has perfected his own form in us. We must be assimilated to the form of Christ in its entirety, the form of Christ incarnate, crucified and glorified.

Christ took upon himself this human form of ours. He became Man even as we are men. In his humanity and his lowliness we recognize our own form. He has become like a man, so that men should be like him. And in the Incarnation the whole human race recovers the dignity of the image of God. Henceforth, any attack even on the least of men is an attack on Christ, who took the form of man, and in his own Person restored the image of God in all that bears a human form. Through fellowship and communion with the incarnate Lord, we recover our true humanity, and at the same time we are delivered from that individualism which is the consequence of sin, and retrieve our solidarity with the whole human race. By being partakers of Christ incarnate, we are partakers in the whole humanity which he bore. We now know that we have been taken up and borne in the humanity of Jesus, and therefore that new nature we now enjoy means that we too must bear the sins and sorrows of others. The incarnate Lord makes his followers the brothers of all mankind. The 'philanthropy' of God (Titus 3.4) revealed in the Incarnation is the ground of Christian love towards all on earth that bears the name of man. The form of Christ incarnate makes the Church into the Body of Christ. All the sorrows of mankind fall upon that form, and only through that form can they be borne.

The earthly form of Christ is the form that died on the cross. The image of God is the image of Christ crucified. It is to this image that the life of the disciples must be conformed: in other words, they must be conformed to his death (Phil. 3.10: Rom. 6.4 f). The Christian life is a life of crucifixion (Gal. 2.19). In baptism the form of Christ's death is impressed upon his own. They are dead to the flesh and to sin, they are dead to the world, and the world is dead to them (Gal. 6.14). Anybody living in the strength of Christ's baptism lives in the strength of Christ's death. Their life is marked by a daily dying in the war between the flesh and the spirit, and in the mortal agony the devil inflicts upon them day by day. This is the suffering of Christ which all his disciples on earth must undergo. A few, but only a few, of his followers are accounted worthy of the closest fellowship with his sufferings – the blessed martyrs. No other Christian is so closely identified with the form of Christ crucified. When Christians are exposed to public insult, when they suffer and die for his sake, Christ takes on visible form in his Church. Here we see the divine image created anew through the power of Christ crucified. But throughout the Christian life, from baptism to martyrdom, it is the same suffering and the same death.

If we are conformed to his image in his Incarnation and crucifixion, we shall also share the glory of his resurrection. 'We shall also bear the image of the heavenly' (I Cor. 15.49). 'We shall be like him, for we shall see him even as he is' (I John 3.2). If we contemplate the image of the glorified Christ, we shall be made like unto it, just as by contemplating the image of Christ crucified we are conformed to his death. We shall be drawn into his image, and identified with his form, and become a reflection of him. That reflection of his glory will shine forth in us even in this life, even as we share his agony and bear his cross. Our life will then be a progress from knowledge to knowledge, from glory to glory, to an ever closer conformity with the image of the Son of God. 'But we all, with unveiled face reflecting as a mirror the glory of the Lord, are transformed into the same image from glory to glory' (II Cor. 3.18).

This is what we mean when we speak of Christ dwelling in our hearts. His life on earth is not finished yet, for he continues to live in the lives of his followers. Indeed it is wrong to speak of the Christian life: we should speak rather of Christ living in us. 'I live, and yet no longer I, but Christ liveth in me' (Gal. 2.20). Jesus Christ, incarnate, crucified and glorified, has entered my life and taken charge. 'To me to live is Christ' (Phil. 1.21). And where Christ lives, there the Father also lives, and both Father and Son through the Holy Ghost. The Holy Trinity himself has made his dwelling in the Christian heart, filling his whole being, and transforming him into the divine image. Christ, incarnate, crucified and glorified is formed in every Christian soul, for all are members of his Body, the Church. The Church bears the human form, the form of Christ in his death and resurrection. The Church in the first place is his image, and through the Church all her members have been refashioned in his image too. In the Body of Christ we are become 'like Christ'.

Now we can understand why the New Testament always speaks of our becoming 'like Christ' (καθὼς Χριστός). We have been transformed into the image of Christ, and are therefore destined to be like him. He is the only 'pattern' we must follow. And because he really lives his life in us, we too can 'walk even as he walked' (I John 2.6), and 'do as he has done' (John 13.15), 'love as he has loved' (Eph. 5.2; John 13.34; 15.12), 'forgive as he forgave' (Col. 3.13), 'have this mind, which was also in Christ Jesus' (Phil. 2.5), and therefore we are able to follow the example he has left us (I Pet. 2.21), lay down our lives for the brethren as he did (I John 3.16). It is only because he became like us that we can become like him. It is only because we are identified with him that we can become like him. By being transformed into his image, we are enabled to model our lives on his. Now at last deeds are performed and life is lived in single-minded discipleship in the image of Christ and his words find unquestioning obedience. We pay no attention to our own lives or the new image which we bear, for then we should at once have forfeited it, since it is only to serve as a mirror for the image of Christ on whom our gaze is fixed. The disciple looks solely at his Master. But when a man follows Jesus Christ and bears the image of the incarnate, crucified and risen Lord, when he has become the image of God, we may at last say that he has been called to be the 'imitator of God'. The follower of Jesus is the imitator of God. 'Be ye therefore imitators of God, as beloved children' (Eph. 5.1).

Indexes

INDEX OF SUBJECTS

Abraham, 82, 88f
Admonition, 261f
Anathema, 264n1
Anxiety, 158ff
Apostles, 182f
Ascension, 218
Asceticism, 77, 152, 153
Atonement, 222
Augsburg Confession, 80
Authority, 235ff, 261

Baptism, 36, 79, 205ff, 215ff, 225f, 230f, 233, 253, 260, 273
    infant, 210 and n1
Beatitudes, 95ff
Body of Christ, 121, 212ff, 223ff, 249f, 252, 255, 256, 263, 272, 274

Celibacy, 121
Chastity, 121, 255
Church, 77, 80, 169, 171, 197f, 201ff, 209, 216f, 225ff, 245ff, 259f, 274
    and world, separation of, 170f, 250f
Church discipline, 36, 260ff
Church order, 227
Communion, 36, 215ff, 225f, 229, 230, 260
    with God, 111, 113, 215f
Confession, 36, 125, 260f
Covetousness, 256
Cross of Christ, 76, 79, 80, 82, 99, 107, 112, 135, 138, 142, 207f, 217, 219, 229, 246ff, 271
    of the Church, 78, 90f, 195, 219

David, 221
Death, 79, 195, 207, 208, 210, 215, 220, 226, 245, 247, 253, 257f, 261, 271, 273
Devil, 171, 182, 185
Divorce, 121

Enemy, 131ff
Eternal life, 61, 170, 195
Evil, 128, 150, 165
Excommunication, 254, 261ff

Faith, 53, 54, 57, 58, 59, 69, 74, 185, 225, 265, 266, 267
Fanaticism, 140, 142, 166, 206n1
Fasting, 151ff
Forgiveness of sins, 41, 80, 113, 149f, 185, 258, 259, 260, 263
Fruit of the Spirit, 256f

Gentiles, 185
Good works, 40, 107, 146, 254, 266ff
Government, 236
Grace, 35ff, 58, 59, 60, 72, 73, 118, 165, 197, 215, 220, 259

Heresy, 228, 264n1
Holy Communion. See Communion
Holy Spirit, 172ff, 208f, 219, 222, 224, 227, 229, 265

Image of Christ, 269ff
Incarnation, 85, 212f, 216, 223, 225, 249, 271ff

Joy, 268
Judgement, 164f, 169, 266, 267
Justification, 41, 42, 87, 185, 208, 247ff
Justitia civilis, 55, 107

Kierkegaard, 43
Kingdom of God, 148, 188, 197, 234, 266

Law, 49, 56, 72, 73, 109, 110, 111, 112, 113, 114, 115, 132, 154f, 219, 232, 267
Legalism, 49, 70, 73, 74

Levi, 48f, 52, 53, 201
Light, 105ff, 154
Liturgy, 228
Lord's Supper. *See* Communion
Love, 132ff, 143f, 163f, 265
Luther, 35, 39, 40, 41, 43, 44, 45, 80, 83, 102n1, 223, 239, 261

Marcion, 109
Marriage, 120, 255
Martyrdom, 38, 79, 80, 81, 192, 273
Mediator, 50, 85, 86, 87, 88, 89, 90, 91, 145, 207
Mercy, 100f
Ministry, 227, 264n1
Monasticism, 38, 39, 40, 239
Mortification, 152

Neighbourliness, 67, 88
Non-violence, 129f

Oaths, 122ff
Obedience, 54, 55, 57, 58, 60, 63, 66, 68, 69ff, 112, 113, 130, 140, 143, 175, 202, 209, 274
Onesimus, 231
Otherworldliness, 239

Party strife, 228
Passion of Christ, 130
Paul, 205f, 218f, 231, 233f, 238
Peacemakers, 102
Pecca fortiter, 43f
Pelagianism, 55
People of God, 132, 229
Peter, 53, 55, 56f
Philemon, 231
Possessions, 72, 97, 154ff, 186
Poverty, 65, 71, 74, 96, 97, 103, 107, 186, 244
Prayer, 134, 136, 145ff, 152, 167
   The Lord's, 148
Preaching, 188, 194f, 224f, 228, 249, 259
Purity, 101f, 121

Reformation, 39, 40, 41, 128
Repentance, 259, 263
Resurrection, 108, 248, 271f, 273, 274
Return of Christ, 192f, 218
Revenge, 126ff
Righteousness, 100, 102, 110, 113, 114, 141ff, 160f, 162f, 247f
   of Christ, 109ff
   of the Pharisees, 113, 114
Roman Catholic Church, 55, 56, 105

Sacraments, 201, 226, 227, 229
Saints, 245ff
Salt, 104f, 249
Salvation, 111, 195, 264, 267
Sanctification, 84, 250ff
Second Coming. *See* Return of Christ
Self-denial, 77, 78
Sermon on the Mount, 95ff, 110, 111, 131, 174, 175, 176
Shepherds and Pastors, 179ff
Sin, 208, 248, 249f, 253, 254f, 259, 262f, 265, 268, 271
Slaves and freemen, 231ff, 238
Solomon, 221
State, 236ff
Suffering, 77, 78, 79, 80, 81f, 98, 99, 102, 127, 138, 190ff, 194f, 216, 220, 244, 257, 273

Teaching, 224, 264n1
Temple, 221f, 246, 250
Theologia crucis, 106
Truthfulness, 122ff

Unbelievers, 162ff

Violence, 127, 128

Whoredom, 255f
Woman, 119ff
Word, ministry of, 201, 226, 227, 229
Word of God, 37, 59, 60, 64, 67, 69, 73, 118, 152, 165, 166, 185, 189, 191f, 212f, 224f

INDEX OF BIBLICAL REFERENCES

Genesis
6.14   251
45.1ff   132

Exodus
15.11ff   245
23.4f   132
30.35   105

Leviticus
16.16ff   246
19.2   246
21.8   246

Deuteronomy
34.1   27

I Samuel
24.7   132

II Samuel
7.5, 11   221
7.12   221
7.13   221
7.14   221

II Kings
6.22   132

Psalms
99   246
109.4   132f
119.45   49

Proverbs
20.27   18
25.21f   132

Isaiah
7.14   249
43.24   187
53.11   187

Isaiah
54.17   249

Jeremiah
33.16   249
ch. 45   11

Ezekiel
16.4   105

Matthew
3.11   208
ch. 5   139, 141,
            142, 144,
            161, 162
5.1-12   95ff
5.13-16   104ff
5.14   252
5.16   141
5.17-20   109ff
5.21-26   115ff
5.27-32   119ff
5.33-37   122ff
5.38-42   126ff
5.43-48   131ff
ch. 6   141, 142,
            144, 161,
            162
6.1-4   139ff
6.5-8   145ff
6.9-15   147ff
6.16-18   151ff
6.19-24   154ff
6.25-34   157ff
7.1-12   162ff
7.13-23   169ff
7.15-20   170ff
7.21   172f
7.22   173f
7.24-29   175ff
8.15-17   213

Matthew
9.35-10.42 179ff
9.35-38   179ff
ch. 10   165
10.1-4   182f
10.5f   184f
10.7f   185f
10.9f   186f
10.11-15   187ff
10.16-25   190ff
10.26-39   194ff
10.40-42   197f
11.28ff   32
16.19   260
16.26   266
18.15f   262
18.17   262, 263
18.18   260
18.18ff   263
18.21ff   259
19.8   120
19.16-22   60ff
19.23-26   74f
19.28   182
22.21   238
25.31ff   268
26.39, 42   81
28.19   206

Mark
1.17   37
2.14   48ff
8.31-38   76ff
9.24   58
9.29   152
10.21   64
10.28-31   90
10.32   91
10.39   207n1
10.42-45   235
10.48   179

INDEX OF BIBLICAL REFERENCES

Luke

2.25	99
2.37	152
4.2	152
4.19	213
6.20	97
6.20ff	96
8.14	155
9.57-62	50ff
9.57ff	110
10.5	188
10.25-29	66
12.50	207n1
14.26	84ff
15.2	213
21.15	192

John

1.1ff	213
1.3	85
2.20ff	221
3.5	208
3.16	88
5.44	156n2
13.15	274
13.34	274
14.26	208
15.12	274
16.12f	209
16.13	208
19.34f	215
20.23	260
21.22	37

Acts

2.42	224
2.42ff	229
2.47	229
4.32ff	229
ch. 5	263
10.47	208
13.2	227
18.1ff	237
19.5	209n1
20.28	227

Romans

1.7	245
1.17	58
1.29	255
1.32	254
2.6ff	266
2.12	216
2.13	266
3.4	248
3.19	216
3.21f	246
3.25	248
3.26	247
3.31	267
5.5	219
5.8	254
5.18ff	215
5.19	214, 254
6.3	206, 215, 249
6.3ff	226
6.4	215
6.4f	273
6.5	215
6.6	215
6.7	208
6.8	215
6.11	210, 249
6.19-22	245
7.5	216
8.1	258
8.2	209
8.2f	271
8.3	213, 216
8.4	209
8.8	216
8.9	216
8.9-11	208
8.10	219
8.14ff	208
8.16	209
8.29	269
8.35ff	220
9.3	264n1
10.3	249
12.2	241, 270

Romans

12.5	217, 218, 226
12.20	134
12.21	237
ch. 13	237
13.1ff	235
13.2	235
13.4	236
13.5	237
13.6	238
13.7	238
13.8	238
15.30	219
16.2	230
16.9	230
16.12	230
16.17	261
16.18	256

I Corinthians

1.1	226
1.2	245, 250
1.11ff	228
1.14ff	226
1.30	249, 265, 268
2.10	208
2.12	208
3.6	228
3.11	222
3.16	222, 249
4.10	220
5.1ff	254, 255
5.5	263
5.9ff	256
5.10	254
5.11	238, 261
5.13	242
6.1-8	243
6.9	254
6.9-11	266
6.10	254
6.11	250, 253
6.13-15	121
6.13ff	255

INDEX OF BIBLICAL REFERENCES

I Corinthians

6.19	222, 249
7.2	255
7.5	152, 243
7.7	242
7.20-24	233
7.22	230
7.29	243
7.29-32a	241
7.33-40	242
7.39	230, 243
8.6	85, 212
9.15	242
10.7	255
10.17	217
11.17ff	226
11.26	226
11.29	260
12.3	172, 219
12.5	227
12.7	227
12.11-13	208
12.12	216
12.12ff	218, 226
12.13	209, 215, 216
12.28	227
12.28ff	227
ch. 13	174
14.32f	227
14.33	245
15.2	216
15.22	215
15.29	207n2
15.31	219, 257
15.45	214
15.47	214, 217
15.49	273
15.58	230
16.22	228, 264

II Corinthians

1.5-7	220
2.17	230
3.17	208, 219
3.18	270, 273

II Corinthians

4.10	220
4.10-12	220
4.16	257
5.1ff	217n1
5.10	266
5.14	215
5.19	248
5.20	220
5.21	213, 216
6.14ff	256
7.3	216
8.9	212
10.3	216
12.21	255
13.4	230
13.5	219
13.9	220
13.14	219

Galatians

1.4	216
1.8	228
1.8f	264n1
1.9	265n1
2.15	254
2.17	254
2.19	273
2.20	144, 219, 257, 274
3.13	216
3.23	251
3.27	206, 215
3.27f	209, 231
3.28	216, 217
4.4	213
4.19	220, 272
5.16	209
5.19	254, 256
5.21	254
5.22	257
5.24	121, 257
6.2	80
6.10	243
6.14	156n2, 273
6.17	220

Ephesians

1.4	213, 245, 265
1.9	208
1.12-14	251
1.13f	251
1.22	218
2.5	215
2.8-10	267
2.15	217
2.20	222, 224, 227
2.21	222
2.22	219
3.6	215n1
3.16f	208
3.17	219
3.19	218
4.1	253
4.3	219
4.11	227
4.12	219
4.19	254
4.22	253
4.24	217
4.28	242
4.30	251
4.32	259
5.1	275
5.2	274
5.3	254
5.5	254
5.8	253
5.9	256
5.25-27	265
5.32	243

Philippians

1.6	268
1.13	230
1.20	220
1.21	274
1.23	230
1.25	220
1.27	253
2.1	230

Phillippians

2.5	274
2.5ff	271
2.6ff	213
2.7	234
2.17	220
3.9	249
3.10	273
4.4	230, 243
4.5	243
4.6	242
4.12f	242
4.13	230

Colossians

1.8	219
1.10	253
1.16	213
1.18	218
1.22	265
1.24	220
2.2	219
2.9	218
2.12	215
2.17	221
2.19	218
2.20	208, 215
2.22	242, 245
3.2	244
3.4	244
3.5	254
3.8	254
3.10	217
3.11	231
3.13	274
3.16	261
3.18–4.1	232

I Thessalonians

2.12	253
2.13	224
4.4ff	254
4.6	243
4.11f	242
4.12	242
5.10	216

I Thessalonians

5.11	261
5.14	261
5.23	251, 265

II Thessalonians

3.6	262
3.8	242
3.11f	242
3.14	261, 262
3.15	262

I Timothy

1.3	264n1
1.10	228
1.15	254
1.20	263
3.2	264n1
4.2	67
4.4	242
4.13	264n1
4.16	228, 264n1
5.20	263
5.21	263
5.22	264n1
5.24	261
6.1	228
6.4	228
6.4f	67, 264n1
6.5	228
6.6–9	242
6.20	228

II Timothy

2.6	228
2.11	217
2.14	264n1
2.15	264n1
2.17	263
2.21	267
2.24	264n1
2.26	262
3.5	261
3.5ff	67
3.6f	264n1
3.7	228

II Timothy

3.8	228
3.10	264n1
3.14	264n1
3.17	267
4.2	261, 264n1
4.3	228
4.15	263

Titus

1.9	228, 264n1
1.10	228
1.13	228
1.16	267
2.1	228
2.14	216
3.1	267
3.4	32, 272
3.8	228, 264n1 267
3.10	228, 263 264n1
3.14	267

Philemon

8–14	231
15	231
17	231
18	231
21	231

Hebrews

1.1ff	213
1.2	85
4.7	188
4.15	213
6.4ff	209
6.5f	249
8.5	221
10.1	221
10.26f	249
11.13	244
12.14	265
12.16	255
13.4	255
13.14	244

James

4.1f	256

I Peter

1.5	251
2.5ff	222
2.11	244
2.21	274
2.24	247
4.1	220

II Peter

1.7	243

I John

1.1	224
1.8–2.1	259
2.6	274
2.12	210n1
2.12ff	210n1
2.15	88
3.2	273
3.9	253
3.16	274
4.3	227
4.15	219
5.3	31

II John

10	264n1
10ff	228

Revelation

2.6	228
2.15ff	228
14.6	195
21.12	183
21.14	183
21.22	222